MAGICAL FRANCE

500 Sacred and Mystical Sites

Rob Wildwood

Dolmen de Kermario, Carnac, p80

MAGICAL
FRANCE

Cave of Mary Magdalene, Opoul-Périllos, p244

CONTENTS

REGIONAL OVERVIEW

Chapelle Saint-Gilles, Montoire-sur-le-Loir, p159

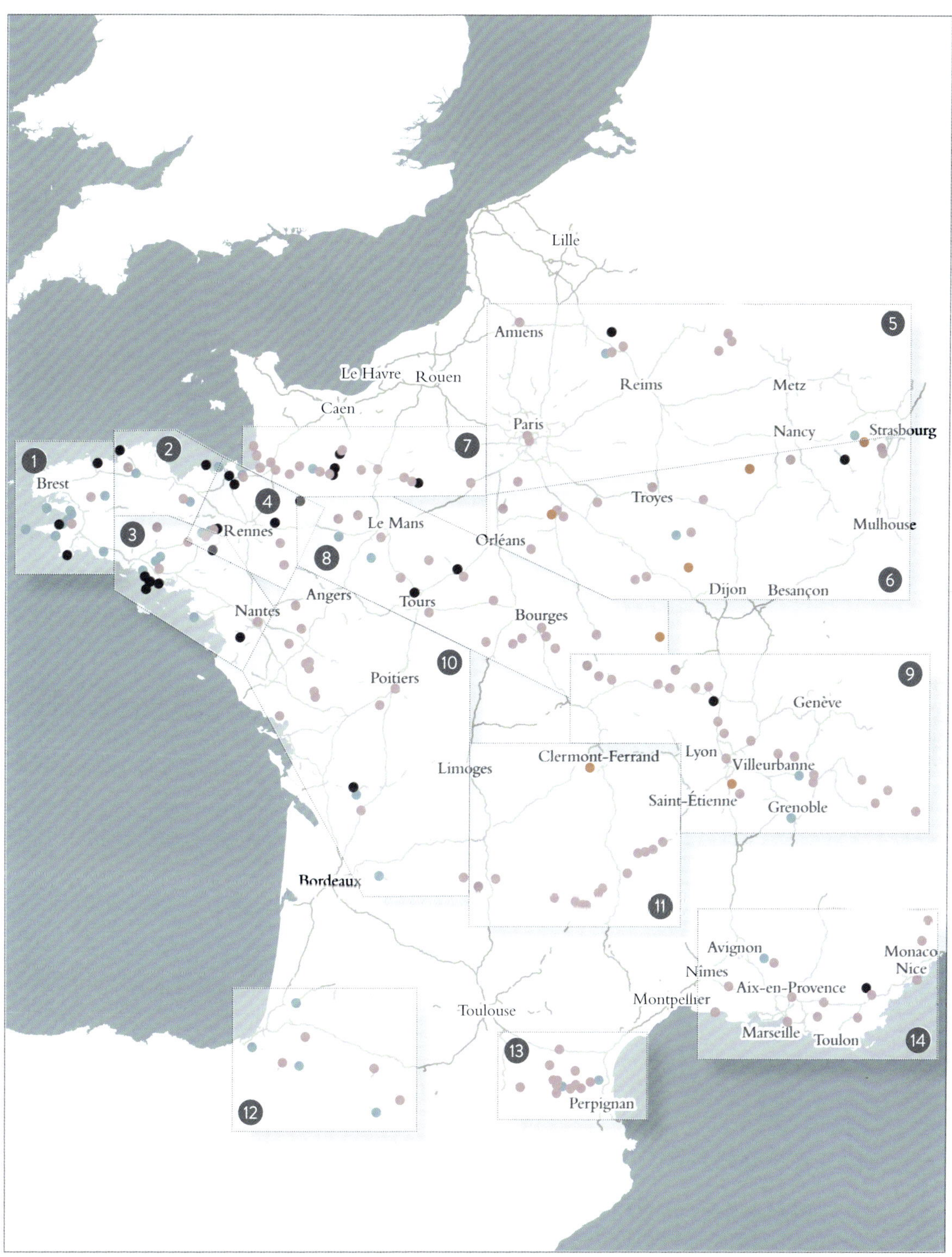

Lille
Amiens
Le Havre
Rouen
Caen
Reims
Metz
Paris
Nancy
Strasbourg
Brest
Rennes
Le Mans
Troyes
Mulhouse
Orléans
Angers
Tours
Nantes
Dijon
Besançon
Bourges
Poitiers
Genève
Lyon
Clermont-Ferrand
Villeurbanne
Limoges
Saint-Étienne
Grenoble
Bordeaux
Avignon
Monaco
Nice
Nîmes
Aix-en-Provence
Montpellier
Toulouse
Marseille
Toulon
Perpignan
1
2
3
4
5
6
7
8
9
10
11
12
13
14

Ti ar C'horriged / House of Korrigans, Douarnenez, p67

FRANCE'S SACRED AND MAGICAL HISTORY

Over millennia, many peoples and cultures have contributed to France's rich legendary history and vibrant folklore, from the earliest Palaeolithic cave dwellers whose memory is preserved in the wonderful cave art they left behind. The oldest paintings are of animals, including mammoths and deer, and include those found in the caves at Arcy-sur-Cure, which are 28,000 years old. For those early inhabitants, the creation of these images can be seen as an act of magic, perhaps to ensure success in hunting, that arose from the liminal place between the imaginal and the physical world.

The mysterious megalithic cultures that existed from the Neolithic to the Bronze Age left menhirs (standing stones), dolmens and other stone monuments in the French landscape. Constructed over a period of thousands of years, they include the immense Cairn de Barnenez in Finistère, built around 6,700 years ago and one of the oldest manmade structures in Europe. The alignments of standing stones at Carnac, the greatest concentration of megaliths in the world, were raised over the course of 2,000 years – an extraordinary cultural continuity. Burial chambers and tumuli were also built for the dead and became portals to the world of spirits and the ancestors. In folklore, these covered structures were the dwellings of korrigans and other fairy folk and were seen as gateways to their realm. Some tall menhirs were said to have been placed or dropped by the giant Gargantua, who plays a cryptic role in France's mythology and magical traditions.

Celtic tribes migrating from the east brought new beliefs to the region. Their priesthood, the Druids, acted as intermediaries between the people and the many gods and goddesses said to preside over the natural world. The Druids held ceremonies in sacred groves called nemetons and believed that everything in nature – forests, rivers and mountains – had its own guardian deity or spirit, with sacred springs especially venerated. Gods in the Celtic pantheon included the thunder god Taranis, Ogmios who guided souls to the afterlife, and Lugus, the chief of the gods, while goddesses included Rosmerta, who governed fertility, Sequana, goddess of the Seine, and the three Matronae, the triple aspects of the Mother Goddess.

The Celtic tribes, who the Romans called Gauls, were powerful and well organised, building hilltop fortified towns called oppida, and constructing extensive road networks that were later adopted by the Romans. Although fiercely independent, the tribes would band together under a single leader when circumstances demanded. The warrior king Vercingetorix led a resistance to the Roman invasion under Julius Caesar which was ultimately unsuccessful, culminating in the Gauls' final defeat at the sacred centre of Alésia in 52 BC.

The major Gallic towns then became Romanised, with amphitheatres, aqueducts and thermal baths, but the culture itself was a hybrid of the two, known as Gallo-Roman. In terms of religion, the Celtic and Roman

Tombeau de Merlin, Saint-Malon-sur-Mel, p100

Chapelle du Saint-Pilon near Mary Magdalene's Cave, p257

pantheons became merged as Romans identified Gallic deities as aspects of their own gods. Temples and sanctuaries were often dedicated jointly to the Roman and Gallic gods.

When in the 4th century the Romans adopted Christianity as their official religion, preachers and missionaries were sent out from Rome in an intensive drive to convert the people of Gaul. Later, these missionaries would be remembered as saints. As the Roman Church became established throughout Gaul, chapels, churches and cathedrals were built on the sites of Gallo-Roman temples and sanctuaries, effectively claiming them for the new faith while also preserving them as sacred sites. Healing springs were re-dedicated to saints with miracles ascribed to them, such as the saint causing the water to flow. Sometimes the saints were reimagined versions of pagan deities. The Celtic Mother Goddess Anu was transformed into St Anne, the mother of the Virgin Mary, who later became the patron saint of Brittany.

In Provence, however, there was an alternative narrative. According to Provençal tradition, Christianity was first brought to Gaul by one of the most enigmatic figures from the gospels, Mary Magdalene, who is said to have arrived at Saintes-Maries-de-la-Mer shortly after the crucifixion. The version of Christianity she preached was believed to be closer to the Gnostic texts than to the one later adopted by the Roman Catholic Church, and some even speak of an 'Underground Church' dedicated to Mary Magdalene in Provence and the Languedoc .

During the gradual decline of the Roman Empire there was a new wave of Celtic migration, this time from the British Isles. These new arrivals settled in Armorica, later to become Brittany, where they established kingdoms that were the origins of the distinctive Breton culture. This was also the era of King Arthur and his knights, the wizard Merlin and Vivian, the Lady of

Chartres Cathedral, p136

the Lake. Although popularly associated with sites in Britain, Arthur is also claimed by the Bretons as their own and places such as the enchanted Forest of Brocéliande and the magical spring of Barenton were incorporated into Arthurian legend. Some even argue that Arthur was based on Rhiothamus, a 5th-century King of the Britons from Armorica (Brittany), who died in a last stand against the Visigoths at Avallon in Burgundy.

The Celtic Christianity that had developed in Britain and Ireland soon permeated Brittany. Welsh and Cornish preachers and hermits, later remembered as saints, spread the new religion and worked miracles throughout the land. Although Brittany later adopted Roman Catholicism, it retains a distinctive religious character with its own saints and traditions, including mass pilgrimages known as 'pardons'.

The collapse of the Roman Empire also allowed in Germanic tribes, most notably the Franks who became the new power in Gaul during the early medieval period. Between 486 and his death in 511 their leader Clovis united the different tribes and conquered most of today's France, making Paris his capital. His conversion to Christianity in 496 marked a watershed in the spread of the religion. Clovis was the first of the Merovingians, often regarded as France's founding dynasty, who ruled for the next 300 years and hold a special place in France's national mythology.

The Merovingians were later overthrown by a new dynasty, the Carolingians, in 751. Their greatest leader was Charlemagne, who was crowned Emperor by the Pope in 800. Charlemagne ruled over most of Western Europe and the Kingdom of France eventually emerged from the western half of his empire. Many myths and legends grew up around him and his paladins (knights), a body of lore that later became known as the 'Matter of France'. Many feature his nephew Roland, a knight whose military exploits made him not only a folk hero but also, according to legend, a giant who wielded the magical sword Durandel.

During the Middle Ages, the Catholic Church attained the full height of its power. The 12th century was the golden age of cathedral building, including the majestic Gothic structures of Chartres, Amiens and Paris' Notre-Dame. They were raised on sites that had long been sacred and many stand on ancient alignments that are places of potent spiritual energy. Pilgrimages developed to these holy sites and also to the most important pilgrimage centre in Europe, Santiago de Compostela in Spain. Many of these trails are still followed by pilgrims today.

Intense religious fervour led to armed pilgrimages, known as Crusades, called to take control of the Holy Land, and from them emerged an order that came to hold a key place in France's magical and esoteric traditions, the Knights Templar. Under the patronage of the eminent St Bernard of Clairvaux this order of warrior monks transformed itself into one of the most powerful and wealthiest organisations of the Middle Ages, an elite fighting force answerable only to the Pope. Mystery surrounds the Templars' story, from their humble origins to their suppression on sensational charges of blasphemy, heresy and idol-worship 200 years later. Yet their legacy endures, and secret societies and magical orders that still claim a Templar heritage exist around the world.

Montségur Castle, p230

Basilica of Ars, Ars-sur-Formans, p177

In France, the medieval Church did not tolerate any deviation from its teaching or questioning of its authority, so individuals and sects holding beliefs considered heretical were ruthlessly suppressed. Most notorious was the brutal Albigensian Crusade against the Cathars of the Languedoc who considered themselves heirs to a simpler and purer form of Christianity that had no need of the organised Church to find communion with the divine.

The Cathars and the Templars have also been linked in mythology to the Holy Grail, the mysterious relic that gave rise to epic poems and romances, the first of which was written in the late 12th century by Chrétien de Troyes. His home town of Troyes was where the Templars originated and became one of their centres. The quest for the Grail was a signature element of the Arthurian romances that developed from British legends, and from the songs and stories of the troubadours who gathered at Eleanor of Aquitaine's court in Poitou. They fostered the concept of courtly love, which later played out in stories such as the romance between Lancelot and Guinevere. Eleanor's eldest daughter Marie of Champagne, who was based in Troyes, continued her mother's patronage through her support for Chrétien.

During the 14th and 15th centuries France was riven by the Hundred Years War with England when Edward II, Charles V and then Henry V claimed the French throne as theirs. Following the Battle of Agincourt in 1415 much of northern France was in English hands, including Paris which was occupied for 15 years. The fightback was famously led by Jeanne d'Arc (Joan of Arc), a teenage peasant girl who believed her mission to save France was divine

and had been communicated to her in visions by several saints, including Archangel Michael. Joan showed a special devotion to Black Madonnas, praying to several of them during her campaigns. She is now France's patron saint and her image can be seen in most French churches and cathedrals.

The French Renaissance, driven by the invention of the printing press, saw a revival of interest in the Arthurian romances and other half-forgotten tales and legends. It also sparked a renewed interest in the magical arts, alchemy and mystical philosophies such as the Cabala, all of which laid the foundation for France's vibrant esoteric subculture that continues to this day. Some of these ancient secrets, however, had not been erased from memory but rather passed on through underground streams of knowledge. They include an awareness of sacred geometry, ancient alignments and earth energies, as the siting of many churches and cathedrals from the Middle Ages through to the 19th century attests.

The French Revolution and ensuing Reign of Terror that swept the nation between 1789 and 1799 had a devastating effect on religious sites, as one of the Revolution's aims was to 'de-Christianise' France. Abbeys and convents were destroyed, churches and cathedrals looted, their precious relics and icons burned or broken up. These included many much-venerated Black Madonna statues that later had to be replaced by replicas.

Through Napoleon Bonaparte, the status of the Catholic Church was restored at the beginning of the 19th century, although it was never to regain the power and privileges it had once enjoyed. Many sites reduced to ruins during the Revolution were eventually rebuilt and pilgrimages were re-established with a renewed vigour. The religious revival also saw the founding of new sanctuaries that became centres of pilgrimage in their own right, most famously at Lourdes following the apparitions experienced by a young village girl, Bernadette Soubirous. The 'white lady' who appeared to Bernadette was declared to be the Virgin Mary.

The 19th century saw a growth of interest in France's Celtic heritage with statues of national heroes such as Vercingetorix being raised in Alésia. The century also experienced a great revival in France's magical traditions, especially in Paris and Lyon, with several ritual magic orders being founded. Many famous painters, composers and writers were initiated into these new orders, a tradition that continued into the modern age. The revival led to a new generation of esoteric scholars and historians who investigated France's magical past, leading to the rediscovery of many forgotten elements that are explored in this book. Among them were Henri Dontenville, who uncovered the esoteric secrets hidden in the legends of Gargantua, and Jean Richer whose work on France's sacred geography was to lead to the discovery of the Apollo alignment.

Since the 1970s there has been a wave of popular interest in mysteries from France's magical past, focused on the Knights Templar, Mary Magdalene, the Merovingians and the enigma of Rennes-le-Château, the Cathars and the Languedoc. A new pagan revival has also seen a renewed interest in the Celtic gods of ancient Gaul, as well as in the beings that inhabit its mysterious Otherworld such as the korrigans and fairy folk who still hide, seemingly just out of reach, within the magical French landscape.

HOW TO USE THIS BOOK

SYMBOLS

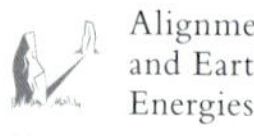 Alignments and Earth Energies

 Korrigans

 Black Madonnas

 Magic

 The Cathars

 Mary Magdalene

 Christianised Pagan Sites

 Pilgrimage

 Creation Stories

 Places of Healing

 Dragons

 Portals – Entrances to the Otherworld

 Fairies

 Saints and Miracles

 Giants

 Water Spirits

 Goddesses

 Wishes and Divination

 King Arthur, Merlin and the Medieval Romances

LISTINGS

Sites fall under one or more categories denoted by symbols (see above and as described in the following pages). The site description then gives a brief overview of the site along with its magical properties, followed by a brief summary of the folklore of the site (for more information see Bibliography at the back of the book or look up the story online). The site description will also include some indication of what it is like to visit the site today and what can be experienced there. A visit to sub-locations highlighted in bold is recommended and most include a photo. For other sub-locations GPS co-ordinates are given for reference purposes only. These sites may still be visited (unless listed as 'private') but might only be of interest to those who wish to explore deeper.

FINDING YOUR WAY

GPS co-ordinates can be typed directly into any map app or website or into a Sat Nav (GPS unit) by setting the Coordinate Format to dd.dddd°. Unless the site is beside the road, GPS co-ordinates are given for the nearest parking area. Trailheads without parking will require you to look for a parking space nearby. The approximate walking distance is given in metres.

ACCESS TO SPECIFIC LOCATIONS

Some locations are on private land in which case this will be clearly stated. Some locations require an entry fee to be paid, shown in multiples of €. Each € = up to €6; e.g. €€ = €6.10 to €12. Parking fees are shown in the same fashion. Coastal sites only accessible when the tide is out are clearly marked 'low tide only'. Always check the tides before walking to these sites and preferably set off when the tide is falling to avoid being cut off by the rising tide.

Path up La Rhune, p220

Menhir de Saint-Uzec, Pleumeur-Bodou, p74

VISITING A SACRED SITE

RESPECT, REVERENCE & INSIGHT

When you visit any of the magical sites in this book, remember that the place is sacred, filled with a spirit and a mystery that deserve both honour and respect. If you want to show your reverence by leaving an offering at a site then please make sure it is made from biodegradable organic material. Plastic ribbons kill trees and modern coins pollute well water. It is better to light a candle, sit in silence, quieten the mind and take time to tune into the energy of the place. Let the stories and folklore guide you to the true 'spirit of place' and what it has to offer in terms of insight and wisdom for our future with the land.

ALIGNMENTS & EARTH ENERGIES

The landscape of France is crossed by ancient alignments, some covering relatively short distances while others extend across the whole country. They include rows of menhirs such as the world-famous alignments at Carnac in Brittany, while others are marked by medieval churches, cathedrals and castles. Some are oriented towards the rising and setting of the sun at solstices and equinoxes, while others are believed to be currents of earth energy, known to the ancient Druids as 'wouivre', which can be traced by dowsers.

The most significant of the energy lines is the Apollo-Athena alignment that crosses France from northwest to southeast, entering France at Mont Saint-Michel on the Normandy coast and leaving through the Alps. It's formed of two currents, one male (Apollo) and the other female (Athena), which cross at key sites to form power points or nodes. Along the Apollo-Athena alignment are important sacred sites, with several significant locations dedicated to Archangel Michael. It is part of a much longer alignment that runs from Skellig St Michael in Ireland through Cornwall's St Michael's Mount, and after leaving France passes through Italy and sites dedicated to Apollo in Greece.

Another long-distance alignment, which also passes through Mont Saint-Michel, is the Ogmios line that begins at the Callanish stone circle in Scotland's Outer Hebrides and runs through Glastonbury Tor in England. After crossing the Channel it continues southwards through western France.

The Grand Meridian of Gaul is a 10km-wide line that runs north–south through France from its most northern point at Dunkirk south to the Pyrenees. It passes through many significant sites including the nation's capital. Meridians follow lines of longitude and are a key part of the earth's energy grid. The Paris Meridian, fixed during the building of the Paris Observatory in the 17th century, falls within the Grand Meridian and connects with other ancient alignments.

These and other alignments form France's sacred geography, sometimes marking out geometric patterns of sacred sites that reflect significant astronomical events – traces of an ancient understanding of the earth and its relationship to the heavens.

BEST SITES

Carnac p80 (pictured)

Menhir de la Haute-Pierre p95

Mont Saint-Michel p145

Alésia p130

Bourges p163

Paris Observatory p104

Butte de Suin p173

Cluny p164

Chapelle Mont Saint-Michel p138

Saint-Michel-Mont-Mercure p194

BLACK MADONNAS

Found throughout Europe, these mysterious feminine icons are especially concentrated in France, where they are known as 'Vierges Noires' (Black Virgins). Most conform to traditional images of the Virgin Mary holding her Child in her arms, except they have black or dark skin. Some are carved from dark wood or stone while others were intentionally painted black or brown. Both figures are often crowned and dressed in ornate robes.

Some were brought back from the Holy Land by pilgrims while others were discovered in France, often miraculously. Healing and other miracles are frequently attributed to them, and many are the object of longstanding pilgrimages, such as the one to Rocamadour. Black Madonna statues once marked the two ends of the pilgrimage trail between Chartres and Mont Saint-Michel, both of them kept in crypts and both known as Notre-Dame de Sous-Terre (Our Lady of the Underground).

Many Black Madonnas were destroyed during the French Revolution and have been replaced by faithful replicas, but originals can still be seen in places such as Arles Cathedral. Some have been repainted in recent times to make them lighter-skinned, although old photographs or depictions show they were originally black or brown.

Black Madonnas are frequently found at sites connected with other mysteries and many of these locations pre-date the coming of Christianity. Several French scholars have argued that the statues, which many consider to be images of the Celtic Mother Goddess, represent a continuity of pagan goddess worship but in a disguised form. The Mother Goddess is also closely identified with the Egyptian goddess Isis, whose cult pre-dated Christianity by many centuries, and statues of Isis holding the child Horus are thought to have been the model for those of the Virgin Mary and Child. Some Black Madonnas, such as Chartres' Notre-Dame de Sous-Terre, are believed to be ancient images of pagan goddesses that were taken to be the Virgin Mary.

Black Madonnas are also found at some sites associated with Mary Magdalene's life in France, linking them to her secret veneration in the Languedoc and the Eastern Pyrenees.

BEST SITES

Arles Cathedral p253

Chartres p136

Mont Saint-Michel p145

Saint-Martin-Vésubie p260

Liesse-Notre-Dame p107

Notre-Dame de l'Épine p154

Moulins p171

Notre-Dame de Fourville, Lyon p179

Notre-Dame-de-Myans p184

Rocamadour p213

Le Puy-en-Velay p204 (pictured)

THE CATHARS

This term describes the followers of an 11th-century religious movement whose heartland was in the Languedoc in southern France, and who consisted of a number of disparate groups. Although their beliefs varied, Cathars shared common ideals, especially the rejection of the authority and dogmas of the Roman Catholic Church, then the dominant religious force in Europe. They believed the Catholic Church had strayed too far from the simple form of worship preached by Jesus. For the Cathars, an individual's spiritual relationship with the divine didn't need the mediation of priests, bishops and popes, or costly churches and cathedrals. They preferred to worship simply, in the open air, and regarded men and women as spiritually equal.

Many of the lords and nobles of the Languedoc adopted the Cathar way, and so the Catholic Church began to perceive the movement as a threat to its authority. Pope Innocent III branded the Cathars heretics, and after various failed attempts to bring them back into the fold, in 1209 he launched a crusade against them, known to history as the Albigensian Crusade. The lords of the Languedoc fought the crusader army, leading to years of brutal warfare during which many of the region's castles were besieged. Eventually, the Cathars' main stronghold, the seemingly impregnable castle of Montségur, surrendered to the crusaders in 1244 after a long siege.

The Cathars hold a significant place in the wider mysteries of the Languedoc. During the crusade, some Cathars were protected and sheltered by the Knights Templar who had a strong presence in the region, while others venerated Mary Magdalene. Great mystery surrounds the 'Cathar treasure', which was said to have been taken to safety by four Cathars who escaped from Montségur. Some believe the treasure contained coded teachings that hid a precious secret, while others believe it contained a priceless sacred artefact, perhaps even the Holy Grail.

BEST SITES

CHRISTIANISED PAGAN SITES

Many of France's Christian churches, chapels and cathedrals are superimposed on other, much more ancient sites, occupying ground that has long been held sacred.

The Church took over temples and sanctuaries where pagan gods and goddesses were once worshipped, building churches and chapels in their stead. Springs identified with the old deities were re-dedicated in the name of saints, and megalithic sites, which were sacred long before the coming of the Celts, were also repurposed. At Chartres, for example, a cathedral was raised over an age-old megalithic structure.

Often the old deities would be transformed into Christian saints, as with the Celtic mother goddess Ana or Anu, who was identified with St Anne, mother of the Virgin Mary. Anne later became the patron saint of Brittany, and a chapel dedicated to her was established at Saint-Anne-la-Palud, the site of her legendary arrival from the Holy Land.

In some places traces of old sacred places, such as Gallo-Roman temples and megalithic monuments, still remain incorporated into Christian buildings. At the Chapelle des Sept-Saints at Plouaret in Brittany, the crypt is an ancient dolmen that predates the church by many centuries.

The suppression of pagan religion and the triumph of Christianity is represented by the story of Archangel Michael subduing the dragon, and its associated imagery can be seen in many of France's churches as well as at Christianised power spots such as Mont Saint-Michel.

BEST SITES

Nevers Cathedral p165

Saint-Michel-de-Brasparts p66

Chapelle de Sept-Saints p70

Menhir de Saint-Uzec p74 (pictured)

Tumulus Saint-Michel p89

Mont Dol p96

Chapelle Saint-Michel p138

Mont Saint-Michel p145

Saint-Michel-Mont-Mercure p194

Chartres p136

CREATION STORIES

Myths explaining how features in the landscape came into being are common throughout the world, and their origin is often attributed to supernatural forces. The Lac d'Aiguebelette in the Alps is said to have been formed when the valley was flooded as punishment for the wicked ways of its inhabitants, while the collapsed face of the nearby Mont Granier is said to have been the work of demons out to destroy the villages in the valley below.

Similar tales are evoked to account for the origin of megaliths. Some menhirs stand where people have reputedly been turned to stone, as with the immense stone alignments of Carnac which were held to be Roman soldiers literally petrified by St Cornelius. The building of dolmens, too, is often ascribed to fairies or other supernatural beings. In the north of France, a number of menhirs are said to owe their origin to the legendary giant Gargantua – usually stones shaken from his shoes or a broken tooth he spat out. Larger landscape features in the region such as hills, rock outcrops, river estuaries and plains, are also said to have been created by this same giant.

Creation legends often evoke folk heroes, such as the huge natural passage, the Brèche de Roland in the Pyrenees, said to have been cut by Roland with his magical sword Durandel. According to local lore, the towering rock pinnacles in Isère known as the Trois Pucelles were three young women who fell in love with Roland and were subsequently turned to stone by his uncle Charlemagne.

The creation of more recent manmade structures such as medieval castles is also sometimes ascribed to supernatural forces. Châteaumur and many other castles in the Western Lowlands, for example, are said to have been built by the fairy Melusine in a single night.

BEST SITES

Carnac p80

Dolmen de la Grotte aux Fées p157

Mortagne-au-Perche p138

Dolmen de la Pierre Levée p159 (pictured)

Alignements de Kerzerho p79

Hottée de Gargantua p107

Lac d'Aiguebelette p184

Châteaumur Keep p192

Brèche de Roland p224

Trois Pucelles p224

DRAGONS

Tales of dragons and great serpents are found throughout France, from the one famously overcome by Archangel Michael at Mont Saint-Michel to the seven-tailed Herensuge of Basque lore who lives in caverns deep under the Pyrenees. They are usually depicted as winged, sometimes with legs and sometimes without, while at other times they are simply large serpents. Dragon lairs are underground caves, often connected to rivers and deep pools.

Although there are legends of knights and other heroes vanquishing dragons, in France's mythology it is more often saints who rid the land of these terrifying monsters. Rather than lances or swords, the saintly weapons are prayer, crucifixes and holy water. St Radegonde overcame the Grande Goule that dwelt in the caves beneath Poitiers by brandishing the latter two, while for St Veranus, making the sign of the cross was enough to defeat the Coulobre of Fontaine-de-Vaucluse in Provence. In these legends the dragon is a symbol of evil, and the tales of its defeat serve to demonstrate the power and superiority of Christianity over the old pagan religions.

Archangel Michael's defeat of the Devil, who had taken the form of a dragon, shares similarities with the legend of St George and both figure strongly in the iconography of France and England respectively. Images of Michael standing on or over the vanquished dragon are found in virtually every church and cathedral in France. Towering statues, such as those at the Basilique Notre-Dame-Fourvière in Lyon and the church in Saint-Michel-Mont-Mercure in Vendée, also show Michael with the dragon pinned to the ground by the archangel's lance.

Sometimes other supernatural creatures take on the characteristics of dragons and serpents, as with Melusine, a key figure in the folklore of western France. Although a fairy woman, she transforms into a winged creature with a serpentine tail.

Dragons also symbolise the serpentine earth energies, known to the Druids as wouivre, that flow through the land. An awareness of the wouivre currents also explains the images of serpents carved in many of the churches and chapels on the Apollo-Athena alignment.

BEST SITES

Église Saint-Vigor p149

Avranches p149

Moulins p171

Saint-Michel-en-l'Herm p194

Notre-Dame-de-Grande, Poitiers p197

Fontaine-de-Vaucluse p248

Saint-Michel-Mont-Mercure p194

La Rhune p220

Mont Saint-Michel p145

Utelle p262 (pictured)

FAIRIES

Fairies are the inhabitants of an Otherworld that can only be accessed at certain magical locations, such as caves and dolmens. Their names and characteristics vary in the folklore of each region, but most common are 'fées', the origin of the English word 'fairy'.

Usually humanoid in form, these beings possess magical powers. Sometimes they inhabit natural places such as springs, pools and forests, such as the Forêt de Huelgoat in Finistère, but often they are associated with megalithic sites, especially dolmens and passage graves ('allées couvertes') that are regarded as their dwellings or gateways to their realm. The fairies emerge from them at night to dance among the stones, sometimes enchanting people who come across them and forcing them to dance.

Fairies can interact with humans in more direct ways, such as becoming godmothers to their children. Some can even take human lovers, the most famous example being the fairy Melusine who plays a significant role in the folklore of the Western Lowlands of France. She married the mortal Raymondin of Poitiers and their children established the prominent Lusignan dynasty.

Unique to Brittany are the Groac'h, fairies who usually take on the guise of old women, while the Groac'h of the coast have walrus-like tusks. The Côtes-d'Armor region, in particular, is the realm of the curiously-named Margot la Fée. These fairies are especially mischievous, cavorting in places such as Mont Croquelien, and well known for taking human children to raise in the fairy realm, replacing them with changelings. In Finistère there is also a type of seawater fairy called a Marie-Morgane.

Some fairies, like Esterelle of Draguignan in Provence, are helpful, giving advice and aid to those who seek her out, while others are mischievous and some, such as the wicked La Gione of Bagnoles-de-l'Orne in Normandy, are positively malign.

BEST SITES

Forêt de Huelgoat p59

Mont Croquelien p75

Melusine's Tower p195

Dolmen de la Salle aux Fées p90

Maison des Fées p95

Lusignan p199

Lit de la Gione p139

Cave à Margot p155

Roche des Fées p112 (pictured)

Pierre de la Fée, Draguignan p259

GIANTS

The figure of the giant Gargantua looms large in the folklore of France. Other countries have legendary giants, but in France this single figure is particularly dominant. The 16th-century writer, François Rabelais drew on existing folk traditions and his tales did much to popularise this gluttonous and pleasure-loving giant. The word 'gargan' frequently appears in Celtic place names and a great many sites, not only megaliths and conspicuous rock formations but also islands and rivers, have legends attributing their origins to Gargantua. However, there's another, deeper level to the often ribald and humorous tales, as many of the giant's sites are also associated with ancient mysteries. A good example is the legendary journey that Gargantua made with his parents Grandgousier and Galemelle, from the mountains in the east of France to Mont Saint-Michel on the Normandy coast, their route following an ancient sacred way. Other Gargantua sites are on alignments that are oriented to sunrise on the summer or winter solstices. Some see the giant as a personification of the forces of nature, perhaps even the distant memory of an ancient sun god.

Other giants have also left their mark on the landscape, especially in Finistère. The immense rock 'chaos' in the Forêt de Huelgoat is reputedly the ruins of a city they created and once inhabited. Out on the Atlantic coast, the headland known as the Château de Dinan was said to be the abode of giants who lured ships onto the rocks.

Some folk heroes, such as the warrior Roland, literally grew in the telling and took on the physical proportions of giants, their actions shaping the very landscape itself.

BEST SITES

Sabot de Gargantua p65

Doigt de Gargantua p72

Affiloir de Gargantua p141

Hottée de Gargantua p107

Dent de Gargantua p94 (pictured)

Laon p108

Vierzeux de Gargantua p108

Brèche de Roland p224

Forêt de Huelgoat p59

Château de Dinan (Grotte des Korrigans) p58

GODDESS

From ancient times to the Gallo-Roman period and even beyond into the Christian era, there have been sites in France sacred to the divine feminine. It's thought that the most ancient religion of prehistoric people was a form of goddess-worship based upon a Mother Goddess who represented the power of the earth and fertility. Her symbols have been found on some megaliths, such as the Cairn de Barnenez – thought to be almost 7,000 years old and a candidate for Europe's most ancient surviving structure. In southwest France, the Basques revered Mari, a supernatural form of the ancient Mother Goddess.

The Gauls had many goddesses, whose worship continued under the Romans. They included Segeta, goddess of the river Loire, whose sanctuary became the Roman town of Aquae Segetae. The Romans also introduced their own goddesses who often supplanted those of the Gauls.

Many Christian holy sites were built on temples and sanctuaries that had previously been sacred to goddesses. Arles Cathedral was raised on a temple to Cybele, the Roman Mother Goddess, and the chapel dedicated to Archangel Michael on Mont-Dol in Brittany was established by St Samson on the ruins of Cybele's shrine.

Some goddesses were even transformed into saints. A notable example is the Celtic mother goddess Ana or Anu who was conflated with St Anne, mother of the Virgin Mary. Sites previously sacred to the goddess were re-dedicated to St Anne, including the major pilgrimage sanctuary of Sainte-Anne-d'Auray, built on the site of the Gallic village of Keranna ('Village of Ana'). Likewise Libera, the Roman goddess of the harvest, became St Libaire, a saint of the Vosges region.

Some see the mysterious Black Madonna statues as representing a continuation of goddess worship beneath the Church's radar. The Black Madonna of Notre-Dame de l'Épine found miraculously at Avioth in northern France is thought to have been a statue of the fertility goddess, Rosmerta, who was venerated by the Gauls. Statues of Rosmerta have been found at other sites that were later dedicated to the Virgin Mary, such as Notre-Dame de Sion at Sion-Vaudémont in northeastern France.

BEST SITES

Cairn de Barnenez p56

Île de Sein p61

Saint-Anne d'Auray p85

Chartres p136

Aquae Segetae p129

Le Puy-en-Velay Cathedral p204

Arles Cathedral p253

Rennes-les-Bains p241 (pictured)

Notre-Dame de Sion p120

Abbaye Saint-Victor, Marseilles p253

KING ARTHUR, MERLIN & THE MEDIEVAL ROMANCES

While King Arthur and his knights are at the heart of Britain's legendary history, they also feature in the mythology of France and especially that of Brittany, where many sites are associated with Arthurian romance, especially those in and around Paimpont Forest, said to be a remnant of the enchanted forest of Brocéliande. They include the Val Sans Retour (Valley Without Return) where Morgan le Fay used her magic to imprison knights who were unfaithful in love, and the Fontaine de Barenton, the spring where the knight Yvain defeated its guardian, the Black Knight. This spring, is also said to be where Merlin met the nymph Vivian. She exploited his passion to learn the secrets of his magic, which she then used to imprison him beneath the Tombeau de Merlin (Merlin's Tomb) on the edge of Paimpont Forest. Outside Brittany, according to local lore, the Fosse Arthour (Arthur's Trench) in Normandy is where Arthur rests with his Queen Guinevere.

The Arthurian literature that emerged in the later Middle Ages also came from northern France. It includes the Grail romances, the first of them written by Chrétien de Troyes in the late 1100s.

Arthur's historical reality has always been hotly debated. Some believe he is entirely fictional while others argue that he was based on a real figure. One historical candidate is Riothamus, a 5th-century King of the Britons who made his last stand near Avallon in Burgundy – a possible inspiration for the Isle of Avalon of Arthurian myth.

The great hero of the 'Matter of France', France's legendary history, was Charlemagne, ruler of the Frankish empire that covered much of continental Western Europe. In later medieval literature Charlemagne was transformed into a hero with supernatural and magical powers, such as turning three sisters to stone to make the Trois Pucelles rock pinnacles in Isère. Many tales were told about Charlemagne's nephew Roland who possessed the magical sword Durandel, given to Charlemagne by an angel. Roland is said to have used it to cut the gap in the Pyrenees known as the Brèche de Roland during his last stand against the Basques.

BEST SITES

Église du Graal p98 (pictured)

Fosse Arthour p142

Avallon p124

Domfront p141

Château de Comper p97

Fontaine de Barenton p99

Tombeau de Merlin p100

Val Sans Retour p100

Brèche de Roland p224

Trois Pucelles p224

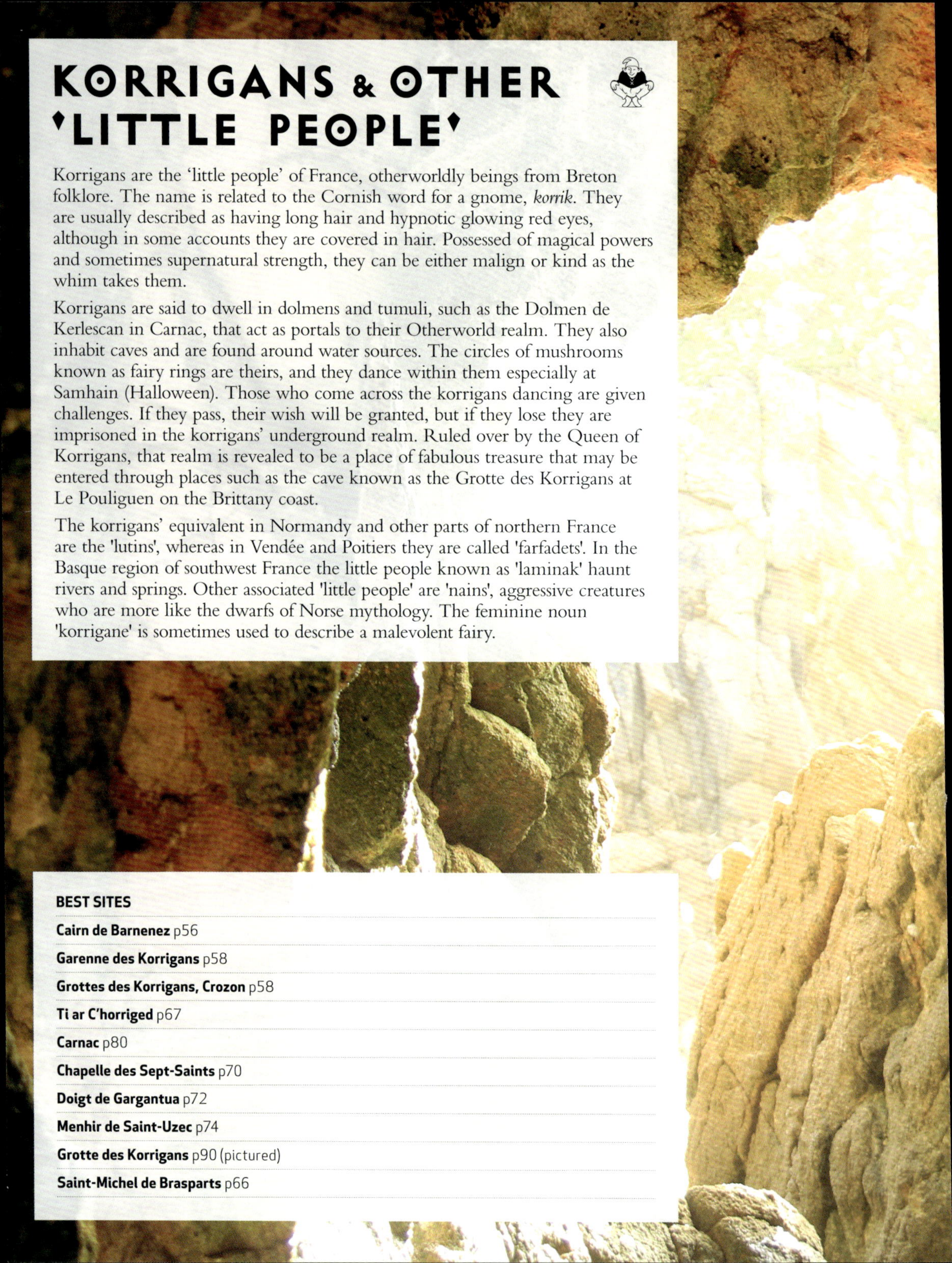

KORRIGANS & OTHER 'LITTLE PEOPLE'

Korrigans are the 'little people' of France, otherworldly beings from Breton folklore. The name is related to the Cornish word for a gnome, *korrik*. They are usually described as having long hair and hypnotic glowing red eyes, although in some accounts they are covered in hair. Possessed of magical powers and sometimes supernatural strength, they can be either malign or kind as the whim takes them.

Korrigans are said to dwell in dolmens and tumuli, such as the Dolmen de Kerlescan in Carnac, that act as portals to their Otherworld realm. They also inhabit caves and are found around water sources. The circles of mushrooms known as fairy rings are theirs, and they dance within them especially at Samhain (Halloween). Those who come across the korrigans dancing are given challenges. If they pass, their wish will be granted, but if they lose they are imprisoned in the korrigans' underground realm. Ruled over by the Queen of Korrigans, that realm is revealed to be a place of fabulous treasure that may be entered through places such as the cave known as the Grotte des Korrigans at Le Pouliguen on the Brittany coast.

The korrigans' equivalent in Normandy and other parts of northern France are the 'lutins', whereas in Vendée and Poitiers they are called 'farfadets'. In the Basque region of southwest France the little people known as 'laminak' haunt rivers and springs. Other associated 'little people' are 'nains', aggressive creatures who are more like the dwarfs of Norse mythology. The feminine noun 'korrigane' is sometimes used to describe a malevolent fairy.

BEST SITES

Cairn de Barnenez p56

Garenne des Korrigans p58

Grottes des Korrigans, Crozon p58

Ti ar C'horriged p67

Carnac p80

Chapelle des Sept-Saints p70

Doigt de Gargantua p72

Menhir de Saint-Uzec p74

Grotte des Korrigans p90 (pictured)

Saint-Michel de Brasparts p66

MAGIC

There are some magical places that don't fit neatly into any category. Rather, they are imbued with a power that radiates from the location itself, attracting or creating wonders of different kinds. With some, such as the Val Sans Retour (Valley Without Return) in the Forest of Brocéliande or the extraordinary alignments of Carnac, to simply visit them is to enter a place of enchantment.

Some are places, often marked by a menhir, where treasure is said to have been hidden by fairies or other supernatural beings. Others are said to be the gathering places of ancient Druids, witches or sorcerers, such as the mountain of La Rhune in Basque Country or the Butte de Champaillaume on the Great Pilgrimage trail. The Île de Sein, an island in the Atlantic off the coast of Finistère, was the domain of nine priestesses known as the Sènes who were skilled in magic. At other magical places, nocturnal processions of mysterious ghostly figures can be seen on significant dates.

Then there are sites where elemental forces, such as storms, can be summoned by magic. Such places often have supernatural guardians, as at the Fontaine de Barenton in the enchanted forest of Brocéliande.

There are places marked out by unearthly sounds, such as the church bells of the drowned city of Ys coming from the waters of the Baie de Douarnenez in Finistère, or the cries of the doomed lovers cast into the waters of the Gouffre de Huelgoat by the enchantress Princess Dahut, who had been schooled in magic by the nine Sènes. The wild hunt can be heard in the night skies above the Plateau des Fées close to the sanctuary of Mont Sainte-Odile in the northeast of France. By contrast, some places of magic are marked out by an unearthly silence, such as the enchanted wood, the Bois de Morphée in eastern France.

BEST SITES

Val Sans Retour p100 (pictured)

Carnac p80

Forêt de Huelgoat p59

Fontaine de Barenton p99

Douarnenez p56

Lumières p249

Bois de Morphée, Butte de Suin p174

Plateau des Fées, Mont Sainte-Odile p119

Île de Sein p61

La Rhune p220

MARY MAGDALENE

This enigmatic figure from the gospels plays a major part in France's religious and national mythology, especially in Provence and the Languedoc. According to tradition, after Jesus' crucifixion and resurrection, Mary Magdalene and others were cast adrift on the Mediterranean in a boat without sails or oars. Miraculously, they survived and came ashore at Saintes-Maries-de-la-Mer in the Camargue.

Until recently, the Catholic Church presented Mary Magdalene as a repentant sinner and reformed prostitute. Yet in the earliest traditions of Provence she was an apostle for the new religion, travelling the region to preach and even perform baptisms.

Mary Magdalene appears in the gospels among Jesus' disciples, but these accounts may not tell the full story. In early texts known as the Gnostic Gospels, which were suppressed as heretical by the early Church, Mary played a much more important role in Jesus' mission and life. There are even hints that they were in a relationship, a belief held by some of the Cathars of the Languedoc. This theory opens up all kinds of speculation, including that Mary and Jesus were married and had children who Mary Magdalene brought with her to France. Their descendants would later become the Merovingian dynasty of Frankish kings. Veneration of Mary Magdalene in the south of France has long been regarded as closer to the Gnostic texts, and it's been argued that secrets about her true significance were passed down through the centuries there.

In the Middle Ages, monks at the abbey at Vézelay in Yonne claimed they possessed Mary Magdalene's relics, which had been brought there for safe-keeping. This resulted in Vézelay becoming a major pilgrimage destination in the mid-11th century. However, what was believed to be Mary's tomb was discovered in the 13th century at Saint-Maximin-la-Sainte-Baume and her relics, including her skull which is displayed in a gold reliquary, can be seen in the basilica dedicated to her.

BEST SITES

Saintes-Maries-de-la-Mer p251

Abbaye Saint-Victor, Marseilles p253

Saint-Maximin-la-Sainte-Baume p254

Mary Magdalene's Cave p257 (pictured)

Rennes-le-Château p237

Rennes-les-Bains p242

Cave of Mary Magdalene p244

Notre-Dame-des-Anges p259

Saint-Martin-Vésubie p260

Vézelay p126

PILGRIMAGE

Pilgrimages to Christian holy places have been at the centre of French religious life since medieval times and four main trails of Europe's greatest pilgrimage, the Camino de Santiago (Way of St James) to the tomb of Santiago de Compostela in Spain, run through France. Starting from Paris, Vézelay, Le Puy-en-Velay and Arles, the trails became established in the Middle Ages and are still followed today. Guided by the iconic scallop shells that are the principal symbols of pilgrimage, today's pilgrims follow the ancient trail and stay at wayside hostels.

France also has its own pilgrimage destinations, such as the Black Madonna shrine at Rocamadour, Saint-Anne-d'Auray in Brittany and, of course, Lourdes, where the Virgin Mary's shrine is the world's most famous Catholic sanctuary. Brittany has its own tradition of local pilgrimages, known as 'pardons', as well as the *Tro Breiz* (Tour of Brittany) taking in the sites associated with the Seven Saints who, according to tradition, brought Christianity to the region.

Yet the practice of undertaking devotional journeys to sacred sites goes back much further. The Romans had their own sacred routes to temples and sanctuaries, as did the Gauls before them whose priests, the Druids, officiated at sacred centres. Worshippers in search of healing or the blessings of the gods and goddesses were drawn to these centres from far and wide. Later, many of these sites became Christian pilgrimage destinations when they were re-dedicated to saints, and so pilgrims continued to follow the old, well-trodden paths. Today, the pilgrimage route between Chartres and Mont Saint-Michel follows the western half of a very ancient trail, the Great Pilgrimage, which crossed France from east to west. Its original purpose is lost in the mists of time.

BEST SITES

PLACES OF HEALING

Since ancient times, those suffering have resorted to springs and wells that were reputed to possess healing powers. Most springs were believed to heal specific ailments, especially of the eyes. In the pagan world, people thought deities and spirits imbued the waters with healing properties and they left votive offerings to them. France has many such water sources, from simple woodland springs to monumental shrines and healing spas still exist from the Gallo-Roman era, such as the hot springs at Dax in southwest France and the baths at Aquae Segetae dedicated to Segeta, goddess of the river Loire.

Many of these sacred places were later Christianised and re-dedicated to saints so their healing powers could be claimed for the Church. Chapels and churches were built beside, and sometimes over, the sacred springs, and legends grew up of a saint miraculously causing the water to flow, often by striking the ground with his or her staff. Healing springs are found at many of the major sanctuaries, such as Mont Sainte-Odile in northeast France and Saint-Anne-d'Auray in Brittany. According to Christian tradition, miraculous water from the spring at Lourdes began to flow during the famous apparitions of the Virgin Mary in the 19th century. The holy water is still used throughout the sanctuary to heal pilgrims who come from all over the world in search of a cure.

Miracle cures were also attributed to religious statues and holy relics, especially statues of the Virgin Mary which often owed their discovery to a miraculous event. The statue of Notre-Dame du Roncier at Josselin was found in a bramble bush ('roncier'), and Notre-Dame de Marceille, Limoux, lay buried in pastureland. In Brittany there were the seven healing saints, each prayed to for the cure of a different ailment. Statues of the seven are housed in the crypt of the chapel of Notre-Dame-du-Haut in Trédaniel.

BEST SITES

Aquae Segetae p129
Fontaine Chaude, Dax p220
Notre-Dame-du-Haut p71
Notre-Dame du Roncier p79
Notre-Dame de Marceille, Limoux p234
Fontaine Saint-Guigner p84 (pictured)
Andlau bear shrine p116
Lourdes p225
Mont Saint-Odile p117
Sainte-Anne-d'Auray p85

PORTALS – ENTRANCES TO THE OTHERWORLD

People throughout the ages have recognised that another world, what we today might call a different dimension or parallel world, exists alongside our own. The Otherworld, as it is known in folklore, is the domain of spirits and magical beings such as the fairy folk. Usually the two worlds are kept apart, but there are places where the boundaries between them are thin, especially at certain times of year, such as Samhain (Halloween). At such times portals or gateways can open up, allowing the denizens of the Otherworld into ours.

Many of these portals are at megalithic sites such as dolmens and tumuli, said to be the haunt of fairies, korrigans and other magical beings. Caves are also often regarded as entrances to the Otherworld, as are enchanted lakes and deep water sources like that of the river Sourge at Fontaine-de-Vaucluse in Provence. Finistère's Baie de Douarnenez, said to be the location of the submerged city of Ys, is believed to be another such gateway. Mountains, too, can be seen as portals, such as Languedoc's Mount Bugarach.

Portals can be opened by the magic of the Otherworld's inhabitants, who can sometimes invite or abduct humans into their realm. Those who are taken there for a night and allowed to return may find that many years have passed in our world, as time flows differently in the two domains. Occasionally the doors can be left open so we can get a glimpse of the secret realm.

Christianity sees some of these gateways not as portals to a magical Otherworld, but to a demonic realm. They include the Grotte du Diable, a cave in Finistère's Huelgoat Forest and the Grand Puits (Great Well) in the city of Carcassonne.

In Arthurian legend, the king lies in the Otherworld in a kind of suspended animation, a magical timeless sleep, until he is needed again. In some versions of the tale he is carried to the mystical Otherworld island of Avalon, while in others he sleeps in an underground chasm, as at the Fosse Arthour.

BEST SITES

Douarnenez p56

Grotte des Korrigans p90

Dolmen de La Contrie p154

Mount Bugarach p233

Dolmen de la Pierre Levée p159

Fosse Arthour p142

Fontaine-de-Vaucluse p248 (pictured)

Dolmen de la Salle aux Fées p90

Grotte du Diable, Forêt de Huelgoat p59

Grand Puits, Carcassonne p233

SAINTS & MIRACLES

Stories of saints performing miracles are found throughout France, especially those from the early Christian centuries when the new religion was striving to establish itself. There are plentiful local tales of saints converting the inhabitants through miracle cures, creating healing springs and freeing the local populace from dragons, monsters or other terrors.

Brittany, with its strong Celtic heritage, has its own saints of Welsh, Irish and Cornish origins, representing the Celtic Christianity that flourished there in the early medieval era. As well as the Seven Saints who are said to have established Christianity in the region, Breton tradition also has seven healing saints who are prayed to for cures of different diseases and ailments. The most celebrated is the blind St Hervé (Herveus), the son of a Druid bard.

While most of the saints who travelled around were male, female saints also performed miracles and they often founded major convents and sanctuaries, such as Mont Sainte-Odile. Many legendary saints are martyrs, and stories of executed saints picking up their own severed heads to wash them in a nearby river or healing spring before dying are fairly common. A number of holy sites are said to have been founded by saints or hermits following direct intervention from angels who appeared to them. These include Mont Saint-Michel, where the Archangel Michael commanded St Aubert to build a chapel. Saints' relics later became the focus of pilgrimages and were themselves credited with miracles of healing or divine protection.

BEST SITES

Fontaine Saint-Corentin p57

Île de Saint-Cado p85

Dol-de-Bretagne p94

Mont Saint-Michel p145

Mont Saint-Odile p117

Crypte Saint-Dagobert p111

Espalion p210

Conques p212

Rocamadour p213 (pictured)

Chapelle Sainte-Roseline p255

WATER SPIRITS

In folklore, France's waters, both fresh and salt, are considered the realm of water spirits. Varied in nature, these spirits are usually female, with water traditionally seen as a feminine element.

For the Gauls and Romans springs, rivers, lakes and waterfalls were the domain of nymphs and water goddesses, such as Segeta who protected the river Loire, Sequana, goddess of the river Seine, or the Nehae, goddesses of rivers and springs to whom the hot springs at Dax were dedicated. At some of the water sources the guardian spirit was transformed into a Christian saint, as at Levroux in central France, where a spring once sacred to the goddess Rodene is now dedicated to St Rodène.

In Arthurian legend Vivian, the Lady of the Lake, was a water nymph. After meeting Merlin by the Fontaine de Barenton, in the enchanted Forest of Brocéliande, she used her charms to learn the secrets of his magic.

Nymphs and fairies are said to bathe in pools at Mortain in Normandy and within Finistère's magical Forêt de Huelgoat, and a nymph guards the source of the river Sourge at Fontaine-de-Vaucluse in Provence. Some water spirits are still honoured by statues such as the 19th-century sculpture of La Naïade who rises from the river at Laignes in Côte-d'Or.

In the sea are the siren-like Marie-Morganes, fairies in the form of beautiful women who haunt the rugged coasts of Brittany, luring in sailors. Dahut, the dissolute daughter of Gradlon, King of Cornouaille in Brittany, was transformed into a Marie-Morgane during the drowning of the city of Ys in Finistère's Baie de Douarnenez. The French coastline is also inhabited by mermaids, maidens with fish-like tails who are sometimes seen sitting on rocks or frolicking in the waters. Carved mermaids (and mermen) are a common motif in France's medieval churches, especially along the Apollo-Athena alignment.

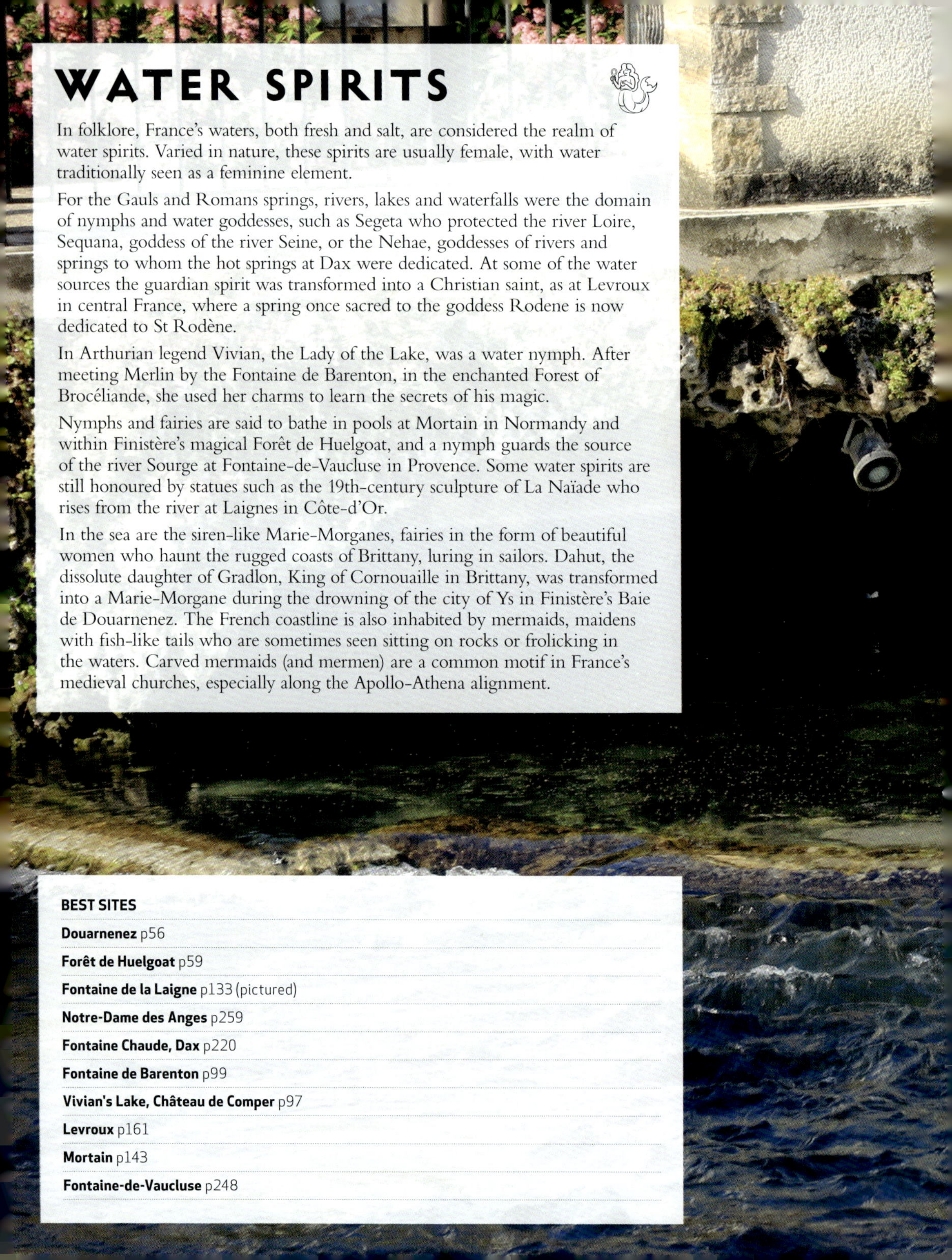

BEST SITES

Douarnenez p56

Forêt de Huelgoat p59

Fontaine de la Laigne p133 (pictured)

Notre-Dame des Anges p259

Fontaine Chaude, Dax p220

Fontaine de Barenton p99

Vivian's Lake, Château de Comper p97

Levroux p161

Mortain p143

Fontaine-de-Vaucluse p248

WISHES & DIVINATION

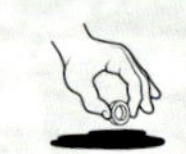

Sacred wells and springs have long been seen as places where wishes could be granted and questions about an individual's future answered. An old custom was to throw votive objects into the waters to seek good fortune from the presiding spirit or deity.

Marriage and fertility were prime concerns, and many local rituals were enacted by young women who were in search of a husband, or to aid conception. At the Chapelle-Sainte-Geneviève in Normandy's Andaine Forest, they would write their name on the wall, while at Locmariaquer near Carnac the May Day custom was for women to slide down one side of the fallen standing stone, the Grand Menhir Brisé d'Er Grah.

For those who wanted to know whether they would be married within the next year, a common ritual was to throw a pin into a sacred spring and see if it floated: if it did the answer was a yes. This was the practice at the Fontaine Miraculeuse in the sanctuary of Sainte-Anne-d'Auray in Brittany and the Fontaine de la Vierge in Finistère's Huelgoat Forest. A similar divinatory ritual took place at the Fontaine de Barenton in the Forest of Brocéliande, where the waters would bubble if the answer was affirmative. To ensure fertility, married women would rub themselves against menhirs or touch a specific part of the stones.

People still leave their written wishes at magical places such as the Tombeau de Merlin in Brittany's Brocéliande. In other places the granting of a wish entails performing a feat, such as throwing a stone onto the top of Carnac's tallest menhir, the 6.5m high Géant du Manio.

Good health was another big concern, with customs either to ensure a trouble-free year or to be forewarned of coming illness. The townsfolk of Locronan would throw a piece of buttered bread for each member of their family into the water of a holy spring dedicated to St Eutropius; if it floated they would remain healthy for the next year.

BEST SITES

Chapelle Saint-Geneviève 140

Locmariaquer p87

Fontaine de Barenton p99

Tombeau de Merlin p100

Carnac p80

Sainte-Anne d'Auray p85

Menhir de Saint-Uzec p74

Fôret de Huelgoat p59

Locronan p62

Pierre de la Fée p259 (pictured)

5

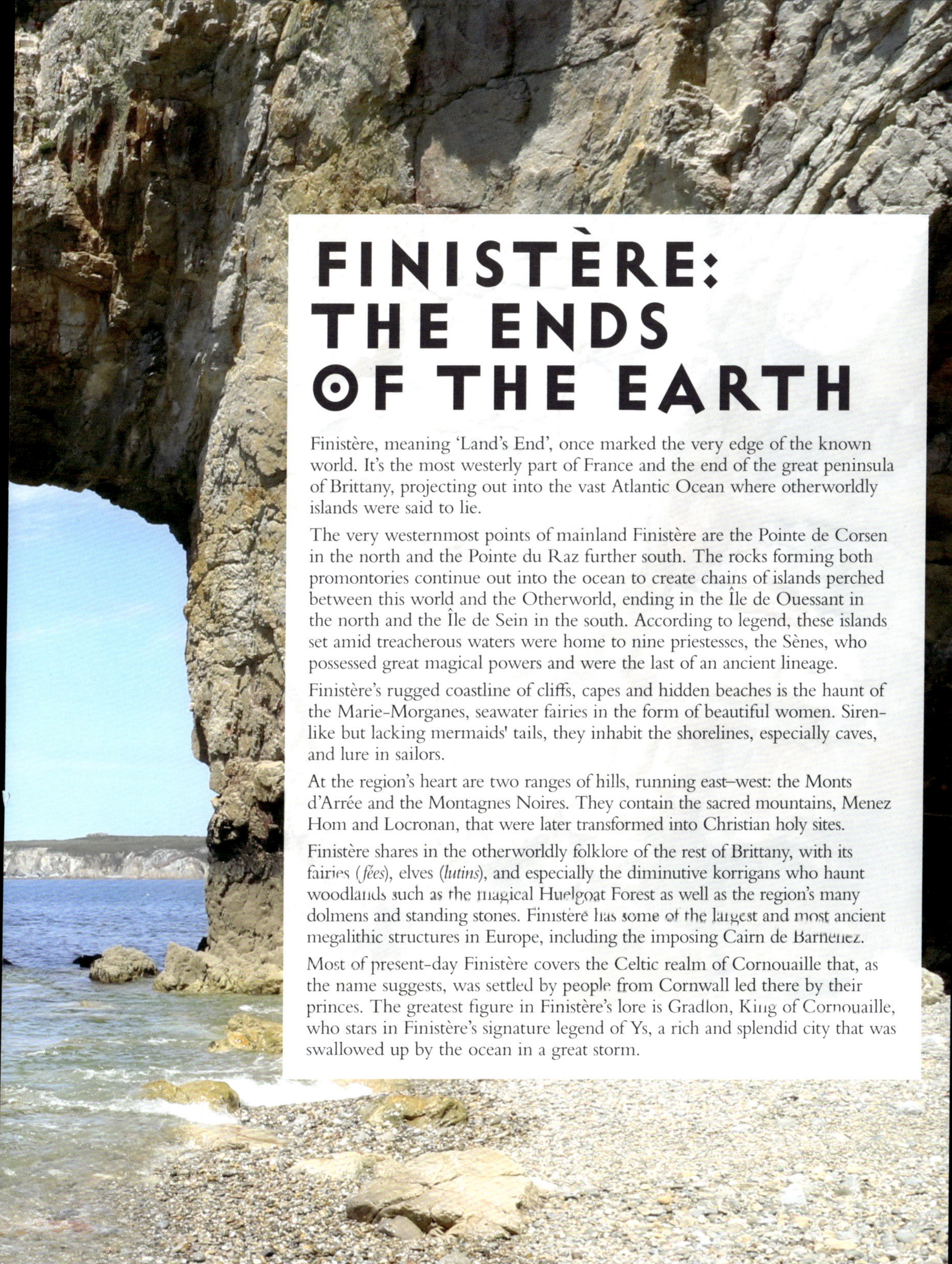

FINISTÈRE: THE ENDS OF THE EARTH

Finistère, meaning 'Land's End', once marked the very edge of the known world. It's the most westerly part of France and the end of the great peninsula of Brittany, projecting out into the vast Atlantic Ocean where otherworldly islands were said to lie.

The very westernmost points of mainland Finistère are the Pointe de Corsen in the north and the Pointe du Raz further south. The rocks forming both promontories continue out into the ocean to create chains of islands perched between this world and the Otherworld, ending in the Île de Ouessant in the north and the Île de Sein in the south. According to legend, these islands set amid treacherous waters were home to nine priestesses, the Sènes, who possessed great magical powers and were the last of an ancient lineage.

Finistère's rugged coastline of cliffs, capes and hidden beaches is the haunt of the Marie-Morganes, seawater fairies in the form of beautiful women. Siren-like but lacking mermaids' tails, they inhabit the shorelines, especially caves, and lure in sailors.

At the region's heart are two ranges of hills, running east–west: the Monts d'Arrée and the Montagnes Noires. They contain the sacred mountains, Menez Hom and Locronan, that were later transformed into Christian holy sites.

Finistère shares in the otherworldly folklore of the rest of Brittany, with its fairies (*fées*), elves (*lutins*), and especially the diminutive korrigans who haunt woodlands such as the magical Huelgoat Forest as well as the region's many dolmens and standing stones. Finistère has some of the largest and most ancient megalithic structures in Europe, including the imposing Cairn de Barnenez.

Most of present-day Finistère covers the Celtic realm of Cornouaille that, as the name suggests, was settled by people from Cornwall led there by their princes. The greatest figure in Finistère's lore is Gradlon, King of Cornouaille, who stars in Finistère's signature legend of Ys, a rich and splendid city that was swallowed up by the ocean in a great storm.

1 Douarnenez

The legendary lost city of Ys was said to have been submerged beneath the waters of the **Baie de Douarnenez**, a name thought to derive from the Breton for 'new land' because the town was founded by survivors of the cataclysm. Locals tell of church bells heard ringing beneath crashing waves during storms, and even of its buildings being glimpsed by sailors and divers, while others consider Ys to be a gateway to an otherworldly realm.

Ys, or in Breton *Ker Is* and meaning 'City Below', was Gradlon's magnificent and wealthy city, founded after the king led an expedition north in search of new lands and encountered the otherworldly Queen of the North, Malgven. Gradlon and Malgven fell passionately in love and she joined his quest, abandoning her husband and her land. She brought with her the magical stallion *Morvarc'h* (Horse of the Sea) that could ride on the crests of waves. Eventually they returned to Brittany, where Gradlon constructed Ys from white stone. However, Malgven was angered when Gradlon was converted to Christianity by Saint Guénolé (St Winwaloe) and vowed to make the king regret his choice. She later died giving birth to their daughter Dahut, who shared her mother's otherworldly heritage, and in some versions was possessed by Malgven's spirit. After Dahut's instruction by the priestesses of the **Île de Sein**, she acquired the power to control the weather and the animals of the forest, as well as shapeshift into animal form. The city of Ys was at that time protected by a great floodgate that was locked during high tides and the key kept by Gradlon. Dahut, possessed by Malgven's spirit, stole it and opened the gate during a great storm but Gradlon escaped by riding the waves on Morvarc'h, taking Dahut with him. When chief minister St Corentin revealed her treachery, Gradlon threw her from the horse as they crossed the **Baie des Trépassés** (Bay of the Departed). Transformed into one of the siren-like Marie-Morganes, Dahut continues to haunt the Baie de Douarnenez.

The legend of a land lost beneath the sea recurs in Celtic folklore and includes the *Cantre'r Gwaelod* (Lowland Hundred) under Cardigan Bay in Wales, and the lost land of Lyonesse off Land's End in Cornwall.

At least part of the Baie de Douarnenez was above water in ancient times. In the 19th century the remains of a dolmen were revealed during an exceptionally low tide near the **Île Tristan** (48.1017, -4.3375), an island connected to the town of **Douarnenez** at low tide and said to be the only part of Ys that survived the cataclysm. With links to another famous Celtic myth, the island was considered the burial place of the lovers Tristan and Iseult of the tales of King Arthur. Their tomb was hidden on the island as protection from the wrath of King Marc'h, Iseult's vengeful husband, and two trees grew from it, their branches intertwining. The Île Tristan is now a protected conservation site that's only open to the public on certain days.

Parking: 48.0964, -4.3351

2 Cairn de Barnenez, Plouezoc'h

The ancient stones of this unique monument, overlooking the waters of the Baie de Morlaix on Finistère's northern coast, conjure up an almost unimaginably distant age. The Cairn de Barnenez (*Kerdi Bras*, Great Cairn in Breton) is one of the oldest structures in Europe and dates from at least 4,700 BC – more than 2,000 years before Egypt's Great Pyramid. Its antiquity makes the immense scale of this 'megalithic parthenon' all the more awe-inspiring: among Europe's Neolithic monuments, only Newgrange in Ireland is bigger.

Originally almost 100m long, 35m wide and 8m high, the Cairn is built of dry stones, 4,000 tonnes in all, including granite that was brought from over a kilometre away. Constructed in a series of steps, it contains 11 chambers with vaulted roofs, each reached by a separate passage. Two have symbols etched into the stone (one thought to represent the Mother Goddess) as well as stylised ox horns and waves. There are also traces of paintings in red and black pigment that originally adorned the chambers, but what they depicted is now impossible to tell. The passages are aligned to the rising and setting of the sun at significant points in the year. The landscape around the Cairn has changed dramatically over the millennia: once it overlooked a grassy plain.

The Cairn was thought to be a tumulus, known locally as the 'House of Korrigans', with associated tales of fairy treasure buried within. However, when a local builder started to dig out stones to use as construction material, the true wonder of the Cairn was revealed and it was soon classified as a national monument and restored.

While the Cairn was clearly sacred to the Neolithic peoples who designed it and devoted so much labour to its construction, its exact function and meaning are lost. Like other cairns, it was probably considered a dwelling place of spirits and ancestors, and a gateway to the afterlife.

48.6675, -3.8586; open to the public all year (closed Mondays October-March), €

3 **Fontaine Saint-Corentin, Plomodiern**

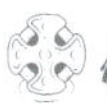 

In a serene glade surrounded by trees, this spring dedicated to St Corentin, whose statue is housed within its stone shelter, has a very curious and unique legend attached. It's by a small chapel dedicated to the hermit saint, one of the Seven Saints credited with establishing Christianity in Brittany in the 4th or 5th century. St Corentin built his hermitage near the mountain of **Menez Hom,** which lies 4km northwest of the chapel and was sacred to the Celts.

St Corentin plays an important part in the Breton folklore of King Gradlon. According to legend, in the spring swam a miraculous fish that sustained the saint in his remote retreat: every day Corentin ate a part of the fish but overnight it would be restored to wholeness. One day King Gradlon, out hunting in the forest around Menez Hom, became lost and, weak with hunger, came across the hermitage. After being fed with

1

2

2

3

some of the fish and witnessing the miracle, the king was convinced Corentin was a truly holy man and made him the first Bishop of his capital of Quimper. He also appointed Corentin as his chief minister, and in that role Corentin plays a part in the legend of the city of Ys (see **Douarnenez**). The chapel was built at the end of the 19th century on the site of the ancient hermitage. It's now the site of a pardon, a form of pilgrimage and a signature of Breton culture, which is held on the third Sunday in July.

48.1896, -4.2106

4 Garenne des Korrigans, Plobannalec-Lesconil

Surrounded by forest is the Mégalithe Quélarn, the remains of a complex known as the Korrigan's Warren. It contains a 5,000-year-old cairn with six chambers reached through low passages and a 2.5m high menhir. Local people believe the cairn to be the home of the diminutive korrigans, who come out at night to dance around the standing stone.

Nearby is the Dolmen de Tronval (47.8129, -4.2488) which lies 300m southeast of the complex. There are many other megalithic sites in the area including the 4m high Menhir de Reun (47.958, -4.2454) by a farm track south of Plogastel-Saint-Germain. It is set into a granite platform which displays a number of cup marks – enigmatic symbols found at megalithic sites across Europe. The Menhir de Léhan (47.7919, -4.2655) has its base in Loc'h Vihan, separated from the sea by a narrow band of sand dunes. It's 4m high, with another 4m below the water and earth, hence the local name of 'les pieds dans l'eau' (feet in the water).

47.8142, -4.2525, Parking: 47.8137, -4.2511, 120m

5 Grottes des Korrigans, Crozon

These large and dramatic rock arches in a sandy cove on the southern shore of the larger Anse de Dinan were home to friendly korrigans who once rid the local area of a band of marauding giants. The giants lived on a headland that was known in folklore as the **Château de Dinan** (48.2333, -4.5667). Legend tells how the giants lit fires to lure ships onto the rocks so they could plunder the cargoes and feed on the bodies of shipwrecked sailors. The local korrigans came to the rescue by putting wet seaweed on the fires, filling the air with smoke. When the giants took shelter in the caves beneath the castle, the korrigans sealed them in by throwing huge boulders down from the cliffs. The grateful people of the Crozon Peninsula have respected the local korrigans ever since.

The headland is connected to the mainland by a ridge of rock that the adventurous can walk across to explore the 'castle' and admire the stunning views across the bay. Beneath the ridge is an immense circular arch, 12m high, where the waves come crashing through at high tide but which can be explored from the shore at low tide. Some call this arch the **Percée des Korrigans** (Korrigans' Breach, 48.2349, -4.5709), and the korrigans themselves lived in the caves that dot the headland.

5

The headland also features two huge arches: the first is wide and low, like a rounded letterbox. Stepping through it at low tide is like entering another world as the small hidden bay beyond is revealed. The second arch is more circular and leads deep into the hidden world beyond. Make sure you leave enough time to make it back before the tide comes in!

48.2361, -4.5667, low tide only; Parking: 48.2334, -4.5637, 400m

6 Forêt d'Huelgoat, Huelgoat

Walking through this lush forest in the river valley of the Argent is an unforgettable and otherworldly experience, dominated as it is by hundreds of colossal boulders. Some are the size of houses and look like they've been thrown together haphazardly, piled on top of each other in angular shapes to form caves and passageways. French geologists call these rock formations a 'chaos' but tradition considered them the work of giants or even the remains of an ancient city they once inhabited. The **Huelgoat Forest** is also said to be haunted by fairies and other ethereal beings, whose domain lies beneath the rocks.

The Argent runs through it, sometimes over, sometimes under the rocks, forming pools, waterfalls and cataracts that add to the sense of being in a world conjured from myth. The river gets its name from the nearby silver mines that have been there since at least Roman times. In the 1500s, the river was dammed to form the Lac d'Huelgoat, which supplied water to the mines. The town of Huelgoat now surrounds the lake.

There are several trails through the forest and along the river that take in the most remarkable sites, all well marked.

A 1km trail begins in Huelgoat beside the **Moulin du Chaos** (48.3654, -3.7467), a watermill built nearly 700 years ago, then immediately descends into the chaos of massive moss-covered boulders behind the mill. There, the river plunges beneath the **Grotte du Diable** (48.3659, -3.7461), a cave formed beneath a great heap of gigantic rounded boulders. Several legends are attached to the cave. According to one, it is the entrance to a succession of subterranean inns where 99 alluring serving girls entice their customers deeper and deeper until they are taken by the Devil ('diable'). In the 18th century, Marion de Faouët, leader of a band of 40 highwaymen and now a local folk heroine, hid her loot there.

Further into the forest of oak, beech and pine trees is a jumble of even more massive

Menhir de Reun

4

Grotte d'Artus

6

Mare aux Fees

6

Roche Tremblante de Huelgoat

rocks known as the **Ménage de la Vierge** (48.3666, -3.7442), named because of their resemblance to household (ménage) items such as a ladle and cauldron. Among the rocks is the Fontaine de la Vierge , a rock basin that, although above the river and protected from rain by an overhang, is always filled with water. According to local custom, throwing coins into the water or floating a pin on the surface will reveal answers to questions about the person's future.

The most famous of the forest's sites is the **Roche Tremblante de Huelgoat** (Shaking Rock, 48.3673, -3.7453), reached either by walking further along the trail from the Ménage de la Vierge or by road (parking 48.3677, -3.7449, 90m). This massive rock, lying on its side at the top of an incline, weighs 140 tonnes and is 7m long by 3m high. Apply a slow but strong rhythmical pressure to one corner of the stone by pushing your back into the rock and pressing upwards, and you'll feel it rock back and forth. It's said that this strange phenomenon is due to the fairies of the forest who enchanted the stone after local townsfolk prevented workmen from breaking it up for building material.

A second trail (48.3664, -3.7349) lies further from the town and covers just over 2km. This leads first to the **Grotte d'Artus** (48.3688, -3.7360, 300m), a shelter formed by massive rocks and a particularly impressive sight. King Arthur (Artus) is said to sleep there along with his knights, awakening when there is a threat to his kingdom. There are also tales of a treasure guarded by will-o'-the-wisp-like elemental beings. According to some the treasure belongs to Merlin, though others say that Merlin's treasure is located under Arthur's Camp further along the trail.

Following the trail another 200m leads to the Mare aux Sangliers (Wild Boars' Pond, 48.3707, -3.7368), its shallow water tinted brown by iron from nearby mines. Another 500m brings you to the **Camp d'Artus** (48.3732, -3.7428) – a Celtic fortified town or *oppidum* on a high point covering 30 hectares and one of the largest known of such sites. The entrance is through a passageway between enormous natural stone blocks.

The third trail, starting at steps down to the Argent, is the most magical and dramatic of all. This takes in the **Gouffre de Huelgoat** (48.3643, -3.7301; Parking 48.3652, -3.7315, 100m) where the river has formed a very narrow chasm (gouffre) and plunges down in a waterfall, its water foaming as it hits the bottom. Folklore associates the chasm with Princess Dahut, daughter of Gradlon, King of Ys (see **Douarnenez**). The **Île de Sein** priestesses (see next entry) had warned her to steer clear of

Baie des Trépassés

7

love as it would bring her misfortune so Dahut pursued her pleasures in secret and in a more debauched way in Kastell Gibel (Chasm Castle). The ruins of this medieval castle, thought to be on the site of an older Celtic oppidum, sit above the waterfall. Here, Dahut used her charms and magic to seduce her conquests, and once satisfied threw her discarded lovers into the chasm. Their cries could be heard coming up from the depths and to this day the sound of the rushing water covers their wailing. Locals call it 'l'eau qui murmure', 'the water that murmurs'. Now a Marie-Morgane (mermaid), Dahut still swims through an underwater tunnel linking the Gouffre to the sea and tries to drown out her lovers' voices with her singing, particularly at the full moon when, siren-like, she tries to lure men down.

Another 120m downstream from the Gouffre is a place of calmer water with a very different atmosphere – tranquil and light. The **Mare aux Fées** (48.3632, -3.7298) is a pond surrounded by trees and with mossy boulders where locals say fairies sit on moonlit nights to comb their long golden hair.

The three trails can be combined into one walk of around 6km starting at the Moulin du Chaos, taking in more of the enchanted forest with its weird and wonderful rock formations.

Parking: 48.3648, -3.7467, 50m from trail

7 Île de Sein

    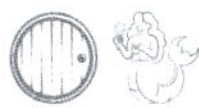

Looking out towards the vast ocean beyond, the Île de Sein feels like a stepping stone to the Otherworld. It's a place of contrasts: in summer vibrant, and renowned for its wonderful light, but in winter windswept and bleak, set amid crashing waves and strong currents that surge around the rocks and reefs. The island is small and serpentine in shape, just 3km long and from 500m to just 30m wide. It's also very flat and treeless. Geologically, it is a continuation of the **Pointe du Raz** (48.0403, -4.7411) 7km away on the mainland and visible on the horizon but separated by the Raz de Sein: *raz* signifying a strong current. The underwater rocks between the Pointe and the Isle make it a notoriously treacherous stretch of water and the scene of many shipwrecks.

Like Finisterra in Spain and Land's End in Cornwall, the Île de Sein is at the end of a sacred promontory that reaches out to otherworldly islands in the western ocean – the place where the sun goes to rest at the end of each day. The Isle was considered the jumping-off point to the afterlife for departing souls, who gathered in the mainland cove just north of the Pointe known as the **Baie des Trépassés** (48.0481, -4.7147). The Isle itself was a sacred site and place of oracle to the Celts, served by nine priestesses called the Sènes. They are first mentioned in texts from about 120 BC and also by the Roman geographer Pomponius Mela who wrote in the middle of the 1st century AD that the priestesses, whom he called Gallizenae, were sworn to perpetual virginity. They could prophesy, conjure the dead and had power over the wind and waves, calming or unleashing storms and tides as they wished. They could also shapeshift into animal forms and taught the secrets of their magic to Dahut, daughter of King Gradlon, (see **Douarnenez**). In the 1790s the Isle was described as 'a place of the fairies, nymphs and dryads', and the seas around it the haunt of Marie-Morganes, the siren-like water fairies that are a feature of Brittany's lore.

The priestesses are also part of an ancient cult of nine priestesses, often sisters, that can be found all over Europe. Elsewhere in Brittany, similar tales are told of the Isle of Ushant (Île de Ouessant, 48.4615, -5.0889) and nine witches were also said to live on **Mont-Dol**. In Dordogne there are tales of the Nine Sorceresses of Larzac (44.7483, 1.0086).

This theme is found particularly in British folklore. In Wales there are the Nine Maidens of Annwn, in England the Nine Sorceresses of Caer Loyw (Gloucester), and

Chapelle Notre-Dame-de-Bonne-Nouvelle

8

in Ireland the Nine Maidens of Donegal. They appear in Arthurian legend too: the Island of Avalon was said to be ruled by nine wise sisters who were healers and shapeshifters like the priestesses of the Île de Sein.

8

Their leader Morgen brought the dying Arthur to Avalon, the Otherworld; in later tales she became the enchantress Morgan le Fay. Several stone circles in Britain are named the Nine Maidens or Nine Stones. These may also be associated with the nine priestesses and are sometimes said to be women who were turned to stone while dancing. Many wells in Britain, particularly Scotland, are dedicated to the Nine Maidens. All these instances suggest that the cult of the nine priestesses is very ancient – and that the priestesses of the Île de Sein may have been some of its last representatives.

Near the centre of the island are two large menhirs known as **Les Causeurs** (The Talkers, 48.0380, -4.8512) as they appear to have their heads together in conversation. Local lore credits them with being able to cure fevers.

At the far western end, near the lighthouse, is the **Chapelle Saint-Corentin** (48.0419, -4.8675), named after the Breton saint who is part of the legend of King Gradlon of Ys (see **Fontaine Saint-Corentin**). Built in the 5th century, although restored in the 20th, the enclosure outside the chapel has a sacred spring beside a menhir, with several smaller upright stones.

The Île de Sein can only be reached by boat, with day trips from the port of Sainte-Evette (48.0060, -4.5571, €€€€€, one hour each way, no cars allowed).

48.0359, -4.8541

8 Locronan

The town of Locronan is famed for the Grande Troménie ('great tour of the sanctuary') held every six years on the second Sunday in July, which attracts people from all over Brittany. The procession starts and ends at the imposing **Église Saint-Ronan** (48.0983, -4.2081), its size reflecting just how important the saint is to the town, which is named after him. Locronan means 'Place of Ronan'.

Irish-born Ronan was raised a pagan in the 4th century. He came to live in Brittany, where the apparition of an angel converted him to Christianity and he withdrew into solitude as a sign of repentance for his old beliefs. He built his hermitage in what is now Locronan, on the site of Chapelle du Pénity (Penitence, 48.0982, -4.2081), which contains the saint's tomb and is adjacent to St Ronan's Church. Ronan became known for his wisdom and cures, including bringing a child back from the dead. As his fame grew, Ronan moved around Brittany, settling in several places. When he died in Laurenan, 125km directly east of Locronan, many places claimed the right to house his relics, which were considered miraculous. To settle the matter, his body was placed on a cart drawn by two oxen which headed for the setting sun, eventually stopping at Ronan's original hermitage in Locronan so his body was buried there. Ronan became one of the most revered saints of Brittany and the Chapelle de Pénity a famous place of pilgrimage.

Ronan's hermitage, and the town that grew up around it, was once at the centre of a vast sacred site of the Druids, a *nemeton*. This open high space that included sacred groves was the arena for their rituals and for making observations of the stars. The nemeton had a perimeter of around 12km, oriented to the sunrise at the solstices and equinoxes, and originally had 12 standing stones placed around it representing the months of the Celtic calendar. These have now been replaced by stone crosses and calvaries, but the memory of the sacred space survives in the Grand Troménie when the Saint's relics are paraded around the perimeter, visiting each of the 12 crosses where there's a short service and a hymn is sung. In the years in between Grand Troménies there is a shorter troménie of 6km. The belief is that St Ronan, to demonstrate his repentance, made the shorter circuit of the land around his hermitage every day, and the longer one every Sunday. The troménie is also known as the 'pardon of the mountain', one of the five major annual mass pilgrimages unique to Brittany.

There are more signs of Locronan's pagan past in the area around the **Chapelle ar Sonj** (Chapel of Remembrance, 48.0991, -4.1816) near the summit of the Montagne de Locronan (48.0975, -4.1828), which at 285m is one of the highest points in Brittany's Montagnes Noires. From both the peak and the town there's a sweeping view to the Baie de **Douarnenez** 6km to the west. A stop on the Grande Troménie, the chapel is on an area of land known as the Plaç-ar-C'horn (Place of the Horn) where one of the oxen pulling the cart bearing St Ronan's body lost its horn. The current chapel was built in 1977, replacing an earlier one that was on the summit itself.

A couple of significant finds were made close by: a stone statue of a goddess, usually described as Venus, and a bronze plaque engraved with a figure of the god Pan, bearing a basket full of fruit and surrounded by fauns and satyrs – the sign of an earlier fertility cult.

The final stop on the Grande Troménie features what may be one of the nemeton's original menhirs, the recumbent **Chaise de Saint-Ronan** (St Ronan's Seat, 48.0908, -4.2067), 13m long and 1.5m high. According to local legend, the saint sat here to contemplate the Baie de Douarnenez and it is also referred to as the 'Barque de St Ronan' – the boat that brought him from Ireland.

A memory of the fertility aspect of Druid religion also persisted here because Locronan women who had trouble conceiving would lay on it to aid pregnancy. The stone is on private land, to which the owner gives special access during the Grande Troménie.

Behind the 15th century **Chapelle Notre-Dame-de-Bonne-Nouvelle** (Our Lady of Good News, 48.1003, -4.2100), 250m from St Ronan's Church, is a spring where water flows into an ornate stone basin. It is dedicated to St Eutropius of Saintes who is said to have travelled from Persia to become a disciple of Jesus. In some versions of Provençal lore concerning Mary Magdalene, Eutropius was on the ship that brought her ashore at **Saintes-Maries-de-la-Mer** in Provençe. During the Grande Troménie, St Ronan's relics are washed in the spring to recharge its power as holy water. In a local custom performed annually, the townsfolk throw a piece of buttered bread into the basin for each member of their family: if it floats that person will remain healthy in the coming year, but if it sinks it's a sign they will suffer illness.

Parking: 48.0995, -4.2056

9 Menez Hom, Plomodiern

One of the modern Druid Orders still holds an ancient midsummer festival on Menez Hom, one of the sacred mountains of Brittany. From the summit there are wonderful views of the whole of the Baie de **Douarnenez**. It's particularly stunning at sunset when the sun is reflected in the waters of the bay.

Old records refer to many megaliths on the mountain but sadly most have disappeared. However a cairn with a pyramid of stones is said to mark the grave of the legendary King Marc'h (Mark) of Cornwall from Celtic and Arthurian lore, part of the shared mythology of Brittany and Britain. He features in the legend of Tristan and Iseult, as the uncle of Tristan. In a Breton version of this legend, Marc'h had the ears of a horse, the result of a spell cast by Princess Dahut (see **Douarnenez**) who he hunted when she'd taken the form of a deer.

Pilgrims going to the pardon at **Saint-Anne-la-Palud** on the last Sunday in August traditionally camp on Menez Hom the night before to welcome the sunrise.

48.2203, -4.2339; Parking: 48.2185, -4.2363 150m to summit.

11

10 Plozévet

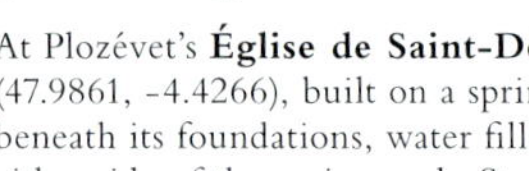

At Plozévet's **Église de Saint-Démet** (47.9861, -4.4266), built on a spring that lies beneath its foundations, water fills wells on either side of the main porch. Stone steps lead down to each of the wells, making for a very unusual entrance to a place of worship. The church is dedicated to a Welsh saint who came to Brittany in the 5th or 6th centuries. Like many churches in the region, St Démet's was built on a site that was sacred to the Celts.

Opposite the rear of the church, on the corner of the Rue du 11 Novembre 1918 and the Rue des Figuiers, is the **Fontaine Saint-Théleau** (47.9866, -4.4262), its healing waters known especially as a cure for fevers. Its stone housing features a carving of St Telio, another legendary Welsh holy man who some believe to be a Christianisation of the Celtic god Cernunnos.

There's another holy spring 4km from Plozévet at the **Chapelle de Saint-Ronan** (47.9894, -4.3728). It, too, was built on a pagan sacred site, with rounded stones thought to be from the ancient sanctuary set by the chapel's entrance. The chapel lies in a tranquil woodland glade, with bushes bursting with colourful flowers around its walls. The spring is in a small stone shrine 150m behind the chapel. Local people seeking a cure for ailments make a pilgrimage to the site three Sundays in a row.

In the grounds outside the chapel is an empty stone sarcophagus. It's said that St Ronan, in his original hermitage at **Locronan**, was wearied by the number of people who flocked to him for help and advice and so threw a stone, vowing to move to wherever it fell. It landed on this spot 20 km away and he built a new hermitage there. The people of Plozéven claim that after his death, the saint's body was first brought back here and only taken to Locronan later, which is why the sarcophagus lies empty.

Parking: 47.9858, -4.4264, 50m

Église de Saint-Démet spring

10

Fontaine de Sainte-Anne

11 Sabot de Gargantua, Pont-Aven

On the east bank of the river Aven, this enormous smooth boulder looks like a giant shoe or sabot (clog) that has been discarded in the river. Named after Gargantua, the infamous giant with an enormous appetite, it's situated near the bank, 60m from the bridge that gives the town of Pont-Aven its name. It's best viewed when the water level is low.

Another site associated with giants, 700m further along the road, is the **Tombeaux des Géants** (Giants' Tombs, 47.8472, -3.7440), an outcrop of rock shaped into three horizontal slabs, two with shallow basins and raised humps at one end. Named for their resemblance to graves with headstones, the slabs appear to be megalithic but their purpose is a mystery.

Among the many other megalithic monuments in the vicinity of Pont-Aven, the **Grand Menhir de Kerangosker** (47.8462, -3.7628) stands out because of its size – a massive 5m tall. A cross was engraved on its eastern side in an attempt to Christianise it. Find it beside the road about 2km southeast from Pont-Aven.

47.8527, -3.7473

12 Sainte-Anne-la-Palud, Plonévez-Porzay

The majestic chapel of St Anne of the Marsh with its healing spring stands on reclaimed marshland. The site has a long history reaching back into the pagan past and is thought to have originally been sacred to the Celtic mother goddess Ana. With the coming of Christianity to Brittany, she was transformed into St Anna, and eventually St.Anne. According to tradition, Anne was the mother of the Virgin Mary. The legend grew that Anne later settled in Brittany, coming ashore at this spot, and this chapel dedicated to her features images that show her teaching her daughter Mary. The most venerated is a statue dating from the 1500s, which is carried in procession to the nearby coast during the Grand Pardon held on the last Sunday in August. Known as the 'pardon of the sea', it attracts people from all over Brittany. Although the religion has changed, the site continues to be devoted to the sacred feminine.

Today's chapel was built in the 1860s and is the fourth in a succession that goes back

13

over 1500 years. Because of the changing coastline, not all were on the same spot. The first was built on the site sacred to Ana by the Welsh Saint Guénolé (St Winwaloe) around the year 500, but it was swallowed up by the sand and sea over the centuries. The **Fontaine de Saint-Anne** (48.1348, -4.2622) is 100m south of the chapel and set in a stone enclosure with a statue of Anne and the young Mary. Fishermen found the statue of St Anne in their nets and tried to take it to their village, but when they reached this spot it suddenly became too heavy to carry. When they put it down, the spring burst forth. The healing water is said to cure all ailments but is especially good for rheumatism – although a sign now warns that it's not for drinking.

A bank of grass-covered sand dunes separates the chapel from the wide and sweeping Plage de Saint-Anne, popular with swimmers and sunbathers, that covers nearly 3km of the eastern shore of **Douarnenez** Bay.

48.1358, -4.2625

13

13 Saint-Michel de Brasparts, Saint-Rivoal

Perched on the highest point of the domed hill of Mont Saint-Michel de Brasparts, which provides 360-degree views over northern Finistère, is the Chapelle Saint-Michel. The Mount is steeped in local lore: korrigans are said to dance at night on its moorlands, and there are tales of a spectral black dog with glowing red eyes. This supernatural creature is common in British folklore, but not French, so is unique to Brittany.

At just over 380m, Mont Saint-Michel de Brasparts is one of the highest of the Monts d'Arrée that run roughly east-west across the heart of Finistère. It's named after the Archangel Michael and, like many high places dedicated to him, the mount has a sacred pagan past and was the site of a Celtic temple to the sun god Belenus. Modern-day Druid orders still hold ceremonies on the summit. The Mount became a place of pilgrimage from early Christian times, with miracle cures credited to St Michael, but it wasn't until the 1670s that a chapel was first built there. It's said that Michael himself appeared to help the workers carry the stones on the long climb to the top. The Pope authorised privileges for all those who made the pilgrimage to the new chapel, a measure of its past importance. Today the interior is undecorated and the furnishings very sparse. Visitors often leave offerings of shells and pebbles, as well as candles, on the simple altar.

According to local belief, when priests exorcise demons or spirits in the vicinity they

14

become imprisoned within an invisible circle on the side of the mountain. Much folklore centres on the **Yeun Elez Marsh** (48.3539, -3.9211), a bowl-shaped depression below the mountain's eastern side that's now partly covered by the Reservoir de Saint-Michel. The marshland has a sinister reputation, with the appearance of the lights of the *feu follets* (will-o'-the-wisps) and sightings of the Dame Blanche (White Lady) whose banshee-like screams can be heard at night. Ankou, the reaper of the dead in Breton lore, is also said to haunt the area and the mountain is even believed by some to be a portal to his realm. The road to the mount from Saint-Rivoal passes by a standing stone, the Menhir de Roquinarc'h (48.3550, -3.9675), also known as the Rocher du Diable (Devil's Rock). It's in a field 1.5km from the chapel.

48.3502, -3.9456; Parking: 48.3501, -3.9470, 150m

14 Ti ar C'horriged / House of Korrigans, Douarnenez

As the name reveals, this 13m long megalithic passage grave is identified with the mischievous korrigans who dwelt within, its flat slabs serving as tables in a game resembling shove ha'penny. The small stones they used as counters litter the woods and fields nearby. It lies amid a small woodland and consists of 18 giant, scale-like slabs that lean together in a way that's been likened to a house of cards, forming a single long tunnel. Also known as the Allée Couverte de Lesconil, its outlines are marked by a second row of 27 stones.

48.0919, -4.3794; Parking: 48.0913, -4.3798, 70m

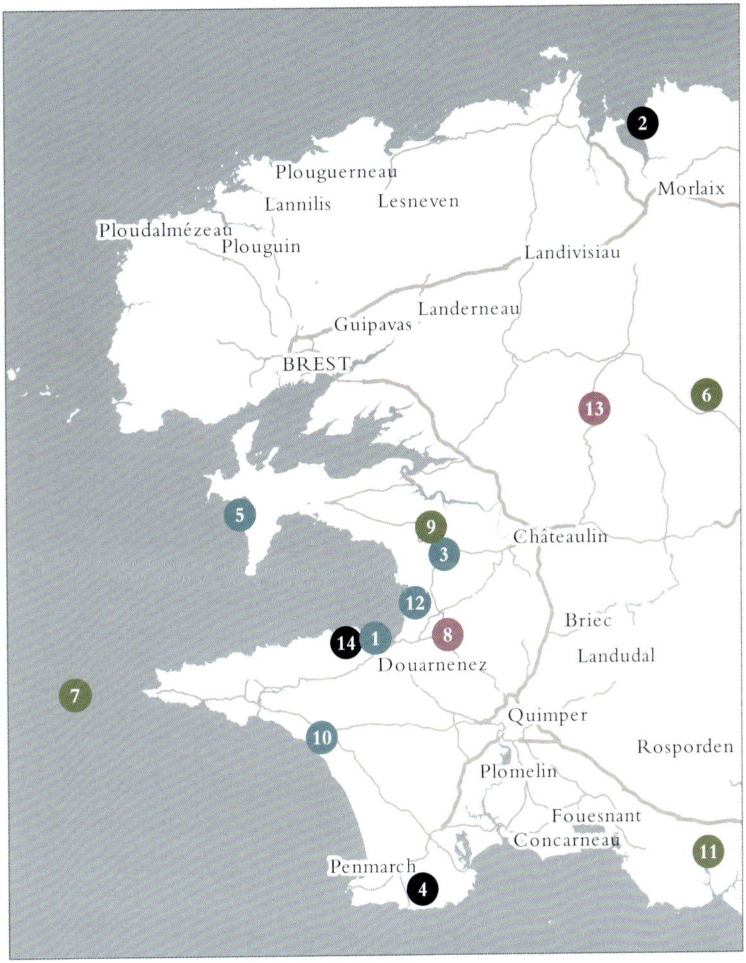

Plouguerneau
Lannilis
Lesneven
Morlaix
Ploudalmézeau
Plouguin
Landivisiau
Landerneau
Guipavas
BREST
Châteaulin
Briec
Landudal
Douarnenez
Quimper
Rosporden
Plomelin
Fouesnant
Concarneau
Penmarch

CÔTES-D'ARMOR AND THE MARGOT LA FÉE

A département of northern Brittany, the Côtes-d'Armor (*ar mor* is 'the sea' in Breton) is known for its spectacular cliffs, headlands and hidden bays, with small islands offshore and some idyllic beaches. East of rugged Cap Fréhel is the Côte d'Émeraude named for the emerald colour of the sea. Inland, the landscape is gently rolling, with some high points such as the sacred hill of Menez Bré.

The region's traditions and folklore are rooted in its Celtic past, which is shared not just with the rest of Brittany but with Wales and Cornwall. The Côtes-d'Armor roughly covers the land of Trégor, founded by settlers from Wales in the 6th century. Celtic saints, such as the blind St Hervé (Herveus), the son of a Welsh bard and one of the Seven Healing Saints of Brittany, feature prominently in local legends. There are many chapels, often with a healing spring nearby, dedicated to the region's Celtic saints.

Standing stones, dolmens and other megaliths are found throughout the region. Some have been turned into Christian monuments, such as the Menhir de Saint-Uzec, while others were seen as places where fairy folk hold sway.

Nature spirits and fairies common to Breton lore include the korrigans, who danced with passers-by on nights of the full moon and could reveal the sex of unborn babies. The Côtes-d'Armor also has its own magical beings, the 'Margot la fée' – a name that refers to the Margot fairies both as individuals and collectively. The Margot la fée have powers of invisibility and shapeshifting, and are known for hiding caches of treasure in caves on the coast or beneath megaliths inland. Like the korrigans, they are said to dance on moonlit nights, especially at magical places such as Mont Croquelien.

Also largely unique to the region are the fées des houles who inhabit caves in cliffs on the coast – *houle* being the local term for a cave. Unlike the Margot fairies who can be vengeful, these cave fairies were well disposed towards people and often became fairy godmothers to human babies, watching over and protecting them until they reached adulthood.

1 Chapelle des Septs-Saints, Plouaret

Set in a calm and peaceful spot within a grove of chestnut trees, the Chapelle des Sept-Saints hides an ancient secret. The chapel's cave-like, dimly-lit crypt is actually a prehistoric dolmen, the Dolmen du Stivel (Spring), a burial chamber made up of four upright stones and two capstones.

When stone statues of the seven saints were unexpectedly found beneath the dolmen in the early Christian era, the dolmen's chamber was converted into a shrine dedicated to them. Later a small chapel was built above it, but that proved unable to accommodate the many pilgrims who came to venerate the saints, so in the 1700s it was replaced with the building we see today.

Adding to the site's mystery, the saints honoured at the chapel are not the Seven Celtic Saints who brought Christianity to Brittany but the Seven Sleepers of Ephesus, a city in modern-day Turkey. According to this very early Christian legend, the seven were fleeing persecution from the Roman Emperor in the 3rd century and took refuge in a cave where they fell into a deep sleep. When their pursuers found them, they walled them up alive but 177 years later when the cave was opened, the sleeping saints awoke. How the cult of the Seven Sleepers reached this corner of Brittany is a puzzle.

The story of the Seven Sleepers is also found in the Koran, where they are known as the 'Companions of the Cave'. Remarkably, the *gwerz* des Sept-Saints, a Breton song recounting the legend, has many similarities to the Koran verses, which explains why in the 1950s the annual pilgrimage to the chapel uniquely became a joint one for both Christians and Muslims. Held on the fourth Sunday in July, it begins with a Christian service in the chapel, for which the seven statues are brought up from the crypt and during which the gwerz is sung. Then follows a procession through woodland to the nearby sacred spring, the **Fontaine des Sept-Saints** (48.6300, -3.4266) where the verses from the Koran are read out. Water from the spring flows into a basin through seven holes arranged in a circle. The spring once served as the local lavoir (washhouse) but sick people in search of a cure would also bathe in it.

Plouaret's local lore includes tales of a type of korrigan known as *danserien noz* (night dancers), who dance in the moonlight at a crossroads near the town. One tells of two half-sisters whose parents, both widowed, had married each other. One girl, Lévènes, was kind-hearted and good-natured, while the other, Margot, was selfish and mean. Margot's mother hated her stepdaughter Lévènes, and one moonlit night she sent her on an errand along the road that would take her past the crossroads, hoping she'd be taken by the night dancers. But Lévènes greeted them politely, accepted their invitation to dance, and received gifts. When she returned home, Margot was sent down the same road, but she insulted the korrigans by refusing to dance so they cursed her.

In the porch of the 16th-century parish church of **Notre-Dame at Plouaret**, (48.6119, -3.4731, Parking 48.6119, -3.4724, 50m) is a damaged and weathered statue of a type known as a 'cavalier à l'Anguipède'. In the Gallo-Roman period, such statues usually depicted the storm god Taranis trampling a malevolent creature whose humanoid form ends in either a serpent's tail or legs in the form of snakes ('anguiped' means 'snake foot'). Unusually, in the Plouaret statue Taranis tramples a female being, who could be a mermaid or siren – it's difficult to make out her exact form.

There's an impressive healing spring in the countryside just over a kilometre south of Plouaret. The **Fontaine de Saint-Jean du Temple** (48.5978, -3.4742) has a large stone enclosure and shrine, the size reflecting its former status as a place of pilgrimage. There was a chapel nearby but it has since disappeared. The spring's water was thought especially beneficial for rheumatism and eye troubles, as well as healing sick sheep. Find it beside the road just past the hamlet of Saint-Jean.

48.6327, -3.4239

2 Notre-Dame-du-Haut, Trédaniel

This dimly-lit and atmospheric chapel houses statues of the seven healing saints of Brittany, each invoked for different ailments: Eugénie (childbirth), Livertin (headache), Houarniaule or Hervé (skin disease and irrational fears), Hubert (wounds and rabies), Lubin (rheumatism and eye troubles), Mamert (colic) and Méen (mental illness).

The stained-glass window behind the main altar depicts the legend of the chapel's founding miracle. A traveller on the road was attacked by a band of brigands, who after robbing him hung him from a tree. He saw in the branches a statue of the Virgin Mary and prayed to her to save him. After vowing to build a chapel to house the statue an angel appeared and cut the rope.

A path opposite the chapel entrance leads to the **Fontaine Notre-Dame-du-Haut** (Our Lady of the Heights, 48.3487, -2.6237), about 150m away in a small wooded valley. It's set in an elaborate stone enclosure and shrine, with the spring water flowing into a rectangular basin. The spring was originally dedicated to St Tujen, a Breton saint whose legend incorporates aspects of a solar cult, then to St Eugénie, and finally to Notre-Dame-du-Haut, with an annual pilgrimage on 15 August. The existence of the spring was largely forgotten until the 1870s when a man from Trédaniel, in pain from rheumatism, asked for help from a local wise woman who told him to bathe in the spring at sunrise.

48.3496, -2.6218

1 Fontaine des Sept-Saints

1

3 Doigt de Gargantua, Plévenon

The twin peninsulas of Cap Fréhel and Pointe de la Latte are linked to stories of the giant Gargantua and of the fairy folk who once dwelt in the caves below. On the east side, Pointe de la Latte ends in the spectacular **Fort la Latte** (48.6683, -2.2847, €€; Parking 48.6646, -2.2923, 750m) built of local pink sandstone. It's surrounded by sea on three sides and overlooks the Baie de St Malo. The fort is often used as a movie location and hosts festivals of Breton music as well as medieval spectacles and re-enactments. It's open to the public from April to mid-November.

Along the path to the fort you pass by the Doigt de Gargantua (Gargantua's Finger), which is perched on a high point overlooking the sea. The tall, thin standing stone at 2.65m high but only 0.5m thick, is linked to the tale of the giant Gargantua who strode across the Channel to England, beginning with a long jump to the Channel Islands 50km away. The prints of his boots and cane are said to be visible in the rock at the stone's base. Another legend says he was killed and dismembered at Cap Fréhel in a battle with the korrigans, his finger forming the standing stone and his body parts the many rocky islands off the coast.

To the west is **Cap Fréhel** (parking 48.6838, -2.3191) with its towering 70m rose-coloured cliffs sculpted into extraordinary rock stacks and pillars. From the clifftop by the cape's famous lighthouse the eye is drawn to a wedge-shaped island 700m out to sea, the **Amas du Cap**. According to local folk memory, the island was once joined to the cape and the land between them inhabited and farmed, but it was all lost long ago beneath the waves.

The cliffs all around the peninsula are full of 'houles' (caves) both above and below sea level, some of which are deep and cavernous, and home to the fées des houles. Appearing as beautiful blonde women, they are usually benevolent and have their own warriors, a type of elf called a Fion. In local lore, the queen of these fairies is Gargantua's godmother.

Although well-disposed to humans, there was a fierce rivalry between the fées des houles of Cap Fréhel and those living on the other side of the peninsula in the caves between the Pointe de Château Serein (48.6402, -2.3077) and the Port de Saint-Géran (48.6505, -2.3002). The fairies on this coast are said to have made spectacular light shows in the sky as they danced over mounds in the woods above the cliffs. However, all the fairies left their caves when one of their human godsons discovered that, although immortal, they were vulnerable if salt touched their lips. Fearing this knowledge would be used against them, the fairies abandoned their caves, leaving behind their treasure guarded by an aggressive gnome-like being known as a nain. An especially large cave with a sinister reputation lies on the headland of La Teignouse, which juts out on the eastern side of Cap Fréhel. Known as the Trou d'Enfer (Hell Hole, 48.6808, -2.3108, no access), it's said to be the lair of a being that emerges to take the souls of drowned sailors. Inside is a flat rock the fairies used as a dining table before they left the cave.

48.6650, -2.2892; Parking 48.6646, -2.2923, 300m

3

4

4 Menez Bré, Louargat

  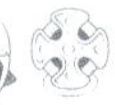

This sacred hill's powerful energy has given it a history steeped in magic and ritual, with a special connection to the ancient bardic tradition. Although Menez Bré is Breton for 'high mount' it's thought the original meaning was 'mount of power' or perhaps 'mount of magic'.

The hill is 300m high with gently rising slopes and stands out from the surrounding flat landscape. There are roads up to the top from north and south, the one from the south being unsurfaced. The summit is open moorland, often windswept, with 360-degree views as far as the coast over 20km away on a clear day.

The blind Druid bard and soothsayer Gwenc'hlan is said to have lived on Menez Bré. He appears in a poem set down in the Middle Ages, 'The Dialogue Between King Arthur and Gwenc'hlan', in which he delivers prophecies to Arthur. According to one tradition, Gwenc'hlan is buried upright beneath the hill, ready to rise again when Brittany has need of him.

Menez Bré is also famous as the place where Brittany's Seven Saints, summoned by St Hervé and including St Samson of **Dol**, met to curse Prince Conomor for killing his latest wife Tréphine. This appears to have been the continuation of an older Druid custom in which a king or lord who had committed a crime was condemned by a council of seven bards, calling for him to be overthrown.

There's been a chapel at the summit dedicated to St Hervé since at least the 6th century, the current one dating from the 16th century. The son of a Welsh bard who had settled in Guimiliau in Finistère, Hervé had healing powers and, like Gwenc'hlan

4

5

was blind. There's a spring, the **Fontaine de Saint-Hervé** (48.5768, -3.3043), in fields 250m east of the chapel that's said to have burst out when Hervé struck the ground with his staff during the gathering of the Seven Saints. It's reputed to cure sick children who are bathed in it.

48.5767, -3.3072

5 Menhir de Saint-Uzec, Pleumeur-Bodou

There are many megalithic monuments around the commune of Pleumeur-Bodou in the west of Clotes d'Armor, but the Menhir de Saint-Uzec is the most famous, both for its massive size and the cross and carvings that were added in an attempt to Christianise it. By the side of a country road, the menhir stands 7.4m high and weighs an estimated 80 tonnes. In the 1670s a stone enclosure was built around it and symbols relating to Christ's Passion and Crucifixion were carved into one face, with a stone crucifix set on top. A painting of Jesus on the Cross also covered the outward face but this has since washed away and only traces of colour remain.

Another Christianised menhir stands 2.5km away outside the **Chapelle de Saint-Samson** (48.7953, -3.5089). It's 1.8m high and has a small cross carved near the top. Women who had difficulty conceiving would rub the stone in the belief that it would aid fertility, and men would do the same to enhance their virility. It also healed ailments, especially of the kidneys, and at one time powder ground from the stone was mixed with water as a cure. There's a healing spring too, set into a stone shrine close to the chapel. Its waters were especially beneficial for eye problems and for helping children to walk.

Another nearby megalith, the 8.5m long **Ty-ar-C'horrandoned** (House of Korrigans, 48.8031, -3.5719; Roadside parking) was a dwelling place of the korrigans. It's on the Île-Grande, an island that can be reached by a short bridge or walked to at low tide, and which is 2km from the Menhir de Saint-Uzec. Several other small islands in the bay are accessible by foot at low tide. In the 1830s an antiquarian proposed that one, the privately-owned Île d'Aval (48.8035, -3.5563), was the Isle of Avalon of Arthurian legends.

Near the Menhir de Saint-Uzec is the Village Gaulois de Pleumeur-Bodou (48.7843, -3.5263), a reconstruction of a village from the Celtic era. It's open May–September, closed on Saturdays in May, June and September, €.

48.7889, -3.5444; Roadside parking

6 Mont Croquelien, Le Gouray

This legendary hillside covered in enchanted woodland and large mossy boulders is home to the Margot la fée of Côtes-d'Armor folklore. Many of the rocks resemble objects, such as a cradle and cattle trough, and bear the Margot fairies' name. Most striking are the three great moss-covered boulders of the **Portefeuille de Margot** (Margot's Purse), beneath which they are said to have buried a barrel filled with gold but anyone who tries to steal it will be turned to stone. The **Baignoire de Margot** (Margot's Bath) has a hollow that fills with rainwater. At the hill's summit, surrounded by gorse and ferns, are great granite slabs polished smooth by the elements – these form **Margot's dance-floor** where the fairies are said to frolic at night. On one is the footprint of one of the human children they swapped for a changeling. Another rock with a smooth slope is used by the fairies as a slide. Traditionally local people avoided passing the place at night for fear of encountering the fairies.

Just outside the village of Le Goulay, 2.5km from the Mont de Croquelien is the **Roche-aux-Fées** (48.3344, -2.4919). Also known as the Allée Couverte de l'Épine, it's another site where the Margot fairies are believed to have buried treasure: in this case a barrel of silver. It can only be found on Easter Sunday, and those looking for it have to remain silent throughout. According to a local story, a group of men from Le Gouray once found the barrel and were hauling it out with ropes when one blurted out "Hold on, I have it!" – and the treasure disappeared. Find it about 0.5km north of Le Gouray in the area of l'Épine. Turn left at the allé couverte sign and walk 90m along a farm track.

48.3224, -2.5230; Roadside parking
48.3235, -2.5250, 200m

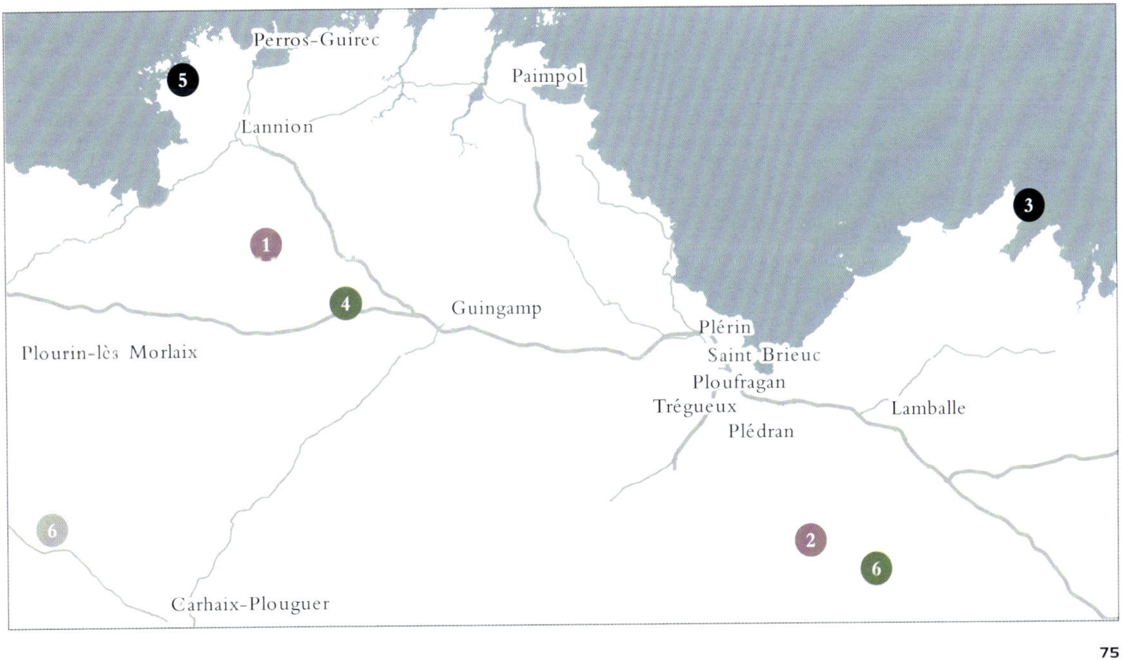

4 Dolmen de Kermario

CARNAC AND SOUTHEAST BRITTANY

The départements of Morbihan and Loire-Atlantique make up the southeastern part of the ancient kingdom of Brittany. Loire-Atlantique is where the river Loire flows through the cathedral city of Nantes and out into the Atlantic Ocean, while Morbihan is most famous for its megaliths, especially the Carnac alignments that stretch for 4km and are made up of nearly 3,000 stones. This region has one of the world's greatest concentrations of megaliths and includes other alignments, such as those at Kerbourgnec on the Quiberon Peninsula that extend out under the sea.

There are also numerous individual megalithic sites, including some of the greatest and most ancient known. In Carnac is what may be the oldest burial mound in Europe, the vast Tumulus Saint-Michel, while the Site des Mégalithes in Locmariaquer includes one of the tallest menhirs ever raised – a staggering 18.5m tall before it fell and broke.

These survivors from an ancient past co-exist with the region's Celtic Christian heritage. Morbihan is home to one of France's major healing shrines at Sainte-Anne-d'Auray, and other magnificent religious buildings such as Nantes Cathedral and the Basilique Notre-Dame de Roncier in Josselin, as well as many humble chapels associated with the early Celtic saints. All have their pardons – annual pilgrimages that bring together people from all over the region. Also associated with holy sites are miraculous springs, often in evocative locations such as the one dedicated to St Cado on the small estuarine island named after him.

The region shares in the fairy lore of Brittany, its dolmens home to korrigans who emerge on moonlit nights to dance among the lines of stones. These beings are also associated with natural sites such as the extraordinary Grotte des Korrigans at Le Pouliguen in Loire-Atlantique. In Morbihan korrigans are called kérions and considered incredibly strong despite their small size: a local saying is 'as strong as a kérion'.

Unique to southern Brittany are the Groac'h – fairies who usually appear as old women but have the power to shapeshift into other forms. Some Groac'h inhabit the coasts and have attributes of water spirits, sometimes being depicted with walrus-like teeth, while others are associated with the region's megalithic monuments. They are usually considered hostile to humans but can on occasion be helpful.

2

MORBIHAN

1 Alignements de Kerbourgnec, Quiberon Peninsula

The remains of megalithic alignments that once equalled those of **Carnac** now lie in a small park in an otherwise ordinary street in the seaside village of Kerbourgnec. It's one of many megalithic sites on the 15km-long peninsula that's connected to the mainland by a sandbank that's just 20m across at its narrowest point. It forms the western arm of the Baie de Quiberon that shelters Carnac.

Similar to Carnac, the Kerbourgnec alignments are oriented west to east. There are 26 visible stones of varying sizes and shapes in five lines that point towards the coast 200m away. They extend for only 60m, but underwater scanning and explorations by divers have found that the alignments continue into the bay, which was above sea level during the Neolithic Age. Like the Carnac alignments, the menhirs were originally said to be soldiers and these individuals were turned to stone when pursuing St Helen, sister of King Conan Meriadoc of Brittany.

Just as unexpected in its urban setting, 170m south of the alignments, is the **Cromlech de Kerbourgnec** (47.5158, -3.1303), an arc formed by 42 menhirs, although there were originally many more. A kilometre to the north, tucked away down a side street on the town's outskirts is the **Dolmen de Roc-en-Aud** (47.5243, -3.1360; parking 47.5241, -3.1367, 90m), 6m across and an impressive jumble of huge stones. It was once the passageway and burial chamber of a tumulus.

There are more megalithic monuments around the town of Quiberon at the northern end of the peninsula. On open moorland with a sensational view over the sea are the **Menhirs de Manémeur** (47.4833, -3.1352; parking 47.4812, -3.1360, 250m), two stones 5m and 3m high. They're 200m from the clifftops of the Côte Sauvage that forms the western side of the peninsula. A third menhir (47.4831, -3.1319) 250m away is in a more unconventional setting – a flowerbed beside houses at the crossing of two streets in the village of Manémeur. It's 3m high and has cup marks on the south face.

Most impressive of all, 3km away on the other side of Quiberon, is the **Menhir de Goulvars** (47.4753, -3.0975, Parking 47.4750, -3.0999, 200m). In open countryside just 200m from the coast, it's a massive 5m high and 2m wide, dwarfing the visitor and radiating a powerful energy.

47.5169, -3.1286

1 Menhirs de Manemeur

1 Menhir de Goulvars

2 Alignements de Kerzerho

The remarkable Kerzerho alignment of menhirs can be found 7km northwest of **Carnac**. As well as being in a more relaxed and pleasant setting than its more famous counterparts at Carnac, it is located conveniently beside the road between Plouharnel and Erdeven, with free access and parking. The 165 stones are arranged in 10 rows oriented west to east, like the Carnac alignments. According to legend, these were the advance guard of the Roman force that pursued St Cornelius and were turned to stone by his prayers.

The menhirs are part of a larger megalithic complex: 200m north along a signposted track is a smaller alignment (48.6364, -3.1482) made up of just 23 menhirs but with much larger stones. Three, known as the **Giants of Kerzerho**, tower between 6 and 7m high. One of the giants is cracked and split, it's thought to be from a lightning strike. Other huge stones are recumbent, with one called the Table du Sacrifice.

There are many other megaliths in the surrounding countryside. Especially striking is the very solid **Dolmen de Crucuno** (47.6242, -3.1264), 2km from the Kerzerho alignment in the village of Crucuno itself. It's 7.6m long with capstones supported by 9 upright stones, one of which bears cup marks. Originally they were part of a much longer burial chamber and passageway but the other stones were used for building by the villagers. Along a narrow lane (follow the sign marked 'Cromlech') 330m exactly due east of the dolmen is the Quadrilatère de Crucuno (Quadrangle, 47.6242, -3.1219; parking 47.6241, -3.1212, 40m), standing stones oriented to the cardinal points and marking out a rectangular area 35m by 25m.

That the megaliths covering this area of Brittany were constructed according to a plan is clearly deonstrated by the **Alignements Mégalithiques de Sainte-Barbe** 1.75km south of Crucuno (47.6089, -3.1333; parking 47.6062, -3.1353, 400m), which are aligned directly with the start of the Carnac lines at Le Ménec, 4.5km away. The Sainte-Barbe alignments are made up of some 50 menhirs, the tallest more than 5m, arranged in 8 lines.

47.6344, -3.1486

3 Notre-Dame du Roncier, Josselin

Stained-glass windows, more than 500 years old, in the south aisle of this beautifully ornate Gothic basilica depict the foundation legend of the old chapel that once stood on this spot. In the year 808, a peasant discovered a wooden statue of the Virgin Mary in a bramble bush (roncier) on the bank of the river Oust and took it home. Miraculously, it restored the sight of his wife who had been blind since birth, but the statue then vanished only to turn up back in the bush. After this happened a few times, the local people realised it was a sign the Virgin wanted a dedicated chapel built on the spot. The chapel was later replaced by a church and then, as its fame as a place of miraculous cures grew and more people flocked to it, by the present basilica dedicated to Our Lady. It was especially renowned for healing blindness and paralysis, and soon Josselin became the second most important place of pilgrimage in Brittany after **Sainte-Anne-d'Auray**. Like many, the original statue was burned during the French Revolution but a replica now stands in its place.

Between Easter and the end of September, visitors can climb the 60m bell tower to take in the views of Josselin, one of the most picturesque towns in France. The tower has its own entrance at the rear of the basilica in the Place de la Mairie. Entry is free but a donation is always welcome.

The **Fontaine de Notre-Dame du Roncier** (47.9533, -2.5431; Parking 47.9533, -2.5437, 50m) is 350m from the basilica and is also called the Fontaine Miraculeuse owing to its healing waters. The well-shrine with its brightly painted statue of the Virgin and Child bears the date 1675 but the spring had been a place of healing long before that. Enhancing the tranquil energy of the spring are the fresh flowers often placed there by the townsfolk. Steps in the stone enclosure lead down to the spring water.

Although Josselin had been a place of pilgrimage for centuries, its fame was given a boost in 1728 when three children from Camors were cured of their epilepsy after drinking water from the spring. This happened during the pardon, the annual mass pilgrimage common to churches and shrines in Brittany. Josselin's is held on the second Sunday in September, when the statue of Our Lady is carried in procession through the town.

Josselin's pardon had a unique element that earned it the name of 'Pardon des Aboyeuses' (Barking Women's Pardon). Accounts from the early 1700s tell of certain women going into a trance and barking like dogs during the ceremony, only stopping when they were either given water from the spring or made to kiss the statue of Notre-Dame du Roncier in the basilica. The source of this phenomenon was said to be a beggarwoman who asked for money from local women washing clothes at the town's lavoir. After they set their dogs on her, the woman revealed herself to be the Virgin Mary in disguise and cursed the women for their bad behaviour. Carvings of dogs inside the basilica reinforce the legend and the last reported occurrence of an 'aboyeuse' was in 1953.

By the basilica are some medieval houses and beside the river stands the 15th century Château de Josselin (Josselin Castle, 47.9522, -2.5472, €€), with its celebrated gardens and three turreted towers.

47.9536, -2.5478; Parking: 47.9541, -2.5461, 50m

2 Dolmen de Crucuno

3

3

4 Carnac

At this truly awe-inspiring place, the ancient stones of Carnac capture the imagination with their presence and the deep sense of mystery that surrounds them. So too does the sheer scale of the site: it's the world's greatest concentration of megaliths, over 10,000 stones at some 150 sites, the most famous being the long alignments of menhirs stretched across the landscape. They are surrounded by many other megalithic monuments such as stone circles, standing stones, dolmens and tumuli. Clearly those who erected the stones thought there was something special and sacred about this part of southern Brittany, especially given the presence of other nearby sites such as the **Alignements de Kerbourgnec**, just 9km across the Baie de Quiberon.

There are three main alignments that together stretch for 4km and are made up of more than 3,000 stones. Each consists of several long rows of menhirs that converge slightly, ending in a cromlech (circle of stones) that formed a sacred enclosure. The three follow on from each other, running roughly from east to west in a band across the moorland and were constructed over an immense period of time, between 6,000 and 4,000 years ago. Their purpose may have been in part astronomical, as there are alignments to the solstices and equinoxes as well as key rising and setting points of the moon, but clearly there are deeper meanings that have been lost to time.

Dowsers believe that the stones are highly charged with energy that flows around the alignments, and many relate it to the earth's energy grid. Some stones are said to draw energy from the ground, others from the sky, perhaps showing that the alignments mark a meeting place of heavenly and earthly energies. Most dowsers find this energy to be a healing one.

Whether looked at from the point of view of archaeology or earth mysteries, many unanswered questions remain, feeding the imagination. It's small wonder that myths and legends have grown up about the origin of these enigmatic stones. In the most well-known legend, the stones were the 'Soldats de Saint Cornély' (St Cornelius' Soldiers), a Roman legion turned to stone by the saint. Pursued by these troops and realising his escape was cut off by the sea, the saint turned to face them and, with a prayer, petrified them. Cornelius was a real figure, an early Pope during the time Christians were still being persecuted, although nothing in the historical record places him in Brittany. Some local traditions connect the stones with the Celtic horned god Cernunnos and as Cornelius is the patron saint of cattle and horned animals – his name derives from 'corne' (horn) - one theory is that in Celtic times Carnac was the centre of a cult to Cernunnos that Christianity later transformed into one devoted to Cornelius.

The **Église Saint-Cornély** (48.5833, -3.0789) in the centre of Carnac is said to mark the spot where the saint turned to face the legionaries and in an annual night-time procession that took place until the 1950s, cattle and other farm animals were brought there to be blessed. After the ceremony they were walked around the menhir alignments. The Church placed Carnac under Cornelius' patronage and during the Middle Ages the alignments were the centre of a great pilgrimage in the region, until the focus shifted to **Sainte-Anne d'Auray** in the 17th century.

In another version of the legend, Merlin turned the legionaries to stone. Other menhirs away from the main alignments are said to be people who were petrified as a punishment for other misdeeds, such as groups of girls who skipped church to dance on the moors. The stones reputedly grew like plants from seeds, while others attribute them to kérions, the local version

Alignements du Menec

4

of the elf-like korrigans, who are still said to emerge from the nearby dolmens to cavort and dance among the lines of stones on moonlit nights.

Treasure is believed to lie beneath some of the menhirs but is protected by supernatural forces. Yet on Christmas Eve when the church bells strike midnight, some of the stones are said to go to nearby streams to drink, revealing the hoards in the holes they've temporarily vacated. Treasure hunters must, however, find it by the end of the twelve chimes, otherwise they'll be crushed by the returning menhirs.

As in many other places, local lore associates the megaliths with fertility and their power was sought out by women unable to conceive or in search of a husband.

Access to the alignments varies during the year. In the summer months they can only be entered as part of a guided tour starting from the visitor centre (see details below), although they can be viewed from footpaths around the perimeters. At other times they are fully open to the public. Each alignment has its own parking area.

Starting from the west, first come the **Alignements du Ménec** (47.5922, -3.0842; parking 47.5910, -3.0874). The very beginning is marked by the Cromlech du Ménec (47.5917, -3.0862), once a circular enclosure of closely placed menhirs, originally around 90m across, of which 70 survive in and around the gardens and lanes of the small village of Le Ménec. From there 11 lines of stones stretch for nearly a kilometre, consisting of nearly 1,200 stones that gradually decrease in size. The highest, which stands at 3.5m, is slightly off the alignment and is thought to have been raised some time before the others were erected.

Local custom links a fallen block known as **Le Vaisseau** (Vessel) with fertility. Newly married couples would visit it at night and, with their family making sure the coast was kept clear, run naked around the stone in the belief that it would ensure they had children. Women who had trouble conceiving would also rub themselves against it.

After a break of 150m through which a road passes, the alignment's name changes from du Ménec to de Toulchigan, although the lines were originally part of the former. Back in Le Ménec itself, 200m from the alignments, is the charming Fontaine du Ménec (47.5902, -3.0866) in its stone housing – an especially picturesque sight in spring and summer when it's surrounded by bright flowers.

Some isolated menhirs can be found to the north of the Le Ménec alignments, including the pointed **Menhir de Crifol** (47.5953, -3.0854), 300m away . Legend has it that the menhir, standing 3m tall, was a rich man turned to stone as punishment for his uncaring extravagance and because his spirit roams

Menhirs de Kerderff

4

Cromlech de Menec

4

Dolmen de Kroez-Moken Cruz-Menquen

4

Geant du Manio

4

around the stone at night, locals avoid it. From the alignments, reach the menhir on a farm track that follows the edge of fields.

The two **Menhirs de Kerderff** (47.5940, -3.0919; parking 47.5917, -3.0922, 350m) stand 50m apart in a field 600m from the alignments. There's no direct path so it's easier to get to them by road. From some angles both appear to have human faces. The tallest, at 6m, is double the height of its companion and known as the Géant de Kerderff.

In the other direction, 500m south of the Le Ménec alignments, is the **Dolmen de Cruz-Menquen** (47.5884, -3.0805), an ancient burial chamber surmounted by a Christian cross. Less than a century ago, the site was open countryside but the dolmen now sits on the outskirts of Carnac itself, along a short track that leads to the town centre, just off the Rue de Courdiec. Nobody knows when the 2.5m high cross was placed on top of the huge capstone to Christianise it. Also known as the Pierre Chaude (Hot Stone), this megalith was the site of marriage and fertility rituals. Young women looking for a husband would sit on it, their skirts held high, on the night of the full moon, and women who wanted to conceive would rub against it.

The second series of alignments, 500m on from those of Le Ménec, are the most famous as they are the longest and have the tallest menhirs. The **Alignements de Kermario** (47.5965, -3.0662; parking 47.5964, -3.0661, 120m) are made up of just under 1,000 stones in 10 rows running for over a kilometre. Again the largest are at the western end, where the land rises. The alignments are interrupted by a pond dug in the 19th century, the continuation sometimes being referred to as the Alignements de Manio. Midway along the lines is a viewing tower repurposed from an old windmill, which also gives a good view of the **Tumulus Saint-Michel** (St Michael's Tumulus) 1.5km to the southwest.

Offset from the beginning of the Kermario alignments is the **Dolmen de Kermario** (47.5956, -3.0669), an ancient burial chamber 9m long by 3.5 wide and made up of 20 stones. Entry to the chamber isn't permitted but it's an impressive sight against the backdrop of stone rows.

A chamber that can be visited lies within the **Tumulus de Kercado** (47.5956, -3.0542, €; parking 47.5970, -3.0300532, 150m), in woods 600m south of the Kermario Alignments. At least 7,000 years old and claiming to be the oldest dolmen in Europe, it's in an amazingly good state of preservation. The

Dolmen de Crucuno

4

ancient mound is 25m in diameter, 5m high and topped by a small menhir. The remains of a small stone circle are close by. Some of the stones of the passageway and burial chamber are engraved with symbols and patterns, and being inside the chamber is a powerful experience. The tumulus is on private property and a small donation is asked for, with an honesty box at the entrance.

The third of the major alignment fields is the **Alignements de Kerlescan** (47.6044, -3.0493; parking 47.6029, -3.0512), with 579 menhirs in 13 rows. These have a more direct west–east orientation than the Le Ménec and Kermario lines, and it's thought they were aligned to the moon's movements and could be used to predict eclipses.

There are some very remarkable sites around the Kerlescan alignments. Two are close together in woodland reached by a path of about 500m from the parking area. The **Géant du Manio** (47.6039, -3.0564) is the tallest standing stone in Carnac, a towering 6.5m. It owes its name not only to its size but on account of the face discernible from some angles. According to a local tradition, if you make a wish and then throw a stone so it lands and stays on the top of the Giant – no easy task – your wish will come true. Around 40m from the Giant is the Quadrilatère du Manio (47.6036, -3.0561), a rectangular enclosure 37m long and 10m wide made up of 1m-high stones.

Just north of the alignments, again in woodland, is the **Dolmen de Kerlescan** (47.6061, -3.0478) which is still partially covered by a mound. Even though it was partly looted for its stones, it's still impressive at 43m long, 7.5 wide and 3m high. Like other dolmens it's believed to be a gateway to the fairy realm from which korrigans and other elemental creatures emerge into our world at night. Follow a path along the edge of the alignments and find the dolmen 700m from the parking area.

A final, smaller set of alignments is often overlooked and, unlike the others, can be freely accessed all year round. The **Alignements du Petit-Ménec** (47.6044, -3.0406, roadside parking 47.6060, -3.0393, 80m) are in woods half a kilometre on from the Kerlescan alignments and may originally have been part of them. There are over 100 stones in 8 rows.

Between April and September Carnac's main alignment fields can only be entered as part of guided tours that start from the **Maison des Mégalithes** (47.5915, -3.0823, €€). This visitor and information centre near the Le Ménec Alignments has a raised terrace with a view over the menhirs. As well as walking tours, there's also a tourist 'train' that visits the alignments.

47.5909, -3.0838

Dolmen de Kermario

4

5

5 Église Saint-Mériadec, Stival

This church and its healing spring are dedicated to St Meriasek (or St Meriadoc), a legendary saint of Brittany celebrated for his miracles and powers of healing. He died in the village of Stival in 570 and the church was built in the 1500s on the site of St Meriasek's hermitage. The church still has original wall paintings of scenes from the saint's life.

Meriasek was the son of Conan Meriadoc, King of Brittany, but he gave up his royal status and privileges to become a monk. He then moved to Cornwall where he gained a reputation for healing and other miracles such as creating the spring at Camborne, of which he became patron saint. He had to return to Brittany because of the persecutions of King Tewdwr (or Tuedar). Supported by the Count of Rohan he founded a chapel at **Josselin** where he performed more miracle cures, healing lepers, the blind and the mute, as well as calming storms and taming a wolf that was terrorising the area. Overwhelmed by the number of people who flocked to him, Meriasek retired to Stival, 35km away, where he built a hermitage close to the Château de Rohan (48.0703, -2.9636). There he helped the Count of Rohan by calling the fire of heaven down to destroy a band of brigands overrunning the count's lands.

The church's most famous holy object is the 'Bonnet de Saint-Mériadec', a copper handbell Meriasek reputedly used to cure deafness and headaches by ringing it then placing it on the sufferer's head, as depicted in one of the paintings. The procedure is still carried out on pilgrims during the pardon held the day before Trinity Sunday.

The **Fontaine Saint-Mériadec** (48.0820, -2.9927) is 400m from the chapel along the main street. It's housed in a large walled enclosure containing a 3m high well-shrine where the water flows into a square basin. The water is known for curing fevers, deafness, ear infections and headaches.

48.0850, -2.9933; Parking: 48.0847, -2.9930, 50m

6 Fontaine de Dévotion Saint-Mériadec, Pluvigner

Unusually, water from this healing spring is used for curing ailments in sick animals as well as people, because Meriasek is also the patron saint of cattle and livestock. It's in woodland just outside the tiny village of Saint-Mériadec, 6km northeast of Pluvigner, and housed in a simple stone shrine. Inside, a niche holds a small statue of the saint and water fills a square basin.

Water from the spring passes beneath the altar of the **Chapelle Saint-Mériadec** (47.8164, -2.9380), 50m away. It was built in the 1500s on the site of a hermitage founded in the 6th century either by Meriasek or one of his followers – more likely the latter as Meriasek spent his last years in Stival, 30km to the north (see **Église Saint-Mériadec**).

The chapel is used only for the annual pardon that takes place on the third Sunday in March, a major event in the area. Accompanied by pipe and drum music, worshippers perform a lengthy song detailing the life of St Meriasek to invoke the saint's blessing and protection for livestock in the coming year. Afterwards, water from the spring is collected and used to cure ailments – it's especially good for headaches – and also mixed in the feed of sick farm animals.

47.8159, -2.9383; Parking: 47.8169, -2.9367, 170m

Fontaine de Saint-Guigner

7

6

7

7 Fontaine Saint-Guigner, Pluvigner

One of the most famous and important healing springs in the region, the Fontaine Saint-Guigner (St Gwinear) is the scene of a major gathering, the Fête des Bannières (Banner Festival). Held on the third Sunday in Pentecost, the fête centres on the relics of Pluvigner's patron saint. These are brought from the **Église Saint-Guigner** (47.7747, -3.0106), 350m away, along with those of six other saints from this part of Brittany. Those suffering from rheumatism drink from the water and pass under the seven reliquaries that are held aloft.

Gwinear was a son of the King of Ireland who was forced into exile after meeting St Patrick and converting to Christianity. He settled at Pluvigner, where a vision and a miracle inspired him to become a monk with a mission to spread the new faith. When out hunting he noticed the stag he was pursuing bore a cross between its antlers. Then, thirsty but unable to find water, he stuck his spear in the ground three times, and each time a spring burst forth: one for himself, his horse and his dog. Taking this as a sign of his calling, he built a hermitage in woodland near Pluvigner, and gathered a band of followers with whom he travelled around Brittany and Cornwall, performing miracles wherever he went to win converts. After he was killed by the tyrannical King Tewdwr of Cornwall in 455, his body was brought back to Pluvigner. Scenes from Gwinear's life, including the hunting of the stag, are depicted in the church's stained-glass windows.

The three miraculous springs are now set into a large stone enclosure on the edge of the town. The main one flows into three large square pools that were once used as Pluvigner's communal laundry but now the sick bathe here during the Fête des Bannières. The two smaller round basins are for drinking: one for people and the other for animals.

There's a second spring dedicated to the saint hidden away in woodland 3km from Pluvigner. The **Fontaine de Saint-Guigner** (47.7819, -2.9657; roadside parking 47.7836, -2.9681, 300m, private), is near the tiny village of Le Moustoir where the saint founded his hermitage, its site now occupied by the Chapelle de la Sainte-Trinité (47.7844, -2.9753). Significantly less well known than the very public monument at Pluvigner, this spring is overgrown with plants and moss and feels hidden and secret.

47.7739, -3.0058; Parking: 47.7735, -3.0064, 50m

8 Île de Saint-Cado, Belz

This delightful and tranquil island, home to a small village, looks out over the estuary of the river Étel. Just 200m across at its widest, it's joined to the mainland by a 125m-long bridge. St Cado is named after Cadoc, a Welsh monk who founded monasteries in Wales and Scotland before withdrawing to become a hermit on this riverine island in Brittany. Before he arrived, an infestation of snakes made it uninhabitable but the saint cast them all out. According to local legend, the Devil offered to build a bridge to the island for Cadoc in exchange for the first soul that crossed it. The saint agreed and the Devil built the bridge in a single night but Cadoc outwitted him by persuading a cat to walk over it first.

The 12th-century Chapelle Saint-Cado (47.6867, -3.1844) is on the site of the holy man's hermitage. Steps lead down from it to the **Fontaine de Saint-Cado** (47.6865, -3.1839), which is in a walled enclosure on the shoreline facing the estuary. Also known as the Fontaine de Dévotion, its waters are noted for healing rheumatism and boils. The spring is covered during high tides.

47.6875, -3.1847; Parking: 47.6849, -3.1857, 150m

9 Menhirs de Monteneuf, Monteneuf

Morbihan's second largest complex of megalithic alignments is set in woodland, and the surrounding trees, gorse and flowering bushes give the Menhirs de Monteneuf a different, lighter atmosphere than those at **Carnac**. So too do the earthy tones of the 400 standing stones, which are purple schist. The woods are said to be the abode of fairies and other elemental creatures that come to dance around the stones at night. Most of the menhirs were knocked down in previous centuries but they were raised up again in the 1980s to create the Site Mégalithique des Pierres Droites (Straight Stones). Between June and September events are held at the site, including re-enactments of raising the menhirs, and workshops and talks on life in the age of megaliths. There are several walking trails through the woods.

47.8822, -2.1858; Parking: 47.8816, -2.1800, 500m

10 Sainte-Anne-d'Auray

    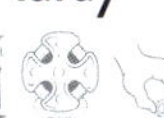

Sainte-Anne-d'Auray began life as the small village of Keranna (Village of Ana, named after the Celtic Mother Goddess) but its sacred places were rededicated to St Anne, mother of the Virgin Mary, following Christianisation. The legend then evolved that St Anne settled in Brittany, coming ashore at Sainte-Anne-la-Palud in Finistère, and some even maintain that Jesus may have come to visit her there. Anne later became the patron saint of Brittany. An early chapel dedicated to St Anne was built in Keranna but it was destroyed by invading Norsemen in the 8th century.

St-Anne-d'Auray's fame as a cult centre began eight centuries later with events that have many parallels to those that were to make **Lourdes** in southern France inter-

nationally famous. Over several months in 1623–24 while working in the fields, an illiterate peasant from Keranna named Yvon Nicolazic had a number of encounters with the figure of a lady dressed in white. His descriptions fit the image of the Dame Blanche found in folklore throughout France who is usually related to the fairy folk. After several appearances, the figure revealed that she was Anne, mother of Mary, and that there had once been a chapel to her on the site, which she wanted rebuilt. Digging at the spot with some of his neighbours, Nicolazic uncovered an ancient wooden statue they identified as St Anne. Like many, the statue was later burned during the French Revolution, but depictions have led to speculation that it was an image of the Roman goddess Bona Dea. Initially the Church was sceptical about the apparitions but was eventually won over, and a new chapel of St Anne was built and consecrated in 1628.

As the humble village grew over the centuries to become Brittany's major pilgrimage centre, several churches and chapels were added along with statues and monuments, culminating in the magnificent basilica that was built in the 1860s–70s. Sometimes known as the 'Lourdes of Brittany', it's now a major Christian sanctuary.

Beside the wide esplanade that leads to the basilica can be found the **Fontaine Miraculeuse** (47.7044, -2.9549), built on the spot where the White Lady first appeared to Nicolazic. At this grand and richly sculpted 19th-century monument topped with a statue of St Anne and her daughter, water flows into three basins for drinking and a larger pool where pilgrims wash. The spring's first reported cure was much earlier in 1660, when a man with paralysed arms was dipped in the water and found he could move his arms again. Since then, many cures for all manner of ailments have been reported. The spring was also used by single women to find out whether they would marry in the next year: if a pin thrown into the pool floated, they would. Despite the crowds, visitors often comment on the peaceful atmosphere around the spring.

47.7042, -2.9533, Parking: 47.7044, -2.9507, 350m

11 Locmariaquer

There's an extraordinary concentration of megaliths around the port and beach resort of Locmariaquer, located on a peninsula that forms the gateway to the Gulf of Morbihan. Several are linked, at least in name, with the Groac'h fairy folk, while one has a specific legend. A number of the most important menhirs and dolmens are in the Site des Mégalithes, forming a kind of megalithic theme park that includes an exhibition centre.

The **Grand Menhir Brisé d'Er Grah** (Great Broken Menhir of the Groac'h, 47.5714, -2.9503) was one of the tallest standing stones ever created before it fell and shattered into four pieces, each still gigantic. Erected around 7,000 years ago, it towered 18.5m with a further 2m below ground. The stone weighed over 300 tonnes and was brought from at least 10km away across the Gulf of Morbihan. Excavations revealed it originally stood at the head of an alignment of at least 18 menhirs. Stretching north, these align with the extreme points of the moon's rising and setting and so are capable of predicting lunar eclipses. Some think the Menhir d'Er Grah is the fabled 'Column of the North' referred to by Greek travellers in the 2nd century BC. During a local rite, observed on the night of the first of May, young women who wanted to marry in the next year climbed on top of the largest of the menhir's four pieces, rolled up their skirts and chemises, then slid down with their bare skin against the stone.

Another exceptional feature of the site is the huge cairn and dolmen known as the **Table des Marchands** (Merchants' Table, 47.5717, -2.9497), its name a French misinterpretation of the Breton which means 'Table of the Horse Path'. It was constructed around 3,000 years after the Menhir Brisé and its companions, indicating that the site was in use over a vast period of time. The cairn is 30m long and 8m high and is oriented north–south. It covers a passageway to a large burial chamber 2.5m high that is carved with geometric patterns and figures of humans and animals, along with symbols of the Mother Goddess. The cairn itself is a reconstruction as the original stones were used by the Romans for building a nearby amphitheatre.

A short distance from the Table des Marchands is the **Tumulus d'Er Grah** (47.5722, -2.9506), also renowned for its size. It's 140m long and built in a series of steps around a burial chamber that was closed off with no passage from the outside. It, too, is a restoration as much of the original stone was taken for building, and as the name implies it was associated with the Groac'h fairy folk.

Outside the Site itself are many other outstanding megaliths, some hidden away in the streets of Locmariaquer. Near the edge of the town is the standing stone now called the **Menhir Men Bronzo** (47.5699, -2.9473, Parking 47.5693, -2.9467, 90m). It appears in older records as Men Bron Sao, 'Raised Stone of the Crow', after the bird that features among its engraved symbols, and is also known locally as the Motte de Beurre (Pat of Butter). The stone fell and broke in two, one part having been re-erected.

Close by is the **Dolmen du Mané-Réthual** (47.5692, -2.9478, Parking 47.5693, -2.9467, 150m one-way), also known as the Tombeau de la Sorcière (Witch's Tomb). Tucked away along a track off the road, it's more complete than most dolmens and still partly covered by its original tumulus. Entry isn't permitted for reasons of safety and the site's preservation. The stones form a passage, 15m long, 3.5m wide and 1.2m high, leading to an antechamber and the semicircular chamber beyond. One of the six stone slabs forming the roof is over 11m long, weighing close to 50 tonnes, and is thought to be a repurposed menhir. There are many engravings on the stones, including images of crosses and axes.

Another remarkable site is the **Tumulus du Mamé-er-Hroëk** (Groac'h's Mount, 47.5627, -2.9385; parking 47.5627, -2.9376, 75m) on the southern outskirts of Locmariaquer. Local legend says that the mound was raised by a widow with the help of a mysterious old woman, one of the Groac'h fairy folk. The widow's son had sailed away and his ship didn't return when scheduled, so every day she went to the Pointe de Kerpenhir, looking to the horizon but in vain. One day an old woman appeared and, hearing her story, told her to make a heap of stones at the end of the point so she would be able to see further. The two women worked together through the night, gathering stones in their aprons and piling them up. In the morning the widow was amazed to see how high the mound was. Climbing to the top she saw her son's ship returning, but when she turned to offer her thanks, the old woman had vanished. Stories of giants dropping mounds of stones from their apron strings are common in folklore but here we have a story of a local woman and a fairy performing this task. The tumulus lies down a track off the main road to the Pointe de Kerpenhir and is 100m long and 8m high. Inside is a 5m-long chamber, which was originally sealed within the tumulus; the entrance and steps down into the chamber are a modern addition. There's an engraved stele just inside the entrance that displays symbols of the Mother Goddess. The tumulus was originally surrounded by menhirs but they're now in private gardens in the neighbouring houses.

On a headland at the end of the peninsula, where it's stood for 5,000 years and with a sweeping view over the Baie de Quiberon, is the **Dolmen des Pierres Plates** (Flat Stones, 47.5567, -2.9508; parking 47.5574, -2.9492, 160m). It consists of a passage over a metre high with a bend leading to a large chamber. The structure is 26m long and partly covered with a cairn, with a standing stone in front of the entrance. Figures etched into the stones are thought to be stylised humans or gods, again including the Mother Goddess. Other strange flowing patterns have been interpreted as representing the phases of the moon and even the cycles of the planet Venus. To protect the monument, visitors aren't currently allowed to enter the passage.

Parking: 47.5716, -2.9520

11 Dolmen des Pierres Plates

12 Tumulus Saint-Michel, Carnac

Dominating the landscape around Carnac this vast and ancient mound, the largest in Brittany, was built around 5,000 BC – long before Egypt's pyramids. Along with the **Cairn de Barnenez** in Finistère, it's one of the oldest mounds in Europe, but unfortunately its central chamber and several galleries holding grave goods are not accessible. Given its scale and the immense amount of labour involved in its construction, the tumulus, at 125m long, 60m wide and 12m high, was clearly of great importance, with a summit almost 50m above sea level. There's an observation deck giving a panoramic view of Carnac from the stone alignments to the north to the Baie de Quiberon to the south. Originally rounded, the mound's top was levelled when a chapel dedicated to St Cornelius, patron saint of Carnac, was built on it back in the 6th century. Later chapels on the same site honoured Archangel Michael, as is so often the case with pagan high places. The current chapel is about a hundred years old. To ensure favourable winds for their husbands' sea voyages from Carnac, it was the custom for sailors' wives to sweep the chapel floor and throw the dust out in the direction they wanted the wind to blow from.

Another custom to invoke Michael's blessing for good winds and safe sailing was to drink from the nearby **Fontaine Saint-Michel** (47.5901, -3.0720), which is housed in a small stone shrine 250m along a woodland path.

47.5878, -3.0733; Parking: 47.5869, -3.0726, 250m

13

LOIRE-ATLANTIQUE

13 Nantes Cathedral

This magnificent Gothic cathedral in what was once Brittany's capital city is home to many celebrated sculptures and paintings. Yet one stands out above all the rest, not only because it is recognised as one of the masterpieces of French Renaissance art but also because of the magical secrets it encodes. The exquisite marble tomb of François II, Duke of Brittany, and his wife Marguerite de Foix was commissioned by their daughter Anne of Brittany, Queen of France, in the first years of the 16th century. Through Anne's marriage to the King of France, the Duchy of Brittany – until then an independent realm – became part of France. One of Brittany's most significant historical figures, Anne was also a great patroness of art and culture. For the design of her parents' resting place she turned to Jean Pérreal, artist, alchemist and magician (also friend and associate of Leonardo da Vinci). His decoration imbues the tomb with alchemical and esoteric meaning, especially the life-sized female figures at the corners, one of whom is gripping a dragon that has burst from a medieval tower. They represent the four cardinal virtues – Prudence, Strength, Temperance and Justice – and the figure of Prudence is modelled on Anne of Brittany herself.

The first cathedral on the spot was erected in the 5th century on the site of a Druid temple to the god Janus. Building of the current cathedral began in 1434 and continued for the next 450 years. The white stone and the immense and lofty space give it a powerful, dynamic energy.

13

Just 200m from the cathedral is the stately **Château des Ducs de Bretagne** (47.2156, -1.5497). Set within high walls and featuring towers, turrets and a huge central courtyard, it's the classic fairytale castle, conjuring up romantic images of jousting and knights in armour. Built in the 15th century, it was the court and centre of power of the Dukes of Brittany, and after the union with France became a royal fortress. Entry to the courtyard and ramparts is free, although there's an entrance fee to the Musée d'Histoire de Nantes housed within the castle (€€, free entry on the first Sunday of each month). In Arthurian legend, Nantes was the city where the lovers Eric and Enide were crowned King and Queen, and where Perceval's sword was forged. Nantes had been famous for its metalworking since the time of the Romans, who dedicated the town to Vulcan, the god of fire and the forge.
47.2183, -1.5508; Parking €€: 47.2142, -1.5490, 550m

14 Dolmen de la Salle aux Fées, La Guinanderie/ Port Faissant

In a field close to the river Tenu can be found what was once an imposing burial chamber, now collapsed and overgrown with bushes and trees, its capstone 2.75m long. One of its stones was engraved with a strange figure that's now too weathered to make out, known as the Bête du Port Faissant (Beast of Le Port Faissant), after the nearby village. Like many dolmens, it was regarded as a gateway to the fairy realm and this one still retains that connection in its name, 'The Fairies' Hall Dolmen'.
47.0792, -1.7914; Roadside parking: 47.0786, -1.7917, 60m

15 Grotte des Korrigans, Le Pouliguen

This enchanted cave, its multicoloured rocks lapped by the wild waves of the Atlantic Ocean, was seen as a gateway to the otherworldly realm of the korrigans. It is the focus of two local legends that reveal the korrigans' dual nature – either sinister or benevolent. In one, the cave was the entrance to a tunnel that led to the town of Guérande, 7km inland, and was the haunt of a malevolent korrigan. Anyone who ventured inside would never be seen again. According to the other legend, a doorway within the cave protected by the korrigans' magic gave entry to their underground realm, its tunnels filled with magnificent treasure. A local man once took pity on an old and unsightly woman who came begging at his door on a freezing winter night. She warmed herself by his fire and after he wrapped her in a blanket and gave her a bowl of hot soup, she revealed herself to be the beautiful Queen of the Korrigans. As a reward for his kindness, she told him the secret words that would open the doorway within the cave. He was also told to help himself to some of the treasure, but only on the condition that he got it home before sunrise, otherwise it would vanish. Once inside the fairy tunnels and beguiled by the magical world and its riches, he lost track of time, then hurrying home along the coast road realised that dawn was nearly breaking. He hid his treasure beneath the **Menhir de la Pierre Longue** (Long Stone, 47.2874, -2.5307) but when he returned the next night to retrieve it the stone wouldn't budge. The Korrigan Queen reappeared and told him that

15

because he'd been greedy in taking so much she wouldn't let him keep the treasure. But as a reward for his earlier compassion she gave him a magic dish that filled with whatever food he desired, so he never went hungry again.
The cave is located in a small cove on the southern side of the town of Le Pouliguen and is reached by steps from the path along the clifftop. Hollowed out by the relentless force of the waves the cave penetrates over 30m into the cliff and is partly flooded at high tide. There are two entrances, a narrow one from the cove and a wider one opening to the ocean. The crashing of the waves sometimes churns up huge amounts of sea foam that, when whipped up by the wind and with the sun beaming through it, seems to dance magically around the entrance.
47.2619, -2.4481; Parking: 47.2637, -2.4485, 300m

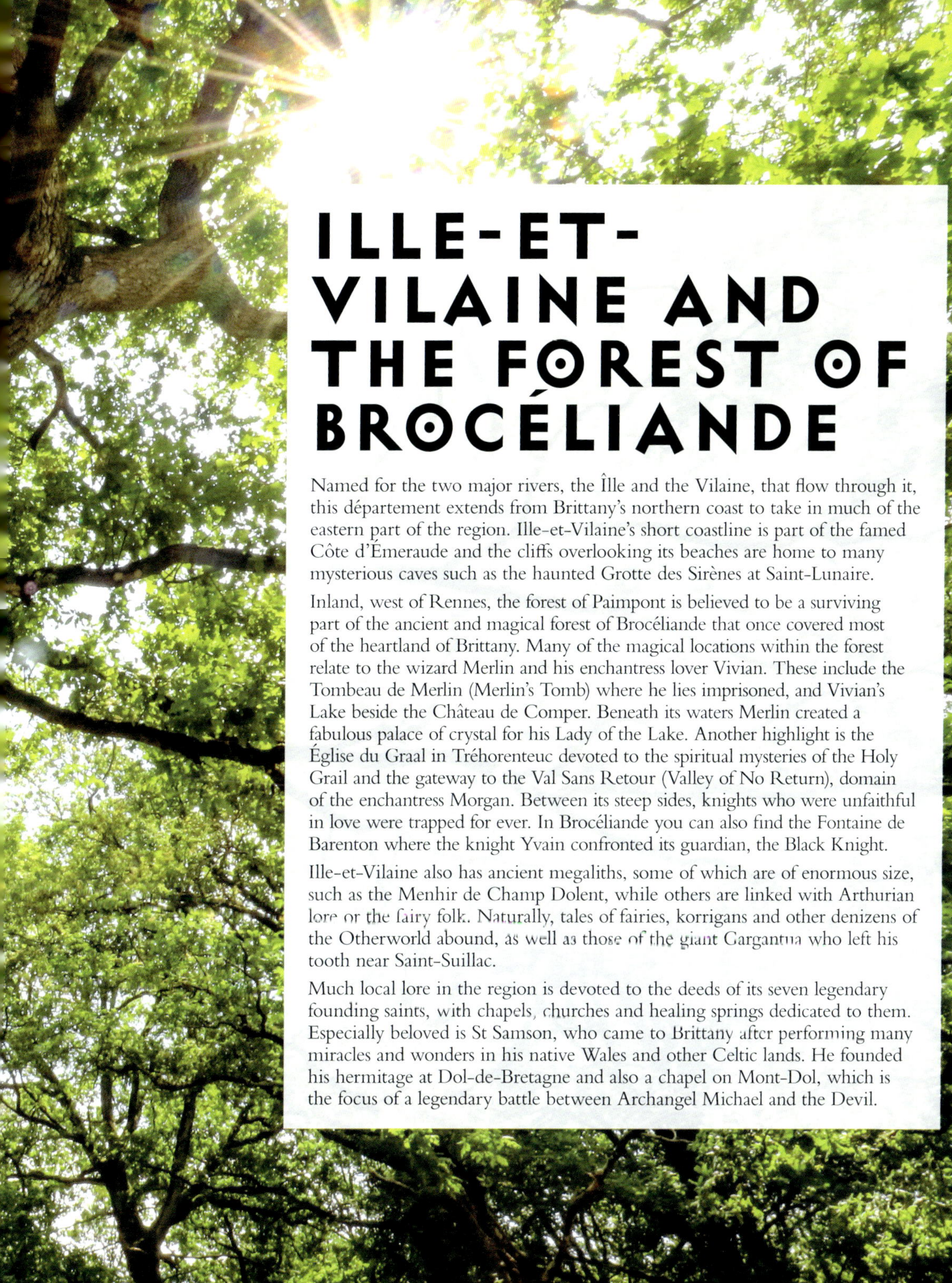

ILLE-ET-VILAINE AND THE FOREST OF BROCÉLIANDE

Named for the two major rivers, the Îlle and the Vilaine, that flow through it, this département extends from Brittany's northern coast to take in much of the eastern part of the region. Ille-et-Vilaine's short coastline is part of the famed Côte d'Émeraude and the cliffs overlooking its beaches are home to many mysterious caves such as the haunted Grotte des Sirènes at Saint-Lunaire.

Inland, west of Rennes, the forest of Paimpont is believed to be a surviving part of the ancient and magical forest of Brocéliande that once covered most of the heartland of Brittany. Many of the magical locations within the forest relate to the wizard Merlin and his enchantress lover Vivian. These include the Tombeau de Merlin (Merlin's Tomb) where he lies imprisoned, and Vivian's Lake beside the Château de Comper. Beneath its waters Merlin created a fabulous palace of crystal for his Lady of the Lake. Another highlight is the Église du Graal in Tréhorenteuc devoted to the spiritual mysteries of the Holy Grail and the gateway to the Val Sans Retour (Valley of No Return), domain of the enchantress Morgan. Between its steep sides, knights who were unfaithful in love were trapped for ever. In Brocéliande you can also find the Fontaine de Barenton where the knight Yvain confronted its guardian, the Black Knight.

Ille-et-Vilaine also has ancient megaliths, some of which are of enormous size, such as the Menhir de Champ Dolent, while others are linked with Arthurian lore or the fairy folk. Naturally, tales of fairies, korrigans and other denizens of the Otherworld abound, as well as those of the giant Gargantua who left his tooth near Saint-Suillac.

Much local lore in the region is devoted to the deeds of its seven legendary founding saints, with chapels, churches and healing springs dedicated to them. Especially beloved is St Samson, who came to Brittany after performing many miracles and wonders in his native Wales and other Celtic lands. He founded his hermitage at Dol-de-Bretagne and also a chapel on Mont-Dol, which is the focus of a legendary battle between Archangel Michael and the Devil.

1

2

ILLE-ET-VILAINE

1 Dent de Gargantua, Saint-Suliac

The huge menhir known as Gargantua's Tooth is said to have fallen from the mouth of the giant. He had met a fairy on the banks of the Rance and they fell in love and married, but when she gave birth to a boy the gluttonous Gargantua wanted to eat him. His fairy wife swapped the infant for a large stone wrapped in a nappy, and when the giant bit it he spat out his broken tooth forming the menhir. Furious, he then kicked the ground, creating a great hollow that flooded to form the estuary of the Rance. As he stormed off in a rage, he felt stones in his boots which he shook out to form the Rocher de Bizeux (48.6281, -2.0267) 8km away in the estuary, and the Rocher de Cancale (48.6815, -1.88265) 16km away in the Baie de Mont Saint-Michel. Gargantua's Tooth itself is now hidden in a field behind farmhouses. Made from quartzite, millennia of exposure to the elements have given it a jagged appearance.

48.5653, -1.9539; Parking: 48.5658, -1.9550, 80m

2

2

2 Dol-de-Bretagne

Founded by St Samson in the 6th century, Dol-de-Bretagne is forever entwined with the mythology of this enigmatic Welsh saint. In his lifetime he travelled through Ireland, Cornwall, the Isles of Scilly and the Channel Islands, establishing monasteries and converting the inhabitants, before arriving in Brittany. He's credited with many miracles, including healing, casting out demons and making a number of holy wells appear. On his travels, Samson also defeated several dragons and witches. A stained-glass window on the east side of the cathedral depicts one of his most famous exploits: taming a fierce dragon that was terrorising the land around Pont-Audemer (49.3550, 0.5147) in Normandy by wrapping his mantle around its neck. To the amazement of the people, he led the cowed beast around before commanding it to leave the land. Samson spent the rest of his years in Dol, and is said to have lived to the age of 120.

In the 9th century, Dol-de-Bretagne became the religious capital of Brittany and a cathedral was built on the site of Samson's monastery. Samson is one of the legendary seven founding saints of Brittany, and the cathedral is one of the stops on the pilgrimage route of the *Tro Breiz* ('Tour of Brittany') that takes in sites associated with each of them: Saint-Malo (founded by St Malo), Saint-Brieuc (St Brioc), Tréguier (St Tudwal), Saint-Pol-de-Léon (St Paul Aurelian), Quimper (St Corentin) and Vannes (St Padarn).

The present cathedral was commissioned by the infamous King John of England to replace the previous one burned down by his soldiers, and was originally designed with two towers. The missing second tower is said to have been knocked off by a stone thrown at the cathedral by the Devil from

Mont-Dol, which landed 2km further on and became the **Menhir de Champ-Dolent** (48.5353, -1.7394). At 9.3m and weighing 50 tonnes, it's one of the tallest standing stones in Brittany and the focus of several legends. In another version of its origin story, the stone burst out of the ground to separate two brothers who were duelling. The best-known legend, though, is that the menhir sinks imperceptibly into the ground every time a local person dies, and when it has completely disappeared the world will come to an end.

48.5508, -1.7558; Parking: 48.5462, -1.7559, 700m

3 La Guerche-de-Bretagne

This historic town sits on the Ogmios alignment of sacred sites and its standout feature is the **Basilique Notre-Dame de l'Assomption** (Our Lady of the Assumption). The oldest parts of the basilica date from the 11th century, and its famous Renaissance-era wood panels depict scenes from the Bible, the seven deadly sins, and mythical creatures such as centaurs and gryphons. On one side of the square outside the basilica is a row of nine half-timbered houses that were built in the 1500s.

La Guerche was one of the Knights Templars' major bases in Brittany, with an important commandery founded by Guillaume II, Lord of La Guerche, who became a high-ranking Templar. Guillaume's mother was from the noble family of **Pouancé Castle**, 22km away on the Ogmios line. The remains of the commandery can still be seen just to the east of the town at Le Temple (47.9458, -1.2177), although it's on private property.

47.9422, -1.2298; Parking: 47.9406, -1.2295, 200m

4 Maison des Fées, Tressé

In local lore this prehistoric passage grave (allée couverte) was known as the Fairies' House as it was said to have been built as their dwelling place. According to one tale, a cow belonging to them escaped and ate some of the local farmer's crops. As compensation the fairies gave the farmer a piece of bread that would stay fresh and never get smaller no matter how much he and his family ate, provided he kept its origins a secret. Inevitably, the farmer didn't keep his side of the bargain and the bread immediately went stale and hard. Atmospherically located in a small clearing deep within the Forêt du Mesnil, the Fairies House has a 12-m long chamber, more complete than most, with its roof slabs intact and forming a narrow passageway. A very unusual feature is that two of the stone slabs have pairs of dome shapes sculpted on them, possibly representing the breasts of the Mother Goddess.

48.4847, -1.8769; Parking: 48.4823, -1.8759, 300m

5 Menhir de la Haute-Pierre, Champeaux

Located by the long-distance Ogmios alignment, the Menhir de la Haute-Pierre (High Stone) is a striking 4m high standing stone that stands isolated in a field. The stone is quartzite, giving it a more angular appearance than most menhirs, and its main faces are oriented east and west. This menhir also forms part of a local alignment with two other nearby standing stones. The nearest is the 2m high Menhir de Villaumur (48.1286, -1.2889), located some 750m away by the road running around the lake of La Cantache. A further 4.5km beyond to the southeast and set in a field near Pocé-les-Bois is the third stone, the 3.7m tall Pierre Blanche (48.1069, -1.2336; roadside parking 48.1066, -1.2351, 120m).

48.1317, -1.2981; Parking: 48.1326, -1.2992, 150m.

4

3

5

6 Mont-Dol

In ancient times this hill, which rises from the flat countryside north of **Dol-de-Bretagne**, was sacred to the goddess Cybele who had a temple there, and also to the Celtic storm god Taranis. The Romans called it Mont Jovis after Jupiter, the Roman equivalent of Taranis. Early texts also refer to the worship of Belenus and Mercury on the mount.

St Samson (see **Dol-de-Bretagne**) built a chapel dedicated to Archangel Michael on the ruins of the temple of Cybele but when the saint first came to Mont-Dol the hill was reputedly the domain of nine witches. They killed one of his followers before the saint expelled them. When the ruined chapel was demolished in the 19th century, the remains of an altar on which bulls were sacrificed to Cybele were found beneath it.

As well as the wonderful views that take in **Mont Saint-Michel** and the surrounding bay, the mount's flat summit also has several standout features. Most prominent is the octagonal **Tour Notre-Dame de l'Espérance** (Our Lady of Hope Tower, 48.5721, -1.7666), surmounted by a statue of the Virgin and Child. It's open for visitors to take in the view from the top. Although it was constructed in 1857, it's said to mark Mont-Dol's ancient power spot. At the same time a new chapel, also dedicated to Notre-Dame de l'Espérance, the patroness of sailors, was built nearby. On the edge of the mount, by the chapel, there's a rock outcrop known as **Le Siège et les Griffes du Diable** (The Devil's Bottom and Claws, 48.5724, -1.7667) that marks the spot where the Archangel Michael threw the Devil onto the rock with such force that the imprint of his buttocks was left. Then as he dug his claws into the rock to save himself from falling they too made their mark. The archangel's footprint is also said to be impressed on one of the rocks. In local legend, the Devil built a magnificent palace on Mont Saint-Michel, in response to which Michael created an even more fabulous one on Mont-Dol made of glass, which he then agreed to swap with the Devil. But when the sun rose on the first morning the Devil discovered Michael's palace was made of ice, and it melted. The water formed the pond on the mount's summit.

Parking: 48.5719, -1.7677

7 Pointe du Décollé, Saint-Lunaire

Cut off from the mainland by a crevasse sometimes known as the Grotte aux Fées, the Pointe du Décollé (Headless Point) can sometimes look like an otherworldly island, especially when fog rolls in and obscures the tip, hence its name. It's said that an army led by King Arthur and his nephew Hywel, King of Brittany, came ashore here to retake Hywel's kingdom after it had been invaded by Saxons.

There are several caves in the cliffs below the point, the most famous of which is the **Grotte des Sirènes** (48.6447, -2.1128, 1.2km, low tide only) accessed by walking along the beach from the Plage de Longchamp (48.6376, -2.1177). There are stories of ethereal female voices singing from the cave on All Saints' Eve, 31 October, and some say they belong to a congregation of young women who were listening to mass in the cave when they were cut off by the tide and drowned. Steps cut into the rock lead down from the entrance into a 21m-deep cavern, where there's a pool even at low tide, lit by a shaft of light from above. A barrier further back prevents visitors accessing the cave's deeper and more dangerous parts.

The nearby town takes its name from St Lunaire (Leonorus), a son of Hywel who, on first landing at the point, encountered fog so thick he had to cut it with a sword. The saint built a chapel in what was then forest and is now the site of the town's Vielle Église (48.6350, -2.1078)

48.6450, -2.1126; Parking: 48.6431, -2.1132, 200m

7

8 Château de Comper, Concoret

The legendary birthplace of Vivian, the Lady of the Lake, this castle is steeped in Arthurian lore. The first fortress there was said to have been created by the huntress goddess, Diana, who gave it to the knight Dionas, Vivian's father. The castle stands by the wide, brooding waters of **Vivian's Lake**, also known as the Étang de Comper (48.0693, -2.1720), its surface concealing her palace from the eyes of ordinary mortals. Schooled in magic by Merlin, Vivian exploited his desire for her to learn all the wizard's secrets, then imprisoned him beneath the **Tombeau de Merlin** at Saint-Malon-sur-Mel. In the castle she raised Lancelot, famous Knight of the Round Table to whom she was fairy godmother.

Several castles have risen and fallen on the spot since the Middle Ages, and the ruins of red stone walls and towers, covered in vegetation, can be seen beside the moat behind the current manor house. Built in the 19th century in the Renaissance style, it's now home to the Centre de l'Imaginaire Arthurien (Centre of the Arthurian Imagination), a cultural association devoted to the history, mythology and artistic exploration of the Arthurian legends. Exhibitions are put on inside and during the summer there are outdoor displays, performances, and storytelling for children in the park.

Growing in a hollow below the lake's bank is the extraordinary **Chêne d'Artus** (Arthur's Oak, 48.0700, -2.1717), which some say marks the place of Arthur's burial. The trunk emerges from a large rock and divides into seven enormous branches. At least 300 years old, it's nearly 30m high and its trunk is 7m around.

48.0700, -2.1723; open May to October, €€

9 Guillotin Oak, Concoret

This vast oak tree, thought to be over 1,000 years old, is a celebrated and much visited landmark that's set in a meadow looking towards the ancient Brocéliande Forest. The oak stands 20m high and the circumference of its gnarled and hollow trunk is 10m. The tree is named after a priest, Pierre Paul Guillotin, who hid precious statues and other items from his church in it during the French Revolution. Beneath it, according to a local legend, lies the treasure of Éon de l'Étoile, a 12th-century monk with a reputation for

6

6

9

10

magic. Étoile proclaimed himself the new Messiah and led his fanatical followers in raids on churches, monasteries and castles, pillaging their treasures and riches. In popular imagination he became a Robin Hood type figure. Today, the tree is reputed to possess a healing energy that can be drawn on by leaning against the trunk. Encircled by wooden benches, it's a popular spot with tourists.
48.0564, -2.2267; Parking: 48.0574, -2.2263, 130m

10 Hollow Oaks of Kernéant, Néant-sur-Yvel

Thought by some to be the remains of an ancient Druid's grove, these hauntingly shaped oak trees are mysteriously hollow on the inside. The Chênes Creux de Kernéant stand on top of a hill beside the small Chapelle Notre-Dame, with a view to the magical forest of Brocéliande below.
The small town of Néant-sur-Yvel lies 3km to the south, close to the edge of the forest. Beside the road just outside town is the healing **Fontaine d'Anne-Toussainte-de-Volvire** (48.0205, -2.3250). Anne, who came from the noble family of the nearby Château du Bois de la Roche (48.0425, -2.3319), was regarded locally as a saint for her piety and good works, especially helping the poor and sick. When she died in 1694 her funeral cortege, drawn by oxen, stopped at this spot and the spring burst forth, its waters soon gaining a reputation for curing illnesses and disabilities. Now set in a small stone enclosure with a flower border, the spring is surmounted by a cross with a statue of St Anne, mother of the Virgin Mary in a niche. St Anne is sometimes equated with Ana, the Celtic Mother Goddess, signifying that this could originally have been a sacred pagan spring.
48.0386, -2.3479

11 Église du Graal, Tréhorenteuc

The unusual Grail Church is decorated with colourful scenes from Arthurian legend and Grail romance giving it an ambience both magical and esoteric. Thanks to the initiative of the village priest, Henri Gillard, the dilapidated church was restored during the 1940s and 1950s and his statue, erected in 1999 now stands outside. The church complements the area's deep connection

11

11

with Arthurian lore but also reflects Gillard's esoteric belief in a universal spirituality that underlies all religion and mythology.

The church's official dedication was to Sainte Onenne, a young noblewoman from Tréhorenteuc who took a vow of poverty and became a goose keeper. One day, a lord of the estate approached determined to violate Onenne but the geese shouted out a warning and she was saved at the last moment by the local people. Geese are now sacred to this local Breton saint and are sometimes driven in procession to her holy well which lies nearby (48.0105, -2.2874).

Above the entrance to the Église du Graal is the enigmatic phrase 'la porte est en dedans' ('the gateway is inside'). The vibrant stained-glass windows, paintings and statues mix Christian iconography with images of the Round Table and the Grail, and there are depictions of legendary scenes such as Lancelot's defeat of Morgan le Fay in the **Val Sans Retour**, Yvain's combat with the Black Knight at the **Fontaine de Barenton** and the fairy Vivian enchanting Merlin in the Forest of Brocéliande. The link between the Christian and Arthurian imagery is, of course, the Holy Grail. A Christian relic that held Christ's blood and was brought to Europe by Joseph of Arimathea, the Grail is also the focus of the Knights of the Round Table's quest. There's other symbolism within the church too, such as a zodiac in one stained-glass window, and the stations of the cross – the ninth depicts Christ and Morgan le Fay. As the notice outside the church says, there are many symbols within to decode. The church has also been likened to the mysteriously decorated church at **Rennes-le-Château** in the Languedoc.

Tréhorenteuc also has an excellent tourist information centre with many books on Breton legend and mythology, some of them in English, as well as multilingual guides and maps of the forest. During the summer months storytelling guides can be hired, too.

48.0078, -2.2872; Parking: 48.0073, -2.2876, 50m

12 Fontaine de Barenton, Paimpont

Hidden deep within the Forest of Brocéliande, lies the Fontaine de Barenton where Merlin is said to have met the water nymph Vivian. She was sitting on a flat stone beside the spring when Merlin fell instantly in love with her.

The stone is now known as the Perron de Merlin (Merlin's Step) and sprinkling water from the spring on this 'rain stone' was said to summon a storm. In times of drought it was the custom for the local priest to lead a procession to the spring to perform the ritual, although unusually the spring has never been assigned to a saint. It's been a sacred site since antiquity, originally dedicated to the Gallic god of healing, fire and light, Belenos or Bel. Its name comes from 'Bel-nemeton', sacred place of Bel.

In several medieval Arthurian romances, including Chrétien de Troyes' *Yvain*, the spring is guarded by the Black Knight, who appears whenever someone attempts to perform the storm-raising ritual and fights them to the death. Yvain, seeking revenge for the killing of his cousin Calogrenant, summons the Black Knight and finally defeats him, becoming guardian in his place.

The hamlet that lies at the beginning of the path to the spring is called Folle Pensée, literally meaning 'mad thought' or perhaps originally 'cure for madness' because the spring waters were said to cure insanity and mental illness. The hamlet is built on the site of a convent and some say it takes its name from a college of druidesses who once used the spring to cure this malady. Healthy people who take the waters are said to be made wise, especially in spiritual matters.

The Fontaine de Barenton is a place of the fairies, too. In the Middle Ages it was the custom to take a newborn child to the spring so that the fairies would give them good fortune. More recently, young women who wanted to know if they would be married within the next year would throw a pin into the spring, and if the water bubbled it was a yes. The effervescent waters remain at a constant 10 degrees throughout the seasons, never freezing even in the deepest winter, and the spring is also often shrouded by mist at dawn – all enhancing Barenton's reputation as a place of fairy magic.

48.0389, -2.2469; Parking: 48.0411, -2.2564, 1.25km

13 **Tombeau de Merlin, Saint-Malon-sur-Mel**

Near the edge of the Paimpont Forest in the dappled shade of an enchanted woodland clearing, a split megalith sits at the centre of a magic circle of small stones. This strange construction is known as the Tombeau de Merlin. Despite the name, it's not thought to be where the wise and powerful wizard of Arthurian lore is buried, but where he was imprisoned by Vivian as he slept by a hawthorn bush. The deceitful fairy, having discovered Merlin's deepest magical secrets, drew a circle around him with her veil nine times, trapping him in an invisible prison. Visitors sometimes leave natural, hand-crafted offerings by the stone, or small tokens after making wishes – all of which adds to the enchanted atmosphere of the place.

Near the parking area is a flat stone known as the Lit de Merlin (Merlin's Bed, 48.0776, -2.1186), while 170m further down the trail past Merlin's Tomb can be found the so-called **Fontaine de Jouvence** (48.07837, -2.1155), a woodland spring that fills a large round pool lined with stones. It's said that at the summer solstice, parents were accustomed to bathing children born during the preceding year in the spring, but it wasn't until the late 19th century that it was given the designation of 'Fountain of Youth'. A local tale says that the fairies of the wood come to drink and bathe there, which is why they never age.

Near to the spring can be found the **Champs de Cailloux** (Field of Stones, 48.0786, -2.1153), an old quarry where visitors pile small stones into cairns of fantastical shapes and sizes, sometimes placing pieces of paper with their wishes wedged between them.

48.0778, -2.1175; Parking: 48.0776, -2.1190, 100m

14 **Val Sans Retour, Tréhorenteuc**

This forested valley has become identified with the domain of the enchantress Morgan le Fay, half-sister of Arthur and leader of the nine sorceresses of the Isle of Avalon. She was the lover of the knight Guiomar, but when she caught him with another woman she turned the pair into stone and created the Val Sans Retour to entrap other faithless knights. Eventually there were 250 knights spellbound there, unable to move. Morgan set these prisoners a number of trials, including defeating a dragon and two knights, as well as passing through a wall of fire, that, if successfully accomplished by an honourable champion, would break the spell and free them. All who tried failed until faithful Lancelot, begged by a maiden to win her lover's freedom, fulfilled the tasks.

The valley features in Arthurian romance under various names such as the Perilous

Vale or Valley of False Lovers. A trail leads up the valley from the **Église du Graal,** and after a welcoming waterfall named the Cascade de Rauco, you come to the **Miroir aux Fées** (Fairies' Mirror, 48.0009, -2.2859), also known as the Lac de Morgane. The lake's surface is so still and clear that the fairies of the forest and even Morgan herself are said to come and gaze at their reflections in the water. It's an enchanting place, with waterlilies floating on the surface and the occasional croaking of frogs.

Nearby is a piece of modern magic, the **Arbre d'Or** (Golden Tree, 48.0013, -2.2862), a chestnut tree covered in gold leaf. Surrounded by five trees blackened by the devastating fire of 1990, it symbolises the indestructibility of the forest and of nature. Jagged stones encircle the tree to prevent vandalism and green ferns flourish all around. Already, folklore has grown up around this tree, said to bear golden leaves at night that the elf-like lutins collect for a magic potion that heals the burnt trees. Glimpsed through the forest, the Golden Tree really looks like it comes from another, more magical realm.

After 400m the trail rises and comes to a large outcrop of rock overlooking the valley, the **Rocher des Faux-Amants** (False Lovers' Rock, 48.0009, -2.2842). Two of the rocks are said to be Guiomar and his lover, turned to stone by Morgan. On the crest of the valley is another ridge of rock, worn smooth by erosion, called the **Siège de Merlin** (Merlin's Seat, 48.0010, -2.2827) where the magician sat to watch over the forest below. Merlin's Seat marks the end of the Val Sans Retour, but trails continuing deeper into the forest lead to other special sites. The **Hotié de Viviane** (Vivian's Hostel, 47.9997, -2.2683), the remains of an ancient burial chamber, can be reached by a circuitous 1.75km trail from Merlin's Seat or an 800m walk from the parking place at La Touche Guérin (47.9950, -2.2670). Just down from a rock crest known as the Échine du Dragon (Dragon's Spine), the chamber is said to be Vivian's dwelling place.

According to local lore, the **Tombeau du Géant** (47.9919, -2.2692, parking as for the Hotié de Vivian, 750m) is the burial place of a giant killed by one of Arthur's knights. At 4m long, it does look very much like an open grave, but it's actually a chamber from a Bronze Age tumulus consisting of stones thought to have been repurposed from menhirs taken from a nearby, even older alignment. Astonishingly, the site was completely forgotten until it was rediscovered in the 1970s. Surrounded by trees and ferns, it's an evocative spot, but is closed during hunting season, September–March.

Parking: 48.0049, -2.2881

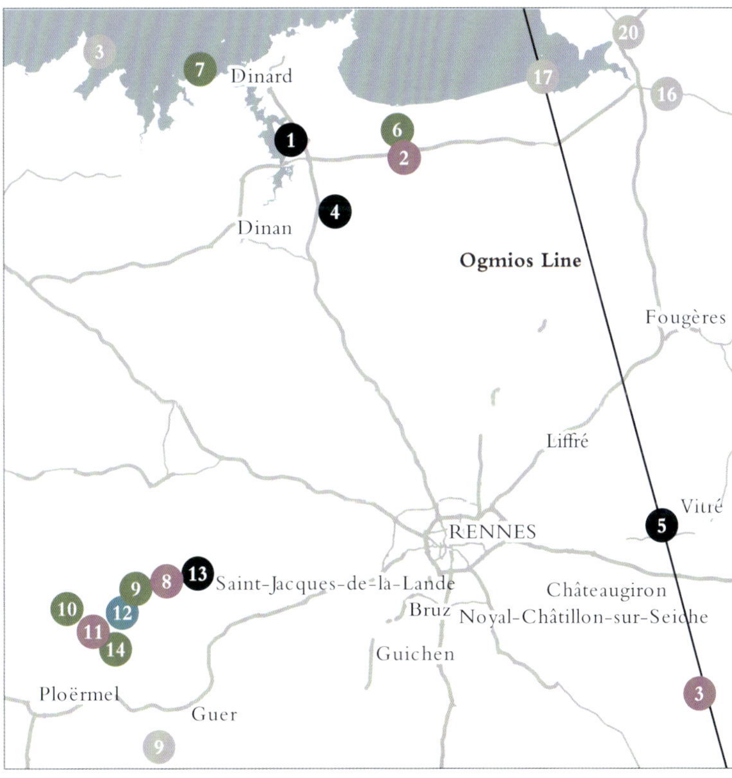

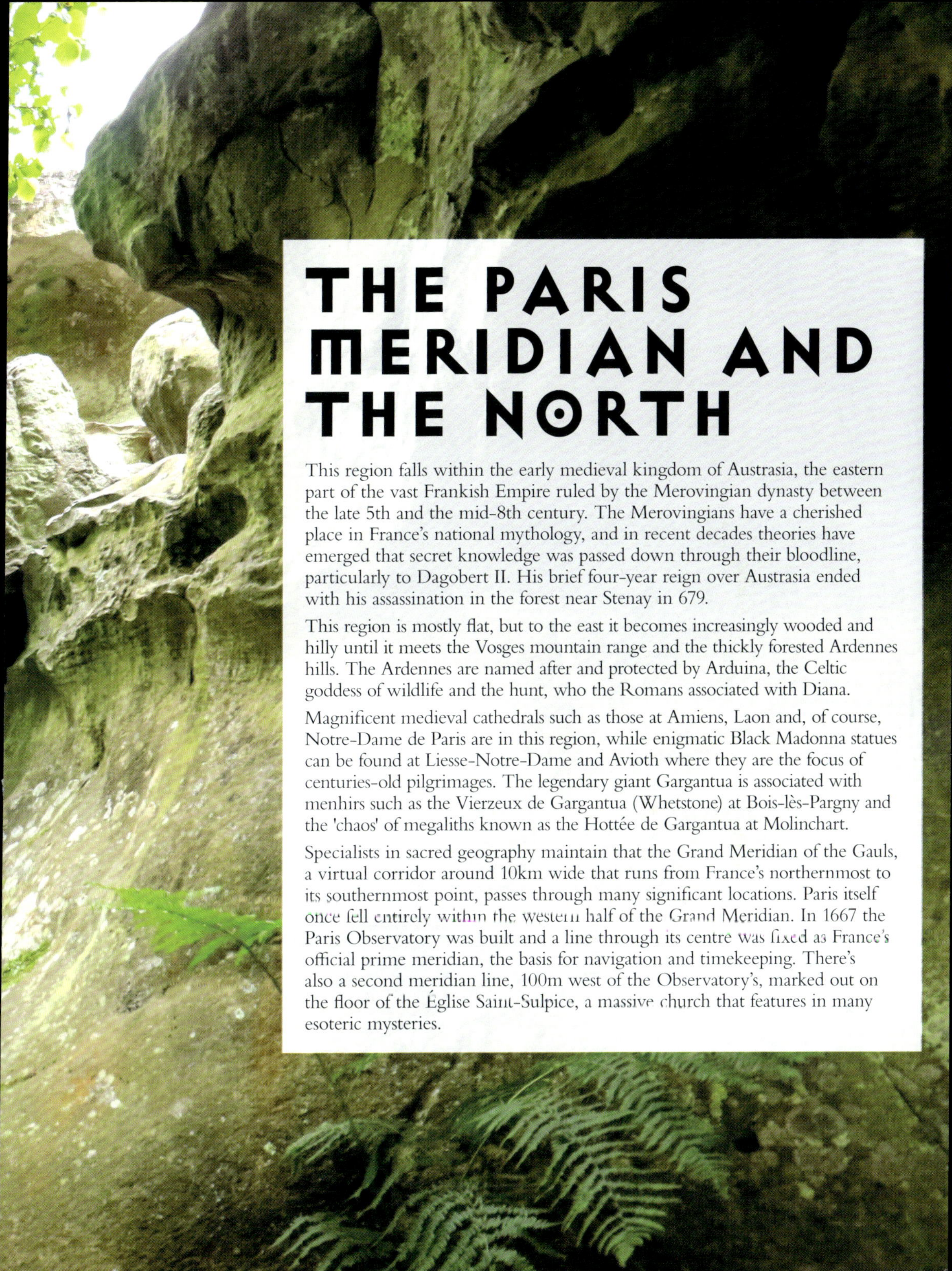

THE PARIS MERIDIAN AND THE NORTH

This region falls within the early medieval kingdom of Austrasia, the eastern part of the vast Frankish Empire ruled by the Merovingian dynasty between the late 5th and the mid-8th century. The Merovingians have a cherished place in France's national mythology, and in recent decades theories have emerged that secret knowledge was passed down through their bloodline, particularly to Dagobert II. His brief four-year reign over Austrasia ended with his assassination in the forest near Stenay in 679.

This region is mostly flat, but to the east it becomes increasingly wooded and hilly until it meets the Vosges mountain range and the thickly forested Ardennes hills. The Ardennes are named after and protected by Arduina, the Celtic goddess of wildlife and the hunt, who the Romans associated with Diana.

Magnificent medieval cathedrals such as those at Amiens, Laon and, of course, Notre-Dame de Paris are in this region, while enigmatic Black Madonna statues can be found at Liesse-Notre-Dame and Avioth where they are the focus of centuries-old pilgrimages. The legendary giant Gargantua is associated with menhirs such as the Vierzeux de Gargantua (Whetstone) at Bois-lès-Pargny and the 'chaos' of megaliths known as the Hottée de Gargantua at Molinchart.

Specialists in sacred geography maintain that the Grand Meridian of the Gauls, a virtual corridor around 10km wide that runs from France's northernmost to its southernmost point, passes through many significant locations. Paris itself once fell entirely within the western half of the Grand Meridian. In 1667 the Paris Observatory was built and a line through its centre was fixed as France's official prime meridian, the basis for navigation and timekeeping. There's also a second meridian line, 100m west of the Observatory's, marked out on the floor of the Église Saint-Sulpice, a massive church that features in many esoteric mysteries.

SOMME

1 Amiens Cathedral

One of the glories of the golden age of cathedral-building, Notre-Dame d'Amiens is the biggest Gothic cathedral in France. The exterior is covered in magnificent carvings, including fantastical creatures and what some have interpreted as alchemical symbolism. The airy and soaring interior is illuminated by a great number of lofty, stained-glass windows. Amid the statues and tombs of eminent individuals the most conspicuous and enigmatic feature is the immense labyrinth laid out on the floor of the nave. It is octagonal in shape and made up of black and white stones. Labyrinths are found in other medieval cathedrals, most famously **Chartres**, but their purpose is a mystery. While they're conventionally explained as symbolising Christ's path to the cross, others see a deeper meaning. Amiens' labyrinth was erased in 1825 as it was thought to be a distraction to worshippers, especially children, but happily it was restored 70 years later.

Amiens became a centre of pilgrimage when what was reputedly the head of St John the Baptist was installed there in 1206, after having been looted from Constantinople during the Crusades. The head, which is on display in the Treasury, is set in a silver-gilt reliquary with a crystal cover and remains the cathedral's most famous relic. The cathedral lies on the Meridian of the Gauls and is only 2km from the Paris Meridian (see **Paris Observatory**).

49.8944, 2.3019; Parking: €€ 49.8965, 2.3008, 200m

PARIS

2 Paris Observatory

This elegant baroque-style building set amid beautiful gardens was one of the first astronomical observatories ever built in Europe, a landmark in the Scientific Revolution of the 16th and 17th centuries. Yet beneath the surface there are clues that magical knowledge, including an awareness of sacred geography, played a part in its foundation and the establishment of the Paris Meridian, which cuts through the building.

The meridian, a straight line between the north and south poles, was fixed by a group of French scientists and scholars on the summer solstice of 1667 as they were laying out the observatory's foundations. It was used as the prime meridian for maps, navigation and timekeeping in France and its colonies for nearly 250 years. Some of the surveying of the line to the south wasn't completed until the early 1800s, when the astronomer and freemason François Arago followed it through the Languedoc and Spain to the significantly named Sa Dragonera (Dragon Island, 39.5839, 2.3214), just off the coast of Majorca. In 1994, a series of 135 bronze medallions marking the path of the meridian were set into the streets of Paris as a memorial to Arago.

Visit the great hall on the observatory's second floor and see the meridian marked with a brass line, over 30m long. At this location, astronomer Giovanni Cassini and his son are said to have traced the sun's path through the year from solstice to solstice by projecting a circle of sunlight through a small opening. Observations were finally completed around 1730. Before he died in 1712, Giovanni Cassini described the meridian line as the 'oracle of Apollo'.

Like all such zero meridians its position was

seemingly arbitrary, chosen only because that's where the observatory was to be built, and its purpose purely practical. However, patterns on the landscape made up of alignments between medieval and even more ancient sites, such as those around **Rennes-le-Château** and **Rennes-les-Bains** in the Languedoc, include the Paris Meridian in their geometry. These sites long pre-date the official fixing of the meridian, indicating that it was known about in past ages. The term 'Rose Line' is now often used to refer to the older, more mystical aspect of the meridian. It was popularised by Dan Brown in his 2003 novel *The Da Vinci Code*, although contrary to popular belief he didn't invent it.

Esoteric scholars also discovered the Grand Meridian of the Gauls (also known as the Meridian of the Omphalos (Navel) of Gaul) that was known to the Celts, and possibly even earlier peoples. This 10km-wide band is said to extend from Dunkirk on the Channel coast to the Pyrenees and the Paris Meridian falls within it, passing just east of **Saint-Benoît-sur-Loire**, regarded by some as the geographical and sacred centre of ancient Gaul.

Beneath the observatory, galleries and tunnels go down to the same depth – around 28m – as the building is high. After visiting them in 1871, famous astronomer Camille Flammarion is said to have seen a statue of the Virgin in an alcove, engraved with the name 'Notre-Dame de Sous-Terre'. It bore the date 1671, the year of the Observatory's completion. Although Flammarion didn't mention its colour, the statue shares its name with the Black Madonnas of **Chartres Cathedral** and **Mont Saint-Michel,** so may have been another Vierge Noire. While the statue is marked on 19th-century plans of the Observatory, its current location is unknown.

1

The road along the east side of the Paris Observatory is one of the main routes of the Camino de Santiago, the pilgrimage trail to the shrine at Santiago de Compostela in Spain. This section, known as the Via Turonensis (Tours Route) was established during the Middle Ages and is still followed by pilgrims today. They set out from the lofty **Tour Saint-Jacques** (St James' Tower, 48.8578, 2.3489, open May-November, €€; parking 48.8569, 2.3497, €), the only remaining part of one of Paris' most important medieval churches. Now set in gardens, the 54m tower was built in the 1500s and is topped by a statue of St James. The pilgrim way crosses to the Île de la Cité in the Seine, passing Paris' iconic **Notre-Dame Cathedral** (48.8531, 2.3497), said to have been built on the site of a temple of Isis. It then heads out of the city along the Rue St Jacques (St James Street) on its long road to join the other trails at **Saint-Jean-Pied-de-Port** before crossing the Pyrenees into Spain.

48.8368, 2.3365 (currently closed for renovation); Metro Denfert-Rochereau

2

3 Saint-Sulpice, Paris

Over the centuries many have seen a hidden meaning in the design and decoration of the vast **Église Saint-Sulpice,** which is comparable in size to Notre Dame and was designed to rival the great cathedral by its founder, parish priest and mystic Jean-Jacques Olier. It replaced earlier churches dedicated to St Sulpice and took almost a century to build. The 20 chapels around its soaring 30m-high interior are filled with acclaimed paintings and sculptures. Especially significant is the Chapelle des Saints-Anges where Eugène Delacroix painted three murals featuring angels in the 1840s. Several esoteric writers believe hidden meanings are encoded in these murals, and for some they are linked with the mysteries surrounding **Rennes-le-Château** and **Rennes-les-Bains** (see ppxxx and xxx) in the Languedoc.

Saint-Sulpice is also famous for its meridian, a brass line set into a marble band marking out a north–south line, similar to that laid out in the **Paris Observatory**. A beam of sunlight shining through a small opening in one of the south windows forms an oval on the floor, which crosses the line at midday. Golden discs mark the spring and autumn equinoxes and a marble plaque on the floor close to the window indicates the summer solstice. As autumn progresses, the light climbs an Egyptian-style obelisk set against the far wall until it reaches a point marking the winter solstice. The meridian features in the novel and movie of *The Da Vinci Code*. For a time in the 1700s Saint-Sulpice's north–south line was considered Paris' second meridian after the observatory's, which is some 100m east. Intriguingly, Saint-Sulpice's meridian passes directly through **Bourges** (see ppxxx), nearly 200km to the south. St Sulpice, a celebrated holy man of the Merovingian era, was Archbishop of Bourges and credited with many miracles. His feast day falls on the day of his death, 17 January – a date that recurs in the mysteries of Rennes-le-Château.

48.8508, 2.3342; Metro Saint-Sulpice; Underground parking €€: 48.8486, 2.3256, 800m

ESSONNE

4 Notre-Dame-du-Fort, Étampes

Among the remarkable interior décor and statuary in this imposing church is a little-known Black Madonna sculpted in stone, which dates from the 1600s. There's also an especially elegant coloured statue of Archangel Michael defeating the dragon, a scene also depicted in one of the stained-glass windows. Founded in the 1020s, the church was originally associated with the nearby castle. It was completely rebuilt a century later and fortified a century after that during the Hundred Years War with England, hence its name 'Our Lady of the Fort'. The crypt of the original church remains, the stone columns and painted ceilings giving it a cave-like atmosphere.

Étampes lies directly east of the great cathedral of **Chartres** and is on the Via Turonensis, one of the routes of the Camino de Santiago to Spain that begins near the **Paris Observatory**, 40km to the north. There are a number of medieval remains in the town, most strikingly the tower, Tour de Guinette (48.4372, 2.1583), the only surviving part of the castle. The Bastille des Portereaux (48.4286, 2.1514) and the Wolf's Tower (48.4305, 2.1540) are part of the medieval ramparts.

A huge menhir that once served as a boundary stone known as the 'Pierrefitte' (or Pierre-Fixe, Fixed Stone, 48.4289, 2.1058, parking 48.4292, 2.1053, 80m), can be seen just outside Étampes in the hamlet named after it. The stone is a towering 4.2m with a further 1.5m underground.

48.4350, 2.1642; Parking outside €

6

AISNE

5 Notre-Dame de Liesse

Named for its celebrated Black Madonna carved from black ebony, the basilica of Our Lady of Joy in Liesse-Notre-Dame – the town named after her – has been the focus of pilgrimage for 900 years. In the Middle Ages its shrine was one of the most important in France, and from the early 15th century three French kings made pilgrimages there. Worshippers pray to Notre-Dame-de-Liesse for the relief of all ailments and misfortunes but, like so many Black Madonnas in France, her statue is a 19th century replica. The original was burned during the French Revolution but its ashes are now in a church in Montreal, Canada.

The Black Madonna is at the heart of the town's foundation legend, that of Isméria and the three Knights of Eppes. Isméria was an Egyptian princess, daughter of the Sultan of Cairo. Some have seen her name as a conflation of Isis and Mary, personifying the divine feminine. During the Crusades three brothers, all Knights Hospitaller and sons of the Lord of Eppes, were taken prisoner. The Sultan sent his daughter to try to convert them to Islam but the Virgin Mary appeared to the knights who carved a statue of her for Isméria. The Virgin then appeared to the princess in her sleep, winning her over to Christianity and she resolved to escape with the knights, taking the statue with her. Miraculously, the gates of the prison opened, then after falling asleep exhausted, the four awoke to find themselves back in France, by a spring some 7km from the brothers' home in Eppes. Vowing to build a chapel in the Virgin's honour in thanks for their miraculous deliverance, they started out for their father's castle but after a short distance the statue became too heavy to carry and the knights realised the Virgin had chosen her own site. The brothers built the chapel to house Notre-Dame de Liesse in 1134, on the site now occupied by the Basilica. Isméria was baptised in nearby **Laon Cathedral**, taking the name Marie, and married one of the brothers. After the chapel was built the spring's waters were found to be healing. Now known as the **Fontaine Miraculeuse** (49.6110, 3.7998), it's on the edge of town 300m from the basilica. The well-shrine housing the spring, topped with a statue of the Virgin and Child, is usually locked but there are two taps nearby from which the water can be drawn, though a notice advises they are only for the use of pilgrims. Beside the spring is the Chapelle Santa Casa (Holy House), a replica of the Virgin Mary's house at Loreto, the site of another famous Black Madonna. Inside is a fresco depicting the legend of Isméria and the Knights of Eppes.

49.6100, 3.8039; Parking: 49.9093, 3.8033, 150m

4

5

5

6 Hottée de Gargantua, Molinchart

This rock chaos, forming a hill-like mound, is said to have fallen from a basket on Gargantua's back when he was building the Butte de **Laon** (Laon's Mound). The tumble of gigantic boulders is now overgrown with trees and shrubs and crisscrossed by small paths through the undergrowth. According to the legend, the giant was standing with one foot on the Butte de Laon 5km to the east and the other on the hill of Saint-Gobain 12km to the west. Rather drunk at the time, Gargantua was startled by a flash of lightning and fell backwards, spilling his load. As he strode off, a cast-off stone formed the **Vierzieux de Gargantua** 23km away. **Saint-Gobain** (49.5967, 3.3758), where Gargantua's left foot was placed, is named after the 7th-century Irish saint who was martyred in his hermitage in the nearby forest. As a result, the town later became a place of pilgrimage.

49.5569, 3.5425; Parking: 49.5600, 3.5403, 400m

Saint-Martin

7 Laon

One of France's most historic cities, Laon is spread around a 100m high mound, the Butte de Laon, which dominates the surrounding Picardy Plain and is said to have been created by the giant Gargantua (see **Hottée de Gargantua**). There's been a settlement on the site since the Gallo-Roman era.

Towering over the city is **Laon Cathedral** (49.5642, 3.6250), work on which began in 1150. Featuring the skilfully carved stonework typical of Gothic architecture, Laon's decoration is unusual in that farm animals feature prominently. Most striking are six life-sized bulls commemorating the legend of the cathedral's building. When the oxen carrying the stone up the steep hill were exhausted and unable to carry on, a huge white bull miraculously appeared to pull the cart to the summit.

There's much of Laon's medieval past to be seen in the old city around the cathedral, including the ramparts, gates and towers of the **Citadelle de Laon** (49.5647, 3.6297). The Knights Templar (Templiers) were a major presence in medieval Laon, you can visit the small but elegant **Chapelle des Templiers** (49.5631, 3.6272) dating from around 1140 and dedicated to St John the Baptist. As with many Templar churches, its octagonal form reflects that of the Holy Sepulchre in Jerusalem. The adjacent buildings of the former Templar commandery now house Laon's Art and Archaeology Museum, which displays artefacts from all eras of the region's past as well as a collection of Mediterranean antiquities. One of the most impressive of Laon's many churches lies on the edge of the city. The **Église Abbatiale Saint-Martin** (49.5625, 3.6119) was built at the same time as the Cathedral and was originally part of an abbey.

Parking: 49.5638, 3.6293

8 Vierzieux de Gargantua, Bois-lès-Pargny

This striking menhir, 4.35m high and broken at the tip, is said to have been a stone Gargantua retrieved and cast out from his shoe as he left the **Hottée de Gargantua**. The megalith's name means 'whetstone' in the local dialect and refers to a second legend of a different giant who used it to sharpen his scythe. It now stands in an isolated location on the edge of farmland and can be reached by a rough farm track. It's little visited although there's a sign in the nearby village of Bois-lès-Pargny.

49.7511, 3.6544; Parking: 49.7502, 3.6533, 125m

ARDENNES

9 Abbaye d'Orval

Mystery surrounds the origin and much of the history of this famous abbey at Orval, just a kilometre over the border into Belgium and set in the Ardennes Forest. In 1070 a small group of monks arrived here from Calabria in the far south of Italy. At what was then a very remote and isolated spot, they built a chapel in a valley close to a sacred spring with a pool. Soon after, the area was visited by Matilda of Tuscany, one of the most powerful rulers of the period who possessed territory in Lorraine. According to legend, she lost her wedding ring in the pool and, distraught, went into the chapel to pray for its return. A trout then surfaced holding the ring in its mouth and Matilda declared 'This is truly a golden valley' ('val d'or' in French), giving Orval its name. In gratitude, she donated money to the chapel for the monks to found a monastery and the trout and ring still feature on the abbey's coat of arms.

However, the Italian monks didn't stay long, leaving the site for unknown reasons after about 40 years. The site was handed over to the Augustinian Order but very soon after the monks decided to switch to the Cistercian Rule. In response, the celebrated St Bernard of **Clairvaux**, head of the growing Cistercian order, sent seven monks there, after which the monastery expanded rapidly. Bernard was one of the most influential figures of his time but also one of the most enigmatic. He had a special reverence for Black Madonna sites as well as for the divine feminine aspects of religion, and famously championed the newly-formed Knights Templar.

Many have seen connections between such powerful individuals and organisations, believing they were all working to a co-ordinated plan of which Orval was the centre. According to some, one of the original group of Orval monks was Peter the Hermit, one of the preachers who is

said to have instigated the First Crusade. It's also been suggested that Orval Abbey guarded potent secrets, and even that Nostradamus later learned his powers of prophecy from an ancient book kept in the abbey's extensive library.

Whatever the truth of these theories and conjectures, Orval's fame as a religious centre grew over the centuries until the French Revolution, when the abbey was looted and burned. Abandoned by the monks, it remained in ruins until 1926, when work began to resurrect the monastery. Over the next 20 years it rose to become a magnificent edifice, the exterior dressed in colossal statues reminiscent of Egyptian temples. However, the modern abbey can only be viewed from a distance as the areas occupied by the monks are off limits. Visitors are allowed to wander around the ruins of the original abbey, where they can also see the circular pool and flowing waters of the magical **Fontaine Mathilde** (49.6404, 5.3480), which commemorates Matilda's legend. There's also a museum and a garden of medicinal plants, as well as a shop where the famous beer brewed by the monks can be bought.

49.6397, 5.3489, €; Parking: 49.6378, 5.3478, 100m

MEUSE

10 Notre-Dame d'Épine, Avioth

The reputation of this pleasant village is far greater than its size, owing to the Black Madonna discovered in a thorn bush (épine) in the 12th century. Each time it was moved the statue would disappear only to be found back in the same spot, which was taken as a sign that the Virgin desired a chapel to be built there. A pilgrimage was soon established in honour of Notre-Dame de l'Épine and its importance grew when St Bernard of **Clairvaux**, a great supporter of Black Madonna sites, came to preach at Avioth. As pilgrim numbers increased, the chapel was replaced by a church and finally, in the 14th century, by today's grand basilica. As with many Black Madonnas, the face and hands were painted a lighter skin tone in the 19th century, when the child was also added. Some researchers considered the statue to be the Gallic fertility goddess Rosmerta, linking it to a spring beneath the basilica believed to cure infertility in women. Statues of this goddess have also been found at **Sion-Vaudémont**.

The basilica was also a rare 'sanctuaire à répit' ('reprieve sanctuary') where stillborn children were brought to be baptised, before being buried in a special area of the cemetery. Outside the basilica, the spot where the Black Madonna was discovered is marked by a singular structure, a carved stone monument known as La Recevresse (The Receiver). A statue of the Virgin was placed inside so that offerings could be left there by pilgrims. She became known as the 'Vierge Recevresse', and the name was transferred to the monument.

49.5667, 5.3914

11 Crypte Saint-Dagobert, Stenay

This dark and atmospheric underground gallery that preserves monuments to one of French history's most enigmatic figures is an unexpected find. Located in the basement of a very ordinary apartment block in the centre of the town of Stenay, it houses an exhibition run by the Cercle Saint Dagobert II, an organisation dedicated to preserving and promoting the memory of this elusive king and martyr – the most mysterious of the Merovingian kings. Above the stairway down to the basement is the stone relief of a bee, the symbol of this dynasty of Kings of the Franks, a Germanic people who between the 5th and 8th centuries extended their rule over vast areas of Europe. They hold a key place in France's national mythology as the founders of what was to become the French nation. Dagobert II reigned over one of the Merovingian kingdoms, Austrasia, which covered today's northern France and parts of Belgium, the Netherlands and Germany. Little is known historically of his life and short reign, although plenty of myths and legends have surrounded Dagobert on account of his assassination following a conspiracy to overthrow him. The king was killed on 23 December 679 when hunting in the Forêt de Woëvre, around 10km from Stenay,

According to local tradition, Dagobert's tomb was discovered beneath Stenay's church in 872. He was declared a martyr saint and the church was rededicated to him and raised to the status of a basilica. Dagobert's relics were displayed there and are said to have repelled a Viking invasion shortly afterwards. However, they were dispersed when the basilica was ransacked during a war in the 16th century, and the building itself was later destroyed.

When the entrance archway to the church was discovered during excavations in 1972, it was moved stone by stone and reassembled in the basement by the Cercle Saint Dagobert II. Above the arch is a carved image of Dagobert and the crypt also houses another stone depicting his assassination.

In recent decades new theories have arisen that consider the Merovingians to be a sacred bloodline, and Dagobert II's murder an attempt to extinguish it. The most widespread theory is that the Merovingians were descended from the children of Jesus and Mary Magdalene, with the Holy Grail representing their bloodline. A bestselling book called *The Holy Blood and the Holy Grail* sets out the theory in great detail.

The spot said to be where Dagobert was assassinated is marked by a stone near the **Fontaine Saint-Dagobert** (49.4335, 5.2855; parking 49.4384, 5.2449; 3.25km), deep within the Woëvre Forest. Visitors still make the trip to honour the king-saint.

Crypte Saint-Dagobert, 3 Place Raymond Poincaré, Stenay. Guided tour only, € by donation.

49.4921, 5.1886; Parking: 49.4924, 5.1893, 80m

MOSELLE

12 Roche des Fées, Lafrimbolle

An impressive rock formation with huge stone pillars forming arches enclosing a cavernous space, this certainly bears an uncanny resemblance to a fairies' grotto hidden in the deep forest. Just 500m north are the evocative ruins of the **Château de Turquestein** (48.5881, 7.0381, 250m), once considered impregnable. Perched on a curious conglomerate rock formation the scattered vestiges of this castle are now cloaked by thick forest. The castle was built around 960 to guard the route to **Mont Donon**, 12km to the southeast, and remained unchallenged for centuries until it was destroyed on the orders of Cardinal Richelieu in 1634 as part of his campaign to reduce the power of the nobility. As the Roche des Fées and the Château de Turquestein are both completely hidden within the forest they are hard to find and not signposted. They can be accessed in a high-clearance vehicle from the Chemin de la Forêt in Lafrimbolle, followed by a short hike; otherwise a longer hike from Lafrimbolle (Parking 48.5941, 7.0161, 3km).

48.5840, 7.0378; Parking: 48.5863, 7.0377, 300m.

12

12

Turquestein

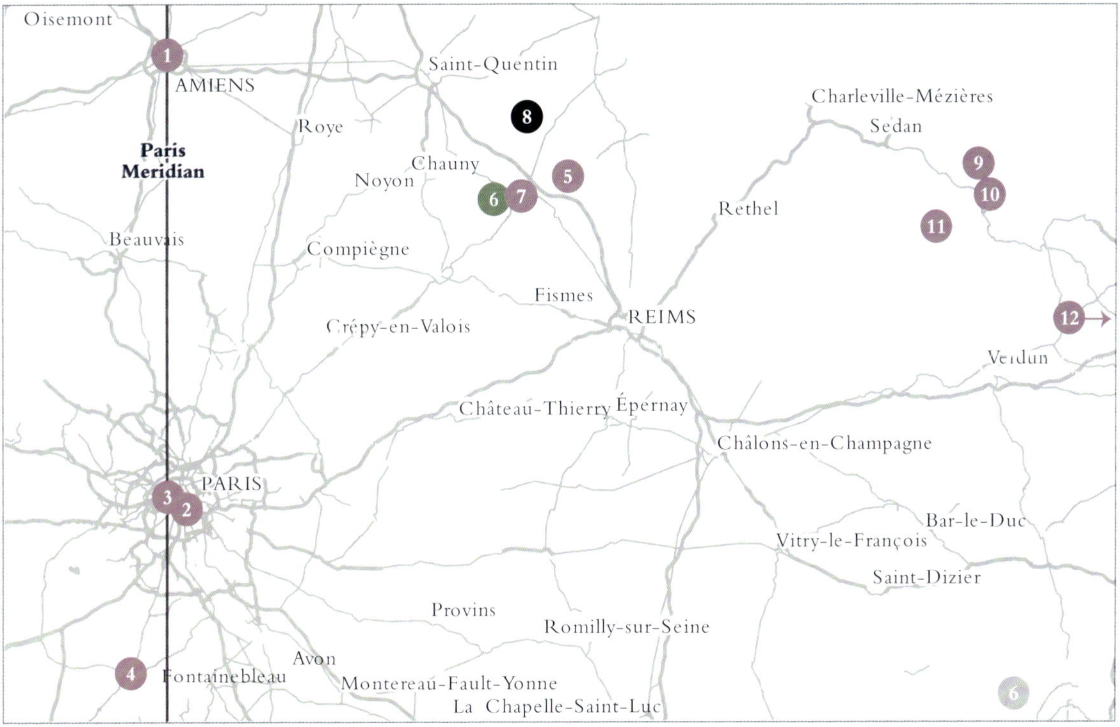

Oisemont
1
AMIENS
Saint-Quentin
Charleville-Mézières
8
Roye
Sedan
Paris Meridian
Chauny
9
Noyon
5
6
7
10
Rethel
11
Beauvais
Compiègne
Fismes
REIMS
12
Crépy-en-Valois
Verdun
Château-Thierry
Épernay
Châlons-en-Champagne
PARIS
3
2
Bar-le-Duc
Vitry-le-François
Saint-Dizier
Provins
Romilly-sur-Seine
Avon
4
Fontainebleau
Montereau-Fault-Yonne
La Chapelle-Saint-Luc
6

2 Pagan Wall

THE GREAT PILGRIMAGE BEGINS

An ancient sacred way once ran across France from east to west, starting in Alsace. Known as the Great Pilgrimage, it visited sites that were sacred in Celtic and Roman times, many of which were subsequently supplanted by medieval Christian places of worship that still attract pilgrims today. In legend, it was the path followed by the giant Gargantua who made the journey as a child with his parents Grandgousier and Galemelle, starting from a 'mountain in the east' and ending at Mont Saint-Michel. Many sites along the way, especially megaliths, have folklore relating to Gargantua, and solar alignments between them also hint at an underlying astrological connection.

The trail begins in the Vosges mountains of Alsace. The Celtic sacred mountain of Mont Donon is exactly east of Mont Saint-Michel and is considered by many to be the mountain from which Gargantua set out. Others think that the mountain may have been Mont Sainte-Odile, 20km to the south and the location of a Christian sanctuary dating back 1,300 years. Mont Saint-Odile is enclosed by a huge and mysterious 'Pagan Wall', showing that it was once of immense importance.

After emerging from the Vosges range, the Great Pilgrimage covers a largely flat landscape, running mainly through former Gallo-Roman settlements, such as Grand (Andesina), Troyes (Augustobona), Sens (Agedincum) and the sacred springs and baths at Aquae Segetae as it heads towards Chartres (Autricum). Stretches of ancient roadways connecting the sites can still be seen in places, such as the Chemin de César (Caesar's Way) between Sens and Aquae Segetae.

Several locations in this region are associated with St Bernard of Clairvaux, the powerful medieval churchman who was behind the rise of the Knights Templar. They include: the abbey of Clairvaux from which he took his name; Troyes, the scene of the Church council he called which officially established the Templars; and the Église Saint-Vorles in Châtillon-sur-Seine whose Black Madonna is said to have miraculously inspired St Bernard's mission.

Further south, on the fringes of the Morvan range, is the major Mary Magdalene pilgrimage centre of the Basilique Sainte-Marie-Madeleine in Vézelay. It's twinned with another nearby place of pilgrimage, Avallon, which has associations with Arthurian legend.

BAS-RHIN

1 Andlau Bear Shrine

Uniquely, the crypt of Andlau's abbey church contains an ancient, damaged statute of a bear. In front of it is a small pit where sufferers stood to cure ailments of the feet. The pit is covered by a trap door which you open to stand barefoot on the earth below.
The magnificent church of Saint-Pierre-Saint-Paul is all that remains of an important abbey founded in 880 by St Richarde of Souabe (Swabia) who was married to the Holy Roman Emperor Charles the Fat. Accused by him of being unfaithful, she volunteered to undergo trial by fire and walked unscathed through the flames barefoot. After she had cleared her name, Richarde withdrew into solitude in the forest. One day an angel appeared and instructed her to found a convent on a spot that would be revealed to her by a bear. When Richarde later came across a bear scratching the ground she knew that was the place. As a result, bears were always special to the abbey and the church is filled with images of St Richarde and the bear. The spot scratched by the bear is directly beneath the small pit.
The church is also a pilgrimage destination where worshippers come to venerate the statue of the Virgin Mary in the church's crypt, which also houses St Richarde's tomb. There's a sculpted frieze depicting Richarde's story along with animals and knightly heroes.
In the town, remains of fortifications peep above the buildings here and there, and there's a walking route around the old ramparts. Silhouetted against the skyline in the tree-covered hills above Andlau are the evocative ruins of two medieval castles, the Château de Spesbourg (48.4019, 7.3973) and the Château de Haut-Andlau (48.4015, 7.4123, 1.25km. Both can be visited along signposted trails from the parking spot at Hungerplatz (48.4054, 7.3983). Further west and 10km along the road from Andlau is the beauty spot of the Cascade du Hohwald (48.4003, 7.3012, parking 48.4003, 7.3065, 400m), a high waterfall cascading down rocks in a serene forest setting.
48.3879, 7.4154

1

1

1

2 Porte de Barr

2 Mont Sainte-Odile

Rising 760m from the Plain of Alsace, Mont Sainte-Odile is one of the possible starting points for the Great Pilgrimage and for Gargantua's highly symbolic journey across France to **Mont Saint-Michel**.
Atop the mountain is the sanctuary of the Abbaye de Hohenbourg, also known as the Convent of Mont Sainte-Odile. It's dramatically situated on the edge of a cliff with a statue of the founding saint looking out over the landscape from the top of a turret. A terrace around the sanctuary gives panoramic views over the Plain of Alsace to the west – on a clear day as far as the Alps and the Black Forest in Germany.
The convent was founded in 680 during the Merovingian period by St Odile, Alsace's patron saint. The daughter of the Duke of Alsace, Odile was born blind and on account of this disability her father ordered that she be killed. Outwitting her husband, Odile's mother had the child taken into hiding in a monastery. When she was baptised at the age of 12 Odile miraculously gained her sight, and as penance for his heartlessness her father gave her his castle of Hohenbourg so she could establish a convent there. It soon became a centre for pilgrimage, especially for those seeking a cure for eye ailments.

The original, simple structure grew over the centuries to become the complex of buildings we see today. The Basilica of the Assumption of the Virgin Mary was built in the elegant Baroque style in the late 1600s. On the terrace, perched on a rock projecting from the cliff, is the square Chapelle des Anges. Built in the 12th century inside are mosaics depicting various scenes in which angels ('anges') play a part. Hollowed from the clifftop beside the terrace are tombs dating from the Merovingian era. The abbey was closed down during the French Revolution and the site sold off in 1796.

2

It was bought 40 years later by the three priestly but mysterious Baillard brothers, who restored the buildings and revived the pilgrimage. They did the same with the Basilique **Notre-Dame de Sion** at Sion-Vaudémont, 100km exactly due west, which they regarded as Mont Sainte-Odile's mystical twin. The relics of St Odile, hidden as protection from the revolutionaries, were returned and her tomb can now be seen in the abbey's Chapelle Sainte-Odile where pilgrims come to pray and light candles. Everywhere is the image of St Odile herself, her two eyes mysteriously peering out from the book she is holding.

Below the sanctuary is the **Source Miraculeuse du Mont Sainte-Odile** (48.4349, 7.4040, 400m), a spring with miraculous waters said to heal eye ailments. According to legend, St Odile made the water burst from the ground by striking it with her staff when she came across a leper faint with thirst. The spring, in a cavity in the cliff, is now behind a metal grille but there's a spout outside from which the water flows into a series of stone basins. It's a stiff 400m walk down the wooded hillside from the abbey, or alternatively you can drive there and park near the spring.

The magic and mystery of Mont Sainte-Odile continues in the forests and hills that surround the summit, especially on coming across the Mur Païen (Pagan Wall) that embraces the area and extends for around 10km. This colossal construction is made up of more than 300,000 huge stone blocks, yet its precise age and purpose are unknown. It was long thought to date from Celtic times or earlier, constructed to mark the mount out as a sacred space. The Church, which gave it the 'pagan' name around the year 1000, considered the wall ancient, even then. However, recent studies have suggested the wall could have been built in the Merovingian period, at around the time of the abbey's founding.

The easiest section of the wall to reach is the **Porte de Barr** (Barr Gate, 48.4290, 7.3985; parking 48.4290, 7.3993, 50m). It lies on the Chemin de Gaulois, an ancient Celtic road that was taken over by the Romans. Some 45m along a path from the Porte are two **Merovingian tombs** (48.4293, 7.3987) dug into the bedrock. A path by the parking spot and heading in the opposite direction to the Porte de Barr path, leads 600m along the course of the wall to the striking **Grotte des Druides** (48.4259, 7.4018). Resembling a megalithic dolmen, this cave is thought to be a natural formation of huge boulders, the massive flat stone across the top forming a cavernous passageway. At night the mischievous fairy folk called 'farfadets' are said to emerge from the cave. A further 60m into the woods to the west of the Grotte des

2 Grotte des Druides

3

Druides is a megalith known as the **Pierre Druidique** (48.4261, 7.4011).
The Pagan Wall also runs over the heavily forested mountain of the Hohenburgerberg to the north of Mont Sainte-Odile, which has several captivating sites including caves and springs – all reached by a network of hiking trails. Close to the wall and facing Mont Sainte-Odile are the ruins of the **Château de Hagelschloss** (48.4494, 7.3894). According to local lore there are tunnels beneath the castle from which processions of ghostly figures emerge on certain nights. A kilometre to the east is the **Plateau des Fées** (48.4521, 7.4036), a weird rock 'chaos' of jumbled boulders with some bearing cup marks, where witches are said to gather at night. According to legend, the plateau is also the scene of a wild hunt led by the Devil himself, when the howls of hunting dogs and the cries of the hunters can be heard passing overhead. The trail to the plateau passes beneath the sheer rock cliff known as the **Rochers des Géants** (48.4478, 7.4033).
48.4378, 7.4047; Parking: 48.4363, 7.4028, 150m

3 Mont Donon

Known locally as Le Donon, the sacred mountain of Mont Donon has been a holy place since at least Celtic times. It was also a Gallo-Roman sanctuary, sacred to the god Teutates and to Mercury whose depiction on a stele with his signature caduceus (winged staff) was found there. Inscriptions invoking Jupiter, Taranis and Hecate have also been discovered, as well as a shrine to an unidentified god wearing an animal hide and touching the antlers of a stag. A number of ancient roads, Roman and earlier, brought pilgrims to the mountain, another sign of its prominence as a sacred centre.
Mont Donon vies with **Mont Sainte-Odile**, 20km to the southeast, as the 'mountain in the east' where Gargantua began his legendary westward journey to **Mont Saint-Michel**, 640km away. It's the most southerly of the great peaks of the Vosges mountain range, just topping 1000m, and lies directly east of Mont Saint-Michel.
This ancient mount and major archaeological site is now an open-air museum. In 1869 a replica Greco-Roman temple, the **Temple-Musée du Donon** (48.5125, 7.1644) was built on the rocky summit to mark the mountain's historical and spiritual importance. There are fantastic views from it over the forested hills and valleys below. According to local legend, visiting the summit guarantees fertility.
There's a 2km walking trail to the summit, becoming steeper towards the top, from the car park at Col du Donon. At the start of the trail is the Rocher à Bassins (48.5088, 7.1586), a massive rectangular stone with several large hollows ('bassins') in which rainwater collects. While it would have been used in rituals, it's uncertain whether the rock is an entirely natural feature or was shaped by human hands. A little further along is a 2m-high menhir (48.5086, 7.1594) that leans to one side. As the path climbs, it passes the foundations of several ancient temples and some stone steles with carved images that have been set upright along the way – all adding to the sense of entering a special, sacred place. The broad, flat summit has a walking trail passing all the sites of interest including statues of

3

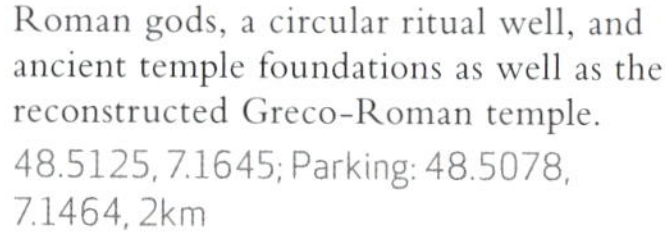

Roman gods, a circular ritual well, and ancient temple foundations as well as the reconstructed Greco-Roman temple.
48.5125, 7.1645; Parking: 48.5078, 7.1464, 2km

MEURTHE-ET-MOSELLE

4 Notre-Dame de Sion, Sion-Vaudémont

A major sanctuary site on the route of the Great Pilgrimage, the Colline de Sion-Vaudémont is steeped in legends and mystery from ancient times to the modern era. The isolated hill lies 100km west of **Mont Sainte-Odile** and exactly due east of **Chartres**, rising 540m from the flat land of Le Saintois. It forms a crescent-shaped crest, 4km long, with the villages of Sion and Vaudémont at either end.
In Celtic times the hill was a sanctuary to Rosmerta, goddess of fertility and abundance who was often depicted with the horn of plenty or cornucopia. When Christianity came and her cult was replaced by that of the Virgin Mary, the site became a centre of pilgrimage, and a sanctuary to the Virgin was built at Sion on its northern end. 'Sion' is the French for 'Zion', evoking the sacred Mount in Jerusalem and marking this out as special to Christians. Yet according to another school of thought, the name derives from a Gallic term, although there's no agreement on what the original was. The earliest parts of the Basilica of Notre-Dame de Sion on the site of the original sanctuary are 14th century, but it's been much enlarged over the centuries. The 45m-tall tower surmounted by a 7m statue of the Virgin, was raised in the mid-1800s. There are a number of chapels and monuments around the sanctuary. An especially eye-catching one is the **Éperon Saint-Joseph** (St Joseph's Spur, 48.4303, 6.0808), a 10m column built of rocks that supports a statue of Joseph and the Child Jesus.
Unique features of the hill that would have added to its sacred aura in the past are the Étoiles de Sion: millions of tiny fossilized marine creatures in the shape of five-pointed stars. A legend explaining their origin centres on the **Saut de la Pucelle** (Maiden's Leap, 48.4149, 6.07497), a steep, thickly-forested escarpment on the western edge of the hill between the two villages. It relates how a daughter of the Lord of Vaudémont, riding to the sanctuary at dusk, was pursued by a knight who emerged from the forest. Fleeing, she came to the cliff edge and praying to the Virgin, urged her horse to jump. It landed safely on a rock where its hoofprints could once be seen, although the rock is now lost. When the knight tried to follow her the Virgin Mary threw a handful of stars at him from heaven. Blinded, his horse plunged over the cliff.
In the 15th century a knights' order, the Brotherhood of Knights of Notre-Dame de Sion, was attached to the abbey. Some have linked it with the controversial secret society, the Prieuré de Sion (Priory of Sion) established in the 12th century to support the Templars. Yolande d'Anjou, Duchess of Lorraine who was married to the Count of Vaudémont, was allegedly the Prieuré's Grand Master at that time.
Like many Christian sanctuaries, Sion was closed down during the French Revolution, but in the 1830s the three brothers Baillard, all Catholic priests, set out to restore it along with Mont Sainte-Odile, which they seemed to regard as its twin. They purchased both sites, renovated the buildings and revived their pilgrimages. However, their story took a strange turn when the brothers became followers of the mystic and occultist Eugène Vintras, turning Sion-Vaudémont from a Catholic sanctuary into a centre for heresy and magic.
The curious story of the Baillard brothers was the basis of a 1913 novel, *La Colline Inspirée* (*The Inspired Hill*) by French writer Maurice Barrès who was also deeply involved in the esoteric scene. Some have seen cryptic references in the novel to another famous French mystery of the time, that of the priest Saunière of **Rennes-le-Château** in the Languedoc (see pXXX), as if Barrès was hinting that there was a hidden connection between the two strange tales. He certainly seemed to consider Sion-Vaudémont to be more than just a Christian holy place. The **Monument Barrès** (48.4086, 6.0703), a 22m high column, was raised in his honour on the southern edge of the Colline de Sion-Vaudémont, its highest point.
48.4308, 6.0839; Parking: 48.4299, 6.0835, 125m

5 Pierre d'Appel, Raon-l'Étape

A group of fairy sites are located on the hill overlooking the valley of the river Meurthe to the south of Raon l'Étape. The **Pierre d'Appel** (Calling Stone) is a triangular outcrop with sheer 12m sides. On the summit are the foundations of a Celtic camp. With a view over the valley 200m below and out to the end of the pass from **Mont Donon**, the site suggests the camp was there to guard the route. Known locally as the Château des Sarrasins (Saracens), it's said to be the dwelling place of fairies who haunt the hill. Some 2km deeper into the forest is an immense hexagonal rock, level with the ground, known as the **Chaudron des Fées** (Fairies' Cauldron, 48.3748, 6.8404). The cauldron consists of three 1.2m-diameter basins that, according to local lore, the fairy folk use for boiling their magic potions. The very chunky 1.8m-high **Menhir des Lèches** (48.3842, 6.8332) is a further 1.25km on.

Although the town of Raon-l'Étape dates back only to the 13th century, it lies on the route of the Great Pilgrimage and the presence of megaliths and other sites around it show the area was much more important in the ancient past. An impressive pink granite menhir 3.25m high known as the **Pierre-Borne** (Boundary Stone, 48.4175, 6.8289; Parking 48.4153, 6.8296, 700m), stands in woodland on the northern edge of the town. Today it marks the boundary of Raon-l'Étape.

48.3764, 6.8629; Parking: 48.3715, 6.6827, 860m

5 Pierre-Borne

6 Grand

This sleepy village had an illustrious past as the thriving Roman town of Andesina, which was described by one historian as 'the mysterious city where a thousand devotees met'. As a measure of its status, it boasted one of the largest amphitheatres in the entire Roman Empire, able to hold 17,000 spectators.

Before the Romans came, the sanctuary was sacred to the Celtic sun god Grannus – the origin of the town's name. The Romans identified Grannus with their solar deity Apollo and erected a temple to him there. This suggests an intriguing link to the giant Gargantua who can also be seen as a personification of the sun, especially in his journey across France from east to west. Grand is another major Roman site on the Great Pilgrimage route.

After the end of the Roman era Grand declined to a small village but vestiges of its past can still be seen. The **Amphithéâtre de Grand** (48.3850, 5.4911, €, open mid-March to mid-November, days and hours vary by season) has been partly restored and is used for performances, with

6

6

the eastern section left as an overgrown mound. Remains of Andesina's ramparts (48.3827, 5.4815) are visible by the roadside on the west side of the town. Other finds, including statues and astrological tablets, are displayed in the **Site Culturel de Grand** (48.3839, 5.4856, parking 48.3837, 5.4860, 40m). Its greatest treasure is the exquisite mosaic covering an area of 232m² that decorated the floor of the Roman basilica. The Gallo-Roman temple to Apollo is thought to have been in the centre of the town on the site now occupied by the **Église Sainte-Libaire** (48.3847, 5.4864). There was a healing spring beneath the church with water running into a well at its side, but it stopped flowing in the 18th century. However, the water-soaked rock and clay made the foundations unstable so the church is no longer open due to the risk of subsidence.

St Libaire was a local martyr who, according to legend, was beheaded during a persecution of Christians in the Roman Empire in 362. She then picked up her head, washed it in the spring, combed the hair and placed it in her burial shroud. However, it's thought the saint may be a Christianised version of Libera, the Roman goddess of the harvest and daughter of Ceres. 48.3861, 5.4867; Parking: 48.3846, 5.4870

AUBE

7 Clairvaux Abbey

One of the most important religious buildings in French history, the Abbaye de Clairvaux is identified with St Bernard of Clairvaux, an intriguing Cistercian monk who plays a significant role in the Western Mystery Tradition. He founded the abbey in 1115, in a remote clearing in the forest beside the river Aube in the Val d'Absinthe on land donated by Hugues of Troyes, Count of Champagne.

Originally sent there by the head of his monastic order, Bernard eventually became head of the Cistercians. He was an astute negotiator between successive popes and heads of state, and presided over the Cistercians' transformation into one of the wealthiest and most powerful religious institutions in Europe. Soon the abbey at Clairvaux expanded and became ever more grand, and it is there that Bernard wrote *In Praise of the New Knighthood*, the foundation document of the Knights Templar. He also organised the Council of **Troyes**, the capital of Count Hugues' lands, which greatly accelerated the Templars' rise to power and influence.

Bernard had a reverence for the sacred feminine in Christianity and especially for Black Madonnas. He was born at a Black Madonna site, Fontaines-lès-Dijon (47.3433, 5.0206) in Côte-d'Or, and it's said that his desire to enter holy orders arose from a miraculous boyhood experience at another Black Madonna site, the **Église Saint-Vorles, Châtillon-sur-Seine**. Aside from the Virgin Mary, Bernard was a devotee of Mary Magdalene and fascinated by Solomon's Song of Songs, which is linked both with the Magdalene and the Black Madonna cult. He went on to deliver a famous sermon calling for the Second Cru-

7

sade from **Vézelay**, then a great shrine to Mary Magdalene.

Clairvaux Abbey was suppressed at the time of the French Revolution and Napoleon ordered that the buildings be turned into a prison – a function that continued until it was closed in 2023. Now under France's Ministry of Culture, the abbey is open to the public for guided tours, with days and times varying throughout the year. The building's many years as a penitentiary have blunted the edge of its spiritual energy, although the light and airy cloisters retain a meditative feel.

A more magical spot is the **Fontaine Saint-Bernard** (48.1369, 4.7586, parking 48.1379, 4.7595, 170m), where the saint was said to meditate. The spring lies 2km along a woodland lane (route forestière) that begins near the abbey and is signposted from the D12. It's a very tranquil spot, with a well-shrine decorated with St Bernard's coat of arms and a cross. Water runs from the well-house into a nearby stream.

48.1471, 4.7884, €€

8 Troyes Cathedral

  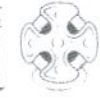

The Great Pilgrimage passed through the important town of Troyes, which in the Gallo-Roman era was known as Augustobona and dedicated to the Emperor Augustus. In the Middle Ages it became the capital of the powerful Counts of Champagne, under whom it flourished as a major centre of learning and culture. Troyes played a big part in the birth of the grail romances, the first of them written by Chrétien de Troyes under the patronage of Marie, Countess of Champagne and the daughter of King Louis VII and Eleanor of Aquitaine. One of the great figures of medieval literature, Chrétien wrote several tales of King Arthur and his knights. It's thought that locations in his stories were inspired by the landscape around **Domfront** in Normandy, the site of Eleanor's court that Chrétien visited with the countess.

An event of historic significance that took place in the capital was the Council of Troyes, called in 1129 by St Bernard of **Clairvaux**. The Council, which had the pope's blessing, marked the official foundation of the Knights Templar because it authorised the Templar Rule, drawn up by Bernard. Its passing transformed a small band of knights into an order of warrior monks that was at the forefront of the Crusades and also became one of the most powerful organisations of the Middle Ages. The mysteries surrounding the order are legion, from its origins to its suppression on charges of blasphemy and idol-worship in the early 14th century. The Templars came to have a key place in Europe's Mystery Tradition as the guardians of great secrets, sacred artefacts and heretical beliefs. The Council of Troyes was held in a church that would later become the site of the Cathédrale Saint-Pierre Saint-Paul, where St Bernard of Clairvaux's skull is now displayed in a silver and enamel reliquary in the treasury.

There are many historic monuments to be seen in Troyes, most in the area known as the Bouchon de Champagne (Champagne Cork) featuring medieval houses and narrow streets such as the Ruelle des Chats (48.2969, 4.0722). Close by, in another very narrow street, is Troyes' oldest church, the stately Église Sainte-Madeleine (48.2978, 4.0711). The garden of the Musée Saint-Loup (48.3008, 4.0807, € - entrance to garden free) houses a number of megaliths gathered from the area around Troyes, including a dolmen and the menhir known as the Grande Borne (Great Boundary Stone).

48.3003, 4.0814

8

YONNE

9 Sens Cathedral

The next major stop on the Great Pilgrimage after **Troyes**, Sens was once the Catholic Church's most important centre in medieval France. The Archbishop of Sens had authority second only to the Pope and controlled bishoprics such as Paris, **Chartres,** Troyes and Orléans.

Sens Cathedral, built on a rise above the river Yonne, is dedicated to St Étienne (Stephen), the first Christian martyr. It's also devoted to the cults of the Virgin Mary and St John the Baptist. It was one of the first Gothic buildings in Europe, with construction beginning around 1130. The cathedral is at the heart of Sens' historic town centre which has many half-timbered houses from the 1400s and 1500s, as well as pleasant squares and parks. Sens was an important Gallo-Roman town, Agedincum, with an amphitheatre and thermal baths. Parts of the Roman walls and

9

9

towers can still be seen along the Boulevard du 14 Juillet (48.1962, 3.2880 and 48.1952, 3.2826), while archaeological finds from the era, including stone steles, are displayed in the Musée de Sens (48.1975, 3.2842, €) beside the cathedral.

Agedincum was on several major Roman roads including the Chemin de César which follows the Great Pilgrimage route to **Aquae Segetae** and beyond; parts of it can still be followed through the countryside, starting from the Île d'Yonne in the middle of the river. Beside the bridge on the isle is the 12th century **Église Saint-Maurice** (48.1978, 3.2756), a half-timbered building that was restored in the 16th century. The bridge leading from the other side of the isle, continuing the Chemin de César, is named the Pont au Diable, reputedly on account of the original bridge's architect. He was in debt to the Devil but requested help from the local priest who banished the demon with holy water.

48.1978, 3.2836; Parking: 48.1997, 3.2833, 250m

9

10 Château-Landon

An impressive fortified town on a ridge, Château-Landon is built on the site of a Gallic fort that was captured by Julius Caesar. The remains of medieval walls can still be seen, including the 9m-high Tour Madeleine (48.1500, 2.7035), the town's oldest building. Château-Landon is also thought to be the birthplace of the first of the Plantagenets, who rose to become England's royal house for over 300 years from 1154 – England's three lions come from their coat of arms.

The giant Gargantua is linked to the town by a local legend which connects him with the village of Sceaux-du-Gâtanais on the site of the Roman spa town of **Aquae Segetae**. It tells how Gargantua stood with one foot on the tower of Abbaye Saint-Séverin (48.1502, 2.7089) and the other on a church tower to the southwest, and shook from his shoe a stone that formed a menhir that stands just outside Sceaux-de-Gâtinais. The giant also came to the aid of Château-Landon's inhabitants who were being terrorised by an invading army. Gargantua defeated it singlehandedly, killing its leader.

Parking: 48.1501, 2.7028

11 Avallon

According to some accounts Riothamus, a 5th-century king of the Britons, retreated from a battle with the Visigoths at **Bourges** and made his last stand near the present town of Avallon. One theory is that Riothamus was the model for King Arthur, and his defeat inspired the story of Arthur's retreat to the Island of Avalon after he was mortally wounded at the Battle of Camlann.

The first story to describe the Holy Grail as

9

a vessel containing Christ's blood was the *Roman du Graal* (*Romance of the Grail*), written by Robert de Boron in the first years of the 1200s. He was a native of the Duchy of Burgundy and some argue that his references to the 'Vale of Avaron', usually taken as Britain's Avalon, point to the area around Avallon in Burgundy.

In the Middle Ages, Avallon was paired with Vézelay, 12.5km to the west, because each held holy relics. Avallon's 17th century church of **Saint-Lazare** (47.4861, 3.9075) has ancient origins and changed its name in the 11th century after the relics of St Lazarus, who Jesus is said to have raised from the dead, were brought there. Lazarus was the brother of Mary of Bethany who many consider to be Mary Magdalene. The monks of the **Basilique Sainte-Marie-Madeleine** at Vézelay claimed to guard her tomb, so pilgrims began to journey from one holy place to the other to venerate the siblings' relics. Pilgrims on the Camino de Santiago (Way of St James), which started in Vézelay, also made the diversion to Avallon.

The **Abbaye Saint-Martin-du-Bourg** (4.4909, 3.9132), the oldest parts of which date back to the 6th century, was built on a pre-Christian sanctuary sacred to the Celtic sun god Belenos. The Romans replaced this with a temple to Apollo, which St Martin ordered to be destroyed when he came to Avallon in 376.

An 18km drive north of Avallon, the village of Saint-Moré has several interesting sites around it. Especially magical is the **Fontaine Saint-Moré** (47.5830, 3.7582, trackside parking 47.5838, 3.7649, 650m), which is set in forest just off a trail that runs beside the wide and tranquil river Cure. The spring is said to mark the spot of the saint's martyrdom, the water beginning to flow where his body hit the ground. The people of the area would make a pilgrimage there to invoke St Moré's blessing, especially in times of drought. However, the spring was previously sacred to Borvo, the Gallo-Roman god of springs. The spring is in a small cave, and the water flows into a stone sarcophagus that serves as a basin. Salamanders can often be seen in the water, especially in the autumn. There's a modern stone cross nearby that has a sculpted salamander climbing up it.

11

The spring's sarcophagus comes from a quarry, the **Carrière des Sarcophages** (47.5840, 3.7572) which is 120m further along the trail. During the Merovingian

10

age, stone for burials was quarried there and taken to the river Cure to be transported. Partly cut sarcophagi can still be seen. At a later date a figure of a 'wouivre', which in this region of France is a supernatural creature in the form of a woman with dragon's wings and a serpent's tail, was carved into the rock by an unknown hand.

The escarpments on either side of the river Cure are penetrated by caves that were first occupied 200,000 years ago, the most famous being the Grottes d'Arcy-sur-Cure, 2km from Saint-Moré. One, the stalactite-filled **Grande Grotte** (47.5917, 3.7667, parking 47.5915, 3.7671, 50m; €€, guided visits only - English available), is open to the public and contains some of the oldest cave paintings in France, at around 28,000 years old. They include depictions of wildlife of the era including mammoths.

Parking: 47.4862, 3.9069

12 Basilique Sainte-Marie-Madeleine, Vézelay

The story of the hilltop town of Vézelay, and the rise and fall of its fortunes, are inextricably linked with Mary Magdalene to whom its basilica is dedicated. The hill on which it stands, known as Scorpion Hill due to its shape, originally housed a monastery that was established in the mid-800s by Girart de Roussillon, the lord of the region who became the hero of a number of medieval romances. Two hundred years later, the monks declared that they possessed the remains of Mary Magdalene, which had been secretly brought from Provence centuries earlier for protection from raids by Saracens. When the Pope endorsed the claim in 1050, pilgrims began to flock to Vézelay and the town prospered and flourished. The pilgrimage was twinned with the one to **Avallon**, 12.5km to the east, where the relics of St Lazarus, believed to be Mary Magdalene's brother, were held.

The magnificent basilica was built between 1120 and 1150. The layout and design are extraordinary, the whole structure expressing a symbolic journey from darkness to light. The area immediately inside the entrance is in almost total darkness, and the interior becomes progressively brighter the nearer it gets to the main altar. The whole building is oriented to sunrise on the summer solstice, which at the time it was built fell on 24 June, the feast day of St John the Baptist. When the sun is at its highest point on the solstice, the windows on the south side project circles of light at regular intervals along the basilica's centre line.

The basilica became the departure point of the Via Lemovicensis, one of the four main pilgrimage trails through France of

the Camino de Santiago to Spain. Marked by the iconic brass scallop shells set into the streets, the trail (now the Vézelay Way) is still followed by pilgrims.

At Easter 1146, St Bernard of **Clairvaux** delivered a sermon from Vézelay calling for the Second Crusade before a huge crowd that included King Louis VII and his Queen Eleanor of Aquitaine. A modern iron cross (47.4694, 3.7508) marks the spot below the hill, 400m from the basilica.

In 1279, after some relics had been discovered at **Saint-Maximin-la-Sainte-Baume** in Provence (see pXXX), the Pope declared them to be the genuine remains of Mary Magdalene, undermining Vézelay's claim. The basilica, the abbey and the town went into decline as a result.

During the French Revolution the abbey was suppressed, then sold and its stone used for building. Restoration began in the mid-19th century and Vézelay once again became a pilgrimage site when more of Mary Magdalene's relics were given to the abbey. These relics, originally discovered in Provence, had been gifted to **Sens Cathedral** but were subsequently moved to Vézelay, and are still on display in a reliquary in the basilica's crypt.

In Roman times there was a temple on the hill to Bacchus, the god of wine, over which the Église Saint-Étienne (47.4636, 3.7428, now private property) was built. Walls with towers and gates, some dating from medieval times, encircle the town.

Midway between Vézelay and Avallon is the **Chapelle Templière du Saulce d'Island** (47.4650, 3.8236), the only remaining part of one of the most important commanderies of the Knights Templar in Europe. It rises close to a farm, Le Saulce. Beside it is the now dry Fontaine Sainte-Anne.

Just south of Vézelay are the remarkable **Fontaines Salées** (47.4492, 3.7767, open April-October, €) that were used for the production of salt from Neolithic to Gallo-Roman times. The oldest wells, lined with oak, date from 2,300 BC. One of the springs was a Celtic sacred sanctuary, and the Romans built their own beside it along with thermal baths. Overlooking one of the neolithic wells is the granite megalith of **Le Poron**, which is thought to be the one mentioned in the medieval epic *Chanson de Girart de Roussillon*. About a kilometre further south is a very striking natural rock formation.

The **Roche Percée** (Pierced Rock, 47.4368, 3.7833, parking 47.4374, 3.7839, 80m) is set on a promontory above the river Cure with a 6m-high arch through the centre.

47.4664, 3.7483; Parking: 4.4661, 3.7442, 500m

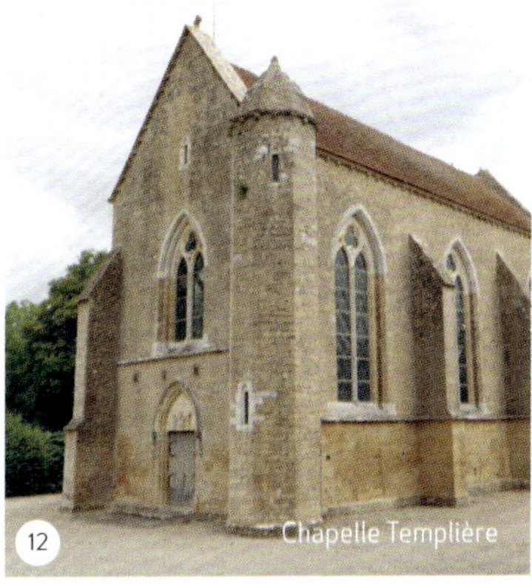

Chapelle Templière

LOIRET

13 Ferrières-en-Gâtanais

A little south of the Great Pilgrimage trail is the town of Ferrières-en-Gâtanais, known for centuries for its historic abbey. According to tradition, it was established by Clovis, 5th-century founder of the Merovingian dynasty and granted special privileges by the King of France and the Pope. In the Middle Ages the abbey with its celebrated library was a major centre of learning that was known as the 'new Athens'.

The abbey was rebuilt nine times during its history, and closed down completely during the French Revolution with only its church, the Église **Abbatiale Saint-Pierre-et-Saint-Paul** (48.0903, 2.7892) surviving, although some of the abbey's original walls and gateways can still be seen. In one of its acclaimed stained-glass windows from the 1500s showing Jesus being placed in the tomb, Mary Magdalene is depicted as Anne of Brittany, Louis XII's Queen and a powerful figure of the era who ruled Brittany in her own right. At that time, some women in authority had themselves symbolically portrayed as the Magdalene, suggesting they saw her not as the humble penitent of Church tradition but as a role model for a woman of power.

The abbey is also linked with the legend of Pope Joan, a woman who disguised herself as a man to take holy orders and rose through the Church's hierarchy to become pope in the 9th century. According to tradition, she began her journey as a monk at Ferrières-en-Gâtinais' abbey.

The feminine energy continues in the **Église Notre-Dame-de-Béthléem** (48.0904, 2.7887) which is right beside the abbey church. It's on the site of a very ancient chapel built on the spot where two 3rd-century missionaries to Gaul, Saints Savinian and Potentian, had a vision of the nativity one Christmas Eve. The church houses a Black Madonna, carved in oak, that's brought out for an annual pilgrimage held on the first Sunday in September, when it's paraded around the town. The rest of the year a replica of a much lighter colour is displayed in a niche in the choir. The Black Madonna was saved from the fate of many others during the Revolution by the wife of Ferrière's prison guard who hid it among her linen. According to the townsfolk, she lived to be nearly a hundred and in good health, which was taken as a sign of the Virgin's gratitude.

13

Parking: 48.0902, 2.7907, 100m

14 Aquae Segetae

Long forgotten by time, this ancient sanctuary on the Great Pilgrimage route was once a famous healing centre. When the Romans arrived they found a sanctuary dedicated to Segeta, goddess of the river Loire, and founded the town of Aquae Segetae. Women with fertility problems would come on pilgrimage, casting votive offerings into the nymphaeum – the sacred spring at the sanctuary's centre. There were two baths within the sanctuary, fed by water from the nymphaeum. Aquae Segetae was a thriving town on the Roman road known as the Chemin de César that ran from **Sens** to Orléans. It boasted workshops, a necropolis and a large forum surrounded by a colonnade for public meetings. Its amphitheatre, a part of which is still visible (48.1168, 2.6232), was one of the largest in Gaul with space for around 14,000 spectators.

The town was abandoned at the end of the Roman era, then in the Middle Ages the village of Sceaux-du-Gâtanais developed 2km southwest of the Roman site. Aquae Segetae wasn't rediscovered until the 19th century when excavations gradually revealed its true extent and importance. It's now a major archaeological site and open to the public. Entry is free but opening times vary, so it's best to phone ahead. The site can be viewed through the fence when it's closed.

There are clues that the area around Aquae Segestae and Sceaux-du-Gâtinais was sacred even before the Celts. Outside the village's **Église Saint-Saturnin** (48.1039, 2.5965) are four megaliths, the highest 1.8m, that once formed an alignment. They were found during excavations in the 1980s at the village of Courtempierre, 1.25km away, then moved to the church.

More intriguingly, in a peat bog ('marais') 2km west of Sceaux-du-Gâtinais is a menhir, the **Pierre du Marais** (48.1092, 2.5700, not accessible). Legend says it was shaken from Gargantua's shoe as he stood with one foot on the tower of the Abbaye Saint-Severin in **Château-Landon** and the other on the tower of the church of St Martin in the village of Beaune-la-Rolande (48.0697, 2.4297). The two towers are 22km apart and the Pierre du Marais is exactly midway between them. While the explanation of megaliths as stones shaken out of his shoe when the giant was astride two significant points is found elsewhere, such as at the **Hottée de Gargantua, Molinchart**, there may be a deeper meaning to this particular tale. The alignment between the towers is oriented to sunrise on 30 April, the eve of Beltane, and when extended in both directions passes through a number of abbeys and megaliths, as well as the centre of Orléans. The first part of Beaune-la-Rolande's name is thought to derive from the Celtic god Belenus who the Romans equated with Apollo, the sun god. Gargantua, too, has been taken as a personification of the sun. These links have given rise to the theory that the legends of Gargantua encode an ancient alignment and that the Pierre du Marais marked a significant point on the line.

48.1156, 2.6228

14

15 Abbaye de Fleury, Saint-Benoît-sur-Loire

Many believe that this small town with its historic abbey stands precisely on the spot that the Gauls considered to be the geographic and sacred centre of their land, its omphalos (navel). Saint-Benoît lies within the Grand Meridian of Gaul and the Paris Meridian passes 2km to the east of the abbey. The present Benedictine abbey dates back to the 11th century, but there's been a monastery on the site close to the river Loire since 650 that had several dependent houses, including one in **Perrecy-les-Forges** in Saône-et-Loire. An important centre of learning, the monastery also owned the land around **Aquae Segetae**, 40m to the northeast. The abbey houses the tomb of King Philip I of France.

47.8094, 2.3056; Parking: 47.8100, 2.3051, 50m

15

16

16

EURE-ET-LOIR

16 Toury

This town on the Great Pilgrimage route lies in the heart of the flat and largely treeless Beauce region between Chartres and Orléans that, according to legend, was cleared by the tail of Gargantua's horse during his journey across France to **Mont Saint-Michel**. The capstone of a dolmen known as the **Pierre de Gargantua** (48.1937, 1.9345) is in a small park in the centre of town, moved there from its original location in a field west of Toury. It's 3.5m long and has a rough, eroded surface. It's said to have fallen from the giant's shoe as he passed by on his way to Orléans.
Toury expanded during the Middle Ages on account of its proximity to the Via Turonensis, the pilgrimage route of the Camino de Santiago that begins in Paris. The stately medieval **Église Saint-Denis** (48.1958, 1.9381) with its grand cloisters was built for the pilgrims.

Parking: 48.1930, 1.9347

CÔTE-D'OR

17 Alésia

A powerful hilltop site once known as the 'mother city of the Celts' is now an evocative and extensive historic site. The Site Archéologique d'Alésia, just outside Alise-Sainte-Reine, contains the foundations and partial reconstructions of the ancient buildings of the oppidum (fortified town). Alésia was the capital of the Gallic tribe of the Mandubii and was said to have been founded by the Greek demi-god Herakles. There he was chosen by Celtine, daughter of the King of the Celts, to father her son Galates, the legendary ancestor of the Gauls.
Alésia is at the centre of a network of ancient sites that aligned to form a complex sacred geography, turning the whole of Gaul into a gigantic solar observatory. Four major lines cross here, including one oriented to the summer solstice that runs across France from southwest to northeast, passing through the capitals of several Gallic tribes as well as **Semur-en-Auxois**, another town said to have been founded by Herakles. The line is exactly parallel to the Via Heraklea (Hercules' Way) that starts on the Sacred Promontory on the Portuguese coast and passes through the Matrona Pass in the Alps (see **Sacra di San Michele**).
Another alignment runs to Alésia through **Bibracte**, 75km to the southwest.
In 52 BC Alésia was the scene of a conflict that holds an important place in France's national mythology. It was where the Roman army under Julius Caesar defeated an alli-

17

ance of Gallic tribes led by the warrior-king Vercingetorix. He had assembled the army at Bibracte but chose Alésia as the battleground because of its sacred nature. In a complex siege that lasted a month or more, the Gauls were eventually defeated and Vercingetorix surrendered to Caesar. It was the decisive victory in the Roman conquest of Gaul.

Vercingetorix was then largely forgotten until the 19th century when there was an awakening of interest in France's Celtic past, and he is now seen as a national hero. As part of the revival, in 1865 a magnificent 7m high statue, the **Monument à Vercingétorix** (47.5386, 4.4906; parking 47.5389, 4.4921, 130m), was erected on the orders of the Emperor Napoleon III.

After taking Alésia, the Romans established their own town adding a forum, theatre, thermal baths and temples. The current archaeological site is Gallo-Roman and includes the foundations of a **Temple to Ucuetis** (47.5397, 4.5017), the Gauls' god of metalwork, and sanctuaries to the goddess Cybele and Jupiter/Taranis.

17

Temple to Ucuetis

The archaeological site is run in conjunction with the **MuséoParc d'Alésia** (47.5358, 4.4689, €€, open mid-February to November), 3km away just outside the town of Les Laumes. This museum and exhibition centre displays artefacts and reconstructions, including a sculpture depicting the battle itself and a model of the Gallo-Roman town. The museum is a striking piece of modern architecture, its design based on the circular wooden defences of the camp constructed by the Romans during the siege.

Alise-Sainte-Reine, on the Plain of Alésia below, takes its name from the legend of the martyrdom of the shepherdess Sainte Reine (St Regina). She is said to have been beheaded in 252, and a spring gushed forth on the spot where her head hit the ground. Its waters were healing and the spring became a place of pilgrimage for those in search of a cure. Find it behind a grille in the outside wall of the small **Chapelle Sainte-Reine** (47.5374, 4.4872) tucked away down one of the village streets. However, the discovery in the late 19th century of ancient offerings, including a stone image of a deity, indicated the spring had been a sacred site since at least Gallo-Roman times. This suggests the Church adopted the legend of Sainte Reine very early on as a means of laying claim to the site. In a centuries-old custom, possibly dating back to 866, a procession is held in Alise on the last Saturday and Sunday of August. It finishes with a performance of a play telling the story of 'Le Mystère de Sainte-Reine', which takes place in the open-air cliffside Théâtre des Roches (47.5381, 4.4925).

Some 13km southwest of Alésia, in the direction of the winter solstice sunset, lies **Semur-en-Auxois** (Parking 47.4903, 4.3351). Your eye is drawn to the towers of the medieval castle and of the church, the **Église Collégiale Notre-Dame** (47.4905, 4.3332) in the cité mediévale, set on a promontory of pink granite overlooking the town and surrounded on three sides by a loop of the river Armançon. Over

Semur-en-Auxois

17

17

the church portal are carvings that include pagan images such as a hair-covered 'wild man' and a green man with plants spewing from his mouth. The four towers of Semur-en-Auxois' castle, including the cracked 44m-high Tour de l'Orle d'Or (Tower of the Gold Chaplet, 47.4908, 4.3298), still stand among the streets and houses. Semur-en-Auxois is often used as a movie and TV location on account of its half-timbered houses, old watermill and bridges.

47.5392, 4.5014, €€, open April-October, entry also gives access to the MuséoPark

18 Église Saint-Vorles, Châtillon-sur-Seine

The first major town the Seine flows through, Châtillon-sur-Seine is pivotal in the life story of St Bernard of **Clairvaux**, the head of the Cistercian monastic order who left his mark on Europe's mystery traditions. His story is bound up with the Black Madonna, Notre-Dame de Toutes-Grâces, whose statue can be seen in the 10th-century church of St Vorles.

St Bernard was educated in the church and according to his legend, he experienced a spiritual awakening there through the 'miracle of the lactation'. While he was praying to the statue, three drops of milk squirted from her breast and into his open mouth. The sense of having been divinely chosen inspired Bernard to take holy orders. Many years later in 1136 and now head of the Cistercians, Bernard founded a monastery in Châtillon-sur-Seine, the Abbaye Notre-Dame (47.8639, 4.5750).

Now kept in Saint-Vorles' underground crypt dedicated to St Bernard, the wooden statue was hidden during the French Revolution and only returned to the church in the 1930s. It's credited with a number of miracles including restoring babies to life. Some 250m from the Église Saint-Vorles is the spectacular **Source de la Douix** (47.8597, 4.5789; Parking 47.8604, 4.5789, 75m) where an underground river erupts from a cave beneath a high cliff, before joining the Seine only 80m away. It varies from a gentle current to a fierce torrent depending on the season and weather. Offerings found in the water reveal that in

the Gallic era it was a healing source sacred to Divona, the Celtic goddess of sacred waters and the origin of the name Douix. A statue of the Virgin and Child is now in a niche in the cliff above the source.
The source of the river Seine itself lies 45km south at the ancient shrine to the river goddess Sequana, **Fontes Sequanae** (47.4860, 4.7169). Those seeking healing or help with fertility visited the source and there's a stone statue of the reclining goddess in a cave.
47.8583, 4.5764

19 Fontaine de la Laigne, Laignes

After disappearing underground 18km to the southeast, the river Laigne re-emerges dramatically in the centre of the small town of Laignes. It surges from a wide, low opening in the rock known as the Fontaine de la Laigne. An arrangement of rocks around the resurgence lends it the appearance of a grotto, and at the centre of the semicircular basin is La Naïade, a captivating life-size statue of a naked waterspirit emerging from the river holding an amphora. It was created in the mid-19th century by a local amateur sculptor named Augustin Husson.
Laignes was at the crossroads of two major Gallo-Roman roads and traces of its medieval past can be seen around the town, such as the Tour de la Maison Dieu (47.8410, 4.3613), the last vestige of the ramparts. Opposite is the small and charming Chapelle de la Maison Dieu, built in the 13th century.
47.8429, 4.3653; Parking: 47.8431, 4.3647, 60m

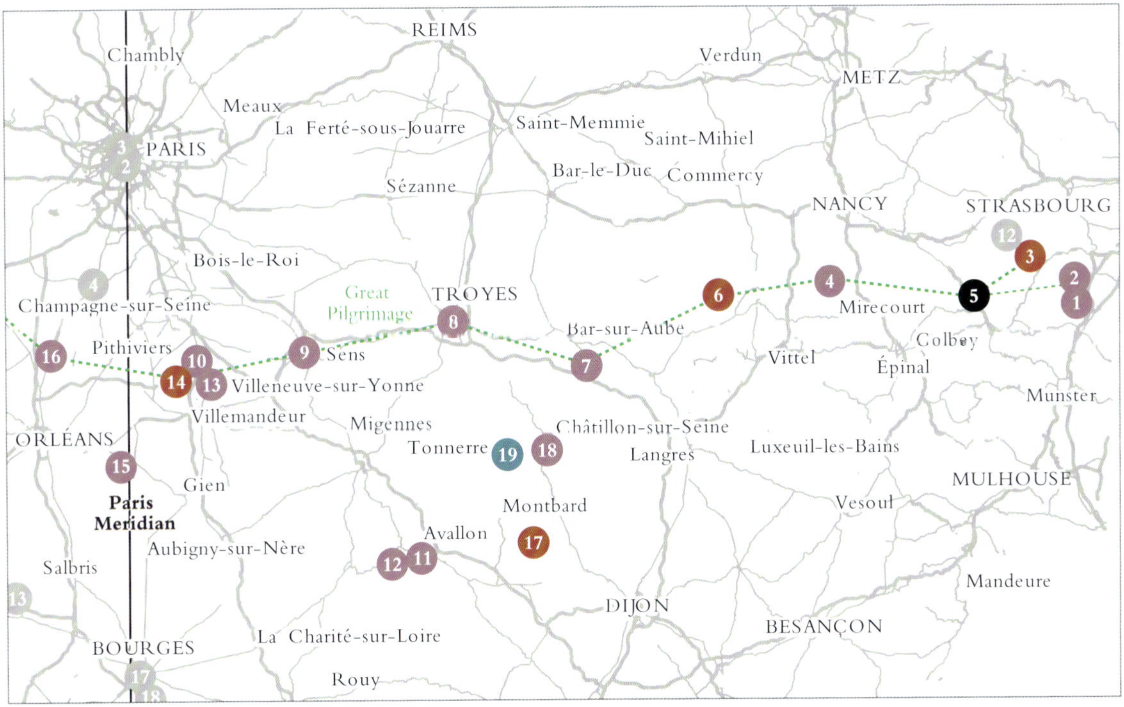

REIMS
Chambly
Verdun
METZ
Meaux
La Ferté-sous-Jouarre
Saint-Memmie
Saint-Mihiel
PARIS
Bar-le-Duc
Commercy
Sézanne
NANCY
STRASBOURG
Bois-le-Roi
Great Pilgrimage
TROYES
Champagne-sur-Seine
Mirecourt
Bar-sur-Aube
Colbey
Pithiviers
Sens
Vittel
Épinal
Villeneuve-sur-Yonne
Munster
Villemandeur
Migennes
Châtillon-sur-Seine
ORLÉANS
Tonnerre
Langres
Luxeuil-les-Bains
MULHOUSE
Gien
Paris Meridian
Montbard
Vesoul
Avallon
Aubigny-sur-Nère
Salbris
Mandeure
DIJON
BESANÇON
La Charité-sur-Loire
BOURGES
Rouy

THE GREAT PILGRIMAGE: CHARTRES TO MONT SAINT-MICHEL

From the far east of France and after passing through Troyes and Sens, the Great Pilgrimage once linked two of France's most important pagan sanctuaries, Autura and Mont Tombe. Autura, a place of 'Druidic assembly' was centred around an ancient megalithic structure where Chartres cathedral now stands. Mont Tombe, a sacred tidal island once associated with giants, later became known as Mont Saint-Michel after the Archangel Michael appeared there in a vision.

Chartres and Mont Saint-Michel are now two of France's most important religious sites, as well as places of powerful spiritual force where it's said that the Earth's vital currents, or wouivre, can be felt. Ancient mystics gave this name to the serpentine energy currents that are thought to snake across the land. Mont Saint-Michel, in particular, is considered a powerful nexus point where these currents meet and cross. The most significant current is the Apollo-Athena line of interweaving male and female energies that travels all the way from Skellig Michael off the southwest coast of Ireland to Mount Carmel in Israel.

Earth forces could be personified as giants, especially the most famous of them all, Gargantua, who is said to have travelled the whole length of the Great Pilgrimage route as a child. François Rabelais' curious 16th-century work, *The Great and Inestimable Chronicles of the Great and Enormous Giant Gargantua,* includes cryptic references to this trail which visits a number of sites with Gargantua legends.

In medieval times this ancient, sacred route was rediscovered and repurposed as a Christian pilgrimage, passing through Chartres to Archangel Michael's shrine at Mont Saint-Michel. At both ends of the trail there were once statues of Black Madonnas in ancient underground chambers, and both bore the name Notre-Dame de Sous-Terre (Our Lady of the Underground), perhaps bearing witness to an ancient connection between the two sites and a reverence for the Earth Mother.

The route passes through landscapes which are thought to have inspired the Arthurian romances, including the very first Grail story. This was written by Chrétien de Troyes who spent time in the region with his benefactor Marie of Champagne, especially at the castle of Domfront.

EURE-ET-LOIR

1 Chartres Cathedral

Built on an ancient sacred site that has long been one of France's most important pilgrimage centres, the huge Gothic structure of Chartres Cathedral is said to encode a deep sacred knowledge. Long before the coming of Christianity, Julius Caesar in his account of the Roman conquest of Gaul records the location, known then as Autura, as being the land's most important Druid sanctuary and the scene of an important annual gathering. The 12th-century cathedral of Notre-Dame de Chartres was built over an underground chamber containing an ancient megalithic structure and there were once other megaliths on and around the mound that have not survived.

The cavernous space inside the cathedral with its soaring columns is lit by over 160 stained-glass windows, including three magnificent rose windows. Many still have their original medieval glass, bathing the interior in a deep blue radiance. Looking towards the west rose window and marked out by black and white stones on the floor of the nave is Chartres' famous labyrinth. At 13m across, its full path covers 260m, although most of it is usually covered with seating making it impossible to follow. People often stand in the centre of the labyrinth to meditate.

Like other Notre-Dame cathedrals the many images of the Virgin Mary, including the rose window devoted to her in the northern transept, give the space a feminine feel. The cathedral's most treasured relic is a piece of Mary's veil, a gift from the Emperor Charlemagne, which is in the Martyr's Chapel. The cathedral also houses two Black Madonnas. In the nave is Notre-Dame du Pilier (Pillar), dating from the early 1500s but recently repainted with light skin. More evocative is Notre-Dame de Sous-Terre, occupying its own chapel in the largest of the two crypts. Wrapping around the cathedral's foundations and extending for 230m, it's the longest crypt in France and is said to incorporate the ancient megalithic structure over which the cathedral was built. Within the dark chapel, in a niche behind the Black Madonna, is a 33m-deep well, the Well of the Strong, which predates the cathedral by many centuries. This ancient Celtic well was only rediscovered in 1901.

The wooden statue of Notre-Dame de Sous-Terre is a replica of the original that, like many others, was destroyed during the

French Revolution. Although the replica is the natural brown of oak wood, it's known that the original was black and that it was housed in the cathedral from at least the early 1200s. According to some historical accounts, however, the original statue was a much more ancient representation of a mother goddess worshipped by the Gauls. It was said to have been found in an underground cave by the first Christians who settled at the site. The current statue can be viewed by joining the afternoon guided tour of the crypt (€) or by attending morning mass in the chapel at 11.30.

The towering cathedral stands on a small hill above the flat lowland plain of La Beauce. It is an awe-inspiring sight, visible for many miles around, and seems to hover above the surrounding city. According to the tale of Gargantua, the plain was once forest but was cleared of trees by the swinging tail of a giant mare that carried the child Gargantua and his parents Grandgousier and Galemelle on their journey from the east of France to **Mont Saint-Michel**. It's one of several signs that Rabelais knew the course of the ancient pilgrimage route.

48.4472, 1.4875; Parking 48.4473, 1.4843, 300m, €

1

Notre Dame du Pilier

1

ORNE

2 Dolmen de la Grosse-Pierre, Bizou

Near the alignment from Chartres to Mont Saint-Michel is an ancient megalithic structure. Its name translates as the 'Dolmen of the Big Stone' and its also known locally as the Druidic Stone. This huge megalith, its surface much gnarled by weathering, sits in the atmospheric setting of a woodland clearing in the Bois de Saint-Laurent. The capstone measures 4.6m long and, although supported by four pillars, is almost on the ground. It is located south of Bizou on the D612, then turn left into the forest at Les Gouptières

48.4664, 0.7503, 15m

2

3 Notre-Dame de Montligeon, La Chapelle-Montligeon

The opulent neo-Gothic basilica of Our Lady of Montligeon is at the heart of a Catholic sanctuary devoted to prayers for the deceased who are in Purgatory awaiting purification. It was built as a pilgrimage centre in the 1890s, a project initiated by La Chapelle-Montligeon's parish priest Paul Buguet. Every Monday he held a mass for the forgotten souls and one day a mysterious woman dressed in blue and wearing a white veil entered, thanked him for remembering them, then disappeared. Buguet took this as a sign that his work should be expanded and through his efforts the basilica was built and filled with statues, paintings, stained-glass windows and mosaics. The white marble main altar, from which a 3.7m tall, 13-tonne statue of a gold-crowned Our Lady of Montligeon rises, is especially majestic. There are pilgrimages to the sanctuary on various Holy Days throughout the year. Beside the road immediately behind the basilica is a small shrine dedicated to St Joseph (48.4839, 0.6563) set into a cave-like niche.

3

The alignment from Chartres to Mont Saint-Michel continues through the small village of **Loisail**, passing the 17th-century **Église Saint-Martin** (48.5006, 0.5914), its very striking and ornate Renaissance-style tower looking somewhat out of place in such a small village.

48.4833, 0.6556; Parking 48.4831, 0.6539, 175m

4 Mortagne-au-Perche

On the approach to this town are two low hills, the Butte de Chartrage (48.5125, 0.5576) and Butte de Champaillaume (48.5208, 0.5858?). According to legend, they were formed from snow the giant Gargantua brushed from his boots as he passed through one winter. The Butte de Champaillaume is said to have been where witches and sorcerers held their sabbats. Among them was believed to be Mathurin Fouquet, a magician notorious in local lore who lived in Mortagne-au-Perche in the 1700s.

Vestiges from this town's rich history are worth seeing, such as the Porte Saint-Denis (48.5219, 0.5469) from the old fortifications, which is just behind the stately Église Notre-Dame (48.5217, 0.5464). Dating from the turn of the 16th century, the church houses some fabulous works of sculpture and painting, including a statue of Archangel Michael defeating the dragon.

After Mortagne-au-Perche, the sacred way passes the **Église Saint-Aubin** (48.5153, 0.4562) in **Boëcé**. This isolated roadside church dates from the 11th century and is dedicated to the Breton St Albinus, a 6th-century Bishop of Angers whose blessing is invoked for sick children.

Parking 48.5226, 0.5472

5 Sées Cathedral

The magnificent twin-towered structure of the Gothic Notre-Dame de Sées graces this historic town. The cathedral dates from the 13th century and is the fourth to be built on the site since around 440 AD, its predecessors having been destroyed by Viking invasions and fire. Sées was said to have been visited by Gargantua on his epic journey to Mont Saint-Michel.

In Gallic times, the town was the capital of the Celtic tribe of the Sagii and was renowned for its wealth, which legend attributed to its possession of a magic golden rooster. There are traces of the town's history all around including, on either side of the Place Saint-Pierre (48.6019, 0.1707), the mound on which the original medieval castle once stood and the scenic ruins of the old Église Saint-Pierre.

48.6053, 0.1731; Parking 48.6050, 0.1726, 75m

6 Chapelle Saint-Michel, La Lande-de-Goult

Dedicated to Archangel Michael, this chapel lies in an open space on the summit of a hill dominating the valley of the river Cance. As a notice outside the chapel details, the

site was once sacred to Belenus, the Celtic god of the sun and healing. The current chapel was erected in 1875, although there's been one on the site since at least the 12th century, which was built by the monks from the Prieuré Saint-Michel (48.6056, -0.0643). The priory's ruins can be seen in the village of Goult below the hill.
La Lande-de-Goult is mentioned as a location on Gargantua's journey from Chartres to Mont Saint-Michel. Grooves in rocks in a nearby forest are said to be ruts made by the wheels of Gargantua's cart on his way back from throwing the rocks into the sea that are said to have formed the islands of **Mont Saint-Michel** and Tombelaine. As well as the hilltop chapel there are also roadside shrines and wells, such as the tiny Chapelle Notre-Dame-des-Champs (48.5894, -0.0457).
48.6033, -0.0638

7 Allée Couverte de la Bertinière, Les Monts-d'Andaine

Also known as the Maison des Fées, this ancient passage grave in a field near the village of Les Monts d'Andaine is one of Normandy's most important megaliths. Oriented west–east, it's 15m long, over a metre high, and made up of 18 upright stones supporting 9 capstones. The burial chamber at the end is partitioned off by two indented stones. Local lore says it is the dwelling of 'nains', malevolent dwarf-like fairy folk who would trap any cattle that came near the stones. Strange sounds coming from the tomb have also been reported at night. The Maison des Fées is along a narrow farm track signposted off the D18, although to avoid blocking the track it's best to park on the main road and walk.
48.6253, -0.4361; parking 48.6291, -0.4391, 600m

8 Lit de la Gione, Bagnoles-de-l'Orne

In local lore this very substantial dolmen was known as the Gione's Bed. It was built as a dwelling by the wicked and hag-like fairy known as La Gione, who must have been giant-sized as she is said to have carried the three stone slabs in her apron. She then bewitched the young lord of the now-

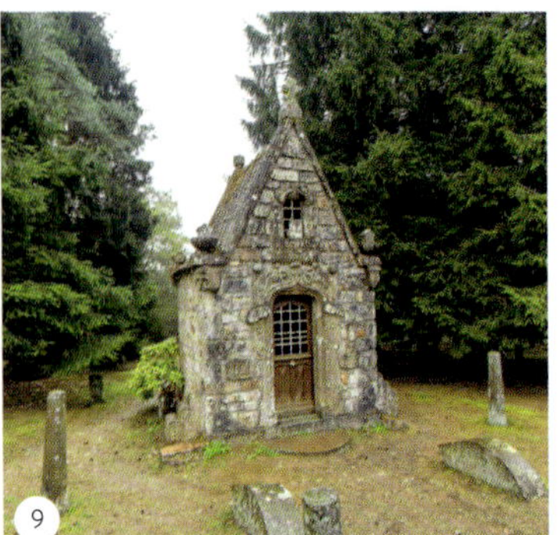

ruined Château de Bonvouloir (48.5642, -0.4992), visiting him every night. On the night he was due to be wedded to another, she lured him to the dolmen and forced him to dance all night. The next morning he was found lying dead on the dolmen's roof from exhaustion. Eventually the local inhabitants drove La Gione away, but even so they still avoid the dolmen after nightfall.

The chamber, which can be entered by crouching, is made up of two large slabs bearing a 3m capstone. It lies in the Forêt d'Andaine along a 16km walking route that runs between Bagnoles-de-l'Orne and Domfront.

Overlooking the town of Bagnoles-de-l'Orne is a spectacular rock spur known as the **Roc au Chien** (48.5548, -0.4186; roadside parking 48.5551, -0.4200, 130m). A legend about its formation tells of a local lord who was notorious for brutally ill-treating those he considered his inferiors, including the nuns of a nearby convent. As divine punishment he was transformed into a creature with the head of a dog ('chien') before being turned into stone. A footpath to the top of the rock gives a wonderful view of the spa town below, which surrounds a gorgeous lake.

The landscape around Bagnoles-de-l'Orne was also believed to have been the setting for Chrétien de Troyes' heroic tale of Lancelot. He was familiar with the area from his visits to the nearby castle at **Domfront**.

48.5655, -0.4635; Parking 48.5610, -0.4458, 1.4km

9 Chapelle Sainte-Geneviève, Juvigny-Val-d'Andaine

This charming little stone chapel is dedicated to St Genevieve, the patron saint of Paris. It occupies a fairytale setting surrounded by stone tables – the remains of old cider presses. The chapel's cramped interior is filled with wooden religious statues including many saints, and young women who wanted to marry within the next year were said to write their names on the wall in the belief St Genevieve would grant their request. The chapel is on the edge of the magical Forêt d'Andaine, said to be filled with fairies and nature spirits and especially beautiful in spring. It's a 3.5km walk along the straight trail from the **Lit de La Gione**, but can also be reached by road, with a parking place opposite. The chapel lies on the straight-line alignment between Chartres and Mont Saint-Michel.

48.5727, -0.5115

10 Domfront

Once the possession of the powerful Eleanor of Aquitaine, Domfront Castle plays an important role in the origins of Arthurian romance. Wace, a poet who popularised tales of Arthur and his knights in the 1150s, was at Eleanor's court. More significantly, Eleanor's daughter Marie of Champagne was the patron of Chrétien de Troyes, who wrote the first ever Grail story in the 1180s. He would accompany Marie during visits to her mother's court in Domfront. Some historians believe that Chrétien used locations in the area in his tales, such as **Barenton**, the landscape around **Bagnoles-de-l'Orne**, the Abbaye Blanche in **Le Neufbourg** and the Forêt de la Lande Pourrie (Forest of the Rotten Land) that once stretched between Domfront and **Mortain**.

Domfront Castle is now an evocative ruin located on a hilltop on the western edge of the historic town centre with dramatic views over the hills and valleys below. There you can also find a 15th-century inn and sections of town walls. The medieval pilgrimage route entered the town by a ford over the river Varenne, beside which stands the 11th century church of Notre-Dame-sur-l'Eau (Our Lady on the Water, 48.5906, -0.6578; Parking 48.5903, -0.6584, 75m). Domfront is mentioned in Gargantua's journey where there was said to be a trouée (gap) associated with him. It also lies on the direct alignment between Chartres and Mont Saint-Michel.

48.5942, -0.6525; Parking 48.5940, -0.6488, 250m

11 Saint-Aubert-sur-Orne

The town is named after Aubert, Bishop of **Avranches,** who in the 8th century founded the first sanctuary on **Mont Saint-Michel**. A stained-glass window in the Église Saint-Aubert depicts the legend of Archangel Michael appearing to Aubert in a dream and instructing him three times to build the abbey to mark his victory over the dragon. The village of Saint-Aubert was relocated to the valley from a nearby hill in the mid-19th century. The ruins of the original church, the Vieux Saint-Aubert (48.7969, -0.3147) can still be seen up there.

48.7896, -0.3310

12 Affiloir de Gargantua, Craménil

According to legend, this 3.3m tall granite menhir known as Gargantua's Whetsone is where the giant Gargantua sharpened his scythe when mowing his fields. It lies in a marshy corner of a field and owes its name to its shape, which resembles a flat stone traditionally used to sharpen blades.

48.7558, -0.3594; roadside parking 48.7549, -0.3590, 100m

MANCHE

13 Fosse Arthour, Saint-Georges-de-Rouelley

Arthur and his queen Guinevere are said to have ended their days in this wooded gorge, named after the legendary king. After his final battle at Camlann, Arthur withdrew here with Guinevere, protected by the fairy who had watched over him since birth. Each lived in their own cave on opposite sides of the river that runs through the gorge, but the fairy warned that they could only visit one another after the sun had set behind the mountain. One day the head-strong Arthur disobeyed, and as he crossed the river it became a rushing torrent and a chasm opened beneath it. The King was swallowed up and the distraught Guinevere, not wanting to be parted from her beloved, threw herself into the abyss after him. They now exist in the timeless realm below. Guinevere's cave is known as the **Chambre de la Reine** (48.6233, -0.7538) and is still visible but Arthur's cave, the **Chambre du Roi** (48.6233, -0.7513), can no longer be seen. The Fosse itself is a spectacular sight: a wide, 70m-deep gorge cut by the river Sonce through the high rock ridge that runs between **Domfront** and **Mortain**. The river cascades down into a deep pool at the bottom of the gorge. Known locally as the 'gouffre', it's said to be bottomless and has a legend attached. If a farmer left a coin on the bank at nightfall, the next morning a pair of enormous black bulls would rise from the water. They were sent by Arthur for a day's ploughing but had to be returned to the bank by the farmer at nightfall, with a bundle of hay tied between their horns. In the valley beyond the Fosse there's a large artificial lake, the Étang de la Fosse Arthour (48.6248, -0.7533), which has picnic areas and hiking trails. The Circuit du Roi Arthur climbs from the waterfall to a calvary, Calvaire du Roc (48.6224, -0.7481) 225m up on the ridge's crest. The gentler Circuit de la Reine Gueniѐvre goes around the lake. The Fosse Arthour is located in the Forêt

de la Lande Pourrie, (Forest of the Rotten Land), so named because the vegetation decays quickly due to high humidity. It's been proposed as the inspiration for the 'waste land' of Arthurian mythology, in particular Chrétien de Troyes' first grail romance. This begins in the 'gaste forêt' ('waste forest') where the hero, Perceval, is raised in solitude by his mother. In the past, the forest stretched for 20km from east to west along the ridge between Domfront and Mortain, but it's now broken up into several smaller woodlands. **Barenton**, a town 6km from the Fosse Arthour, is another resonant placename in Arthurian legend on account of the magical spring, the **Fontaine de Barenton,** in the enchanted Forest of Brocéliande. In the town's elegant 16th-century Chapelle Notre-Dame-de-Bonté (Our Lady of Goodness, 48.6028, -0.8317) a stained-glass window commemorates Barenton's most famous son, the extraordinary occult philosopher and visionary Guillaume Postel. Born in the town in 1510, Postel was a great influence on later esoteric tradition.

Parking 48.6224, -0.7531

14 Mortain

The town of Mortain lies at the western end of the ridge from **Domfront**, an area once covered by the Forest of the Rotten Land (see **Fosse Arthour**). Within the town can be found the **Collégiale Saint-Évroult** (48.6486, -0.9419), which dates back to 1230 and was built on the site of a pagan temple. The church is famed for the treasures it houses, which include a gold-covered container for holy oil with runic inscriptions, indicating that it originated in northern England. There's also a reliquary containing the skull of the patron saint of Mortain, the 11th century St Guillaume Firmat. Évroult (Ebruf), to whom the church is dedicated, was a soldier who became a monk and converted the region around Mortain. He is invoked to cure fevers and diseases of the blood and skin, as well as for the protection of livestock.

The **Petite Chapelle Saint-Michel** (parking 48.6467, -0.9328, 450m) is on the site of an old hermitage, with a statue of Michael and the dragon inside. It's on a spur of the Colline de la Montjoie (Mountjoy), a name that may derive from *Mons Jovis* ('Jupiter's Mount'), indicating the hill was once sacred to the god. A viewpoint on a rock outcrop gives sweeping vistas of the lowlands to the south, from eastern to western horizon, and as far as **Mont Saint-Michel** on a clear day.

Legend links this area with Velléda, a member of Mont Saint-Michel's ancient coven of nine priestesses who took refuge here when the Romans suppressed her cult. To the east of the town, atop the 320m cliff of the Rochers du Grand-Noë (Great-Noah) that rise up from the forest is a formation known as the priestess's seat, the **Chaire de Velléda** (48.6440, -0.9241). The clifftop is inaccessible but the outcrop can be seen from the road below.

Adjoining Mortain but separated by the river Cance, Le Neufbourg is a spread-out rural community in a valley, surrounded by forest and high rocks. Its church, the **Église Saint-Hilaire** (48.6530, -0.9467) features a modern, rather abstract, stained-glass window depicting the local saints Vital and Adeline, who were brother and sister. Around the year 1110, Adeline founded the **Abbaye Blanche**, a Cistercian convent

14

Petite Chapelle Saint-Michel

14

14

14

16

15

around which Le Neufbourg grew. The abbey has been linked to the story of Elaine, mother of Lancelot, Knight of the Round Table. In some versions of the tale, after her husband Ban died and her son was taken by the enchantress Vivian (see pXXX), the grieving Elaine became a nun at the Abbaye Blanche.

The old abbey no longer exists, while the unattractive modern abbey lies to the west of the village, at the entrance to the gorge of the river Cance. The gorge contains the entrancing Grande Cascade (48.6554, -0.9432; parking 48.6558, -0.9428, 100m), its waters rushing down through a cleft into a rock-lined pool.

There are more outstanding natural features on the southern side of Le Neufbourg, best reached from the car park in Mortain. The Petite Cascade (48.6505, -0.9476) is a delightful spot where the river Cançone, also known as the Golden River, flows down 20m over the rocks. The river carries on around the towering 30m high **Rocher d'Aiguille** (48.65006, -0.9472) to meet the Cance. Steps have been cut beside the river and there's a small bridge across to the rock. According to a local legend, long ago there was a pool here where nymphs bathed, well away from the eyes of mortals. When a young warrior named Léonix came there to spy on them, a furious nymph stabbed him with her needle ('aiguille'). As Léonix fell, the ground swallowed him up and the protruding needle formed the rock.

Above the Petite Cascade is an old arched bridge, no longer used, known as the **Pont du Diable** (48.6508, -0.9478). Every bridge that was built across the river here would be brought down by storms and floods, so the story goes, but one day a man dressed in black appeared and declared that he could build a stout bridge for free. All he asked in return was that the first to cross his bridge would become his slave. The very next morning the bridge had miraculously been built so eventually a young man came forward carrying a sack. He opened it, a cat ran across the bridge and the man followed it, immediately placing a cross on one of the pillars. Furious at being cheated, the man in black revealed himself to be the Devil and tried to bring rocks and trees crashing down onto the bridge but it was protected by the cross.

The **Trail des Cascades**, one of several walking trails in the area, leads from the Petite Cascade 250m to the Chapelle Saint-Vital (48.6499, -0.9498), dedicated to Le Neufbourg's local saint. It was built in the 19th century between two large rock outcrops beside the Grotte Saint-Vital, the cave where he came to pray and meditate in solitude. Steps from the trail lead to the top of the Rocher Brûlé (48.6496, -0.9491), from where there's a superb view over the valley.

Parking 48.6486, -0.9453

15 Saint-Hilaire-du-Harcouët

As with many sites on the way of the Great Pilgrimage, the giant Gargantua features in the local lore of this market town. A stone is said to have been dropped there by him, and it was the custom for women who wished to become pregnant to rub themselves against it. Little now remains of the town's ancient past and only one tower survives from the medieval church, itself replaced by an imposing 19th-century one (48.5753, -1.0926). Like the town itself, both are dedicated to the celebrated 4th-century St Hilary of Poitiers.

48.5762, -1.0909

16 Église Saint-Pair, Ducey

The 19th-century church in Ducey is known for its stained-glass windows, including one of the Virgin who, carrying her child, is defeating a dragon above an image of **Mont Saint-Michel**. The Welsh St Padarn or Paternus, to whom the church is dedicated, was one of the seven founding saints of Brittany and the first Bishop of **Avranches**. Renowned for his healing abilities, included curing blindness, he's said to have travelled to Jerusalem accompanied by St Teilo and Wales' patron saint, David. After leaving Britain, the three found they were able to speak in tongues, which meant people heard them in their native language. Padarn appears in the legends of King Arthur as the holy man who converts Arthur to Christianity by invoking divine aid for his victory at the Battle of Badon.

Ducey's imposing Château des Montgommery (48.6211, -1.2942, open April–October, €) sits on the banks of the river Sélune close to the Vieux Pont (48.6192, -1.2958). The bridge was built in the early 1600s for pilgrims on their way from **Chartres** to **Mont Saint-Michel**.

48.6170, -1.2904

17 Mont Saint-Michel

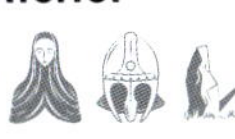

At the end of the ancient pilgrimage trail from **Chartres** lies one of the most magical places in Europe. The pyramid-shaped island of Mont Saint-Michel appears like a vision from myth or fable, with the spires of the medieval Abbey that cling to its peak pointing skywards. Delving into its history, it soon becomes clear that enchantment penetrates deep into the mount: it truly is an ancient place of magic, mystery and power. Walking out to the island and exploring its narrow streets and, above all, the intricate and labyrinthine levels of the Abbaye du Mont Saint-Michel is an unforgettable experience.

Mont Saint-Michel is a circular island formed from a granite outcrop that rises up nearly 100m from the bay to which it gives its name. The island is capped by the heavily fortified abbey, which completely envelops its peak. On the landward side are medieval streets that are today filled with gift shops and cafés. The island is over a kilometre from the mainland, but at low tide the sea recedes several kilometres leaving the mount exposed in a vast expanse of sand. Further out into the bay is the smaller, flatter island of **Tombelaine** (46.6601, -1.5130), which is frequently paired with the mount in legends. It can be visited at low tide on a guided tour. When the tide turns, the water comes rushing in at speed and there are patches of quicksand, so walking to either of the islands across the sand is perilous without a guide. There's a long bridge connecting Mont Saint-Michel to the mainland to take visitors across. It's one of France's busiest tourist attractions, with over 2 million visitors a year.

Mont Saint-Michel is most famous as the legendary location of Archangel Michael's victory over the Devil in the form of a

17

great dragon or serpent. Their battle is said to have begun on **Mont-Dol**, 20km away, and ended with the dragon being vanquished on top of Mont Saint-Michel. These two high points are connected in several legends and myths.

This legend made the mount a major centre of Christian pilgrimage with trails leading to it from all over Europe, followed by pilgrims who became known as 'miquelots'. Yet long before the advent of Christianity, this was a sacred mount. It lay at the end of an ancient trail that began in Alsace and Lorraine in the far east of France, passing through **Chartres** along the way. The fabled giant Gargantua is said to have travelled with his parents along that same path and, at the end of the journey, his father Grandgousier was buried on Mont Saint-Michel and his mother Galemelle on Tombelaine.

Giants also feature in a story about King Arthur defeating a fearsome giant who lived on the mount. When the giant kidnapped King Hywel of Brittany's niece, the King appealed to his relative Arthur for help. Arthur confronted the giant who countered the King's sword with a club made of oak that he'd set on fire. After a fierce battle, Arthur finally vanquished his adversary, beheading him to show Hywel the giant was no longer a threat.

The Romans called the mount the 'Portus Hercules' (Gate of Hercules). Many consider Hercules the equivalent of Ogmios, the Celtic warrior god – an indication that in pre-Roman times, the mount was probably sacred to him. In Celtic mythology, Ogmios was locked in rivalry with his brother Taranis (Roman Jupiter), to whom Mont-Dol was dedicated.

According to a curious legend, the mount was once a sacred oracle presided over by nine priestesses known as the Sènes who could divine the future, shapeshift into animal form, make themselves invisible and travel on the wind. A very similar legend is told of the **Île de Sein** in Finistère, suggesting that they were part of the same cult. The Sènes practised their rites in a circular temple deep within the mount, where people came to consult them. At night they went to Tombelaine, an even more secret place forbidden to ordinary mortals. When the Romans came they suppressed the cult but one of their priestesses, Velléda, took refuge in **Mortain**, a site on the ancient trail from Chartres.

Legend also says that Mont Saint-Michel Bay was once a vast forest called Forêt de Scissy, named after Sessia, the Gaulish goddess of sowing and growing crops. Mont Saint-Michel was then a hill known as Mont Tombe that rose above the forest until 709, when a great cataclysm brought the sea rushing in, turning Mont Tombe and Tombelaine into islands.

It was around this time that the island became identified with Archangel Michael. The change came after St Aubert, the Bishop of Avranches, was commanded by Michael to build a chapel to mark the spot of his final victory over the Devil. The archangel appeared to Aubert in his sleep three nights running, but on the first two occasions Aubert dismissed the apparition as merely a dream. The third time, to convince him otherwise, Michael touched Aubert's forehead with his finger, leaving a hole in it. The saint's skull, with the hole clearly visible, is now in the Basilique Saint-Gervais-et-Saint-Proteus in **Avranches**. Michael decreed that the chapel should be built at the spot where Aubert would find a white bull tethered, and when he found it the bull was tethered to a menhir, which the saint cast down. After the chapel was built he assigned 12 monks to it and Mont Tombe was renamed Mont Saint-Michel.

Aubert sent two of the monks to Michael's main sanctuary in Europe at Monte Sant'Angelo in Gargano, Italy – a unique site in that it was said to have been consecrated by Michael himself. They returned with relics that included a piece of the archangel's cloak. The relic was venerated by pilgrims, miraculously curing blindness and other ailments. In the following centuries a pilgrimage trail developed between the two sites, following the Way of St Michael. This same route would later be known to dowsers as the Apollo-Athena alignment.

This alignment can be extended to the island of Skellig Michael off the coast of Ireland and also connects Mont Saint-Michel to its namesake, St Michael's Mount in Cornwall. In legend, the two mounts

18

were formed from rocks thrown across the sea by two battling giants. From Monte Sant'Angelo in southern Italy the alignment can also be extended to sites associated with the god Apollo in Greece and then further on into Israel. Mont Saint-Michel lies on a number of these long distance alignments including the Ogmios line, which passes through the Callanish stone circle in the Outer Hebrides of Scotland, Glastonbury Tor and, after passing through the mount, continues southwards through France. According to the legend, it was while the monks were treading this path from Monte Sant'Angelo that the sea engulfed the Scissy Forest, and on their return they were stunned to see that their hill rising from trees was now an island in a bay.

As Mont Saint-Michel's fame as a pilgrimage centre grew, so did the chapel, and in 965 a Benedictine abbey was founded in its place. The abbey too was expanded over the centuries, gradually enclosing the Mount's entire peak. The present abbey is on three levels, featuring a complex of stairways, chapels and crypts, with a great terrace behind the main church.

In the oldest, deepest part of the abbey, on the site of St Aubert's original chapel, is the **Chapelle Notre-Dame de Sous-Terre** (Our Lady of the Underground Chapel, 48.6360, -1.5119). It once housed a Black Madonna, Notre-Dame de Sous-Terre, which fell victim to the French Revolution. Significantly, the Black Madonna at the start of the trail in **Chartres Cathedral** bears the same name. It's thought that Mont Saint-Michel's Black Madonna was brought back from the Holy Land by the abbey's monks who made a pilgrimage there in the 860s. The ancient underground chapel is where the male and female currents of the Apollo-Athena line are said to cross the chamber and meet, forming a node. The chapel has two altars side by side which the respective currents pass through – the male one dedicated to Archangel Michael and the female to the Virgin Mary. The chapel was covered by the abbey's nave and forgotten about until rediscovered during excavations in 1906. It can only be visited as part of a special two-hour long guided tour (in French) of areas normally off-limits to visitors (contact the abbey for dates).

In the 1850s a new Black Madonna was placed in the Crypte des Gros-Piliers (Crypt of the Large Pillars) beneath the choir, as part of the revival of her cult. A similar action took place at Chartres Cathedral, forging another connection between the two sites.

48.6361, -1.5114; Parking 48.6114, -1.5025, €€€, 3km walk or free shuttle bus. Abbey €€

19

19

18 Église Saint-Vigor, Carolles

This church in the coastal town of Carolles lies on the Ogmios alignment of sites. Inside, a statue depicts the legend of St Vigor, 6th-century Bishop of Bayeux, who was called on by a lord named Volusien to deal with a dragon that was terrorising his lands. He not only tamed the beast but demonstrated his power over it by leading it around on a simple cord made of wool. A stained-glass window shows the miraculous discoveries of various statues of the Virgin Mary, including that of **Notre-Dame du Cap Lihou**. Outside the entrance is an ancient yew tree that's believed to be over 700 years old.
The deep cleft of the **Vallée du Lude** (48.7484, -1.5676, parking for trail 48.7476, -1.5639) in the forest between Carolles and the coast is said to have been cut by a stroke of the Archangel Michael's sword in one of his battles with the Devil. His opponent hid behind the Rocher du Diable (48.7488, -1.5719), also known as the Rocher du Sard, a prominent outcrop on the cliff overlooking Mont Saint-Michel Bay.
48.7506, -1.5585

19 Notre-Dame du Cap Lihou, Granville

This stately church's centrepiece is the statue of Notre-Dame du Cap Lihou that fishermen found in their nets in 1113 and for which a chapel was built. The current church, which replaced the original chapel, is set high up on Cap Lihou, a peninsula overlooking the port of Granville and Mont Saint-Michel Bay. Granville lies on the Ogmios alignment of sites. When the sea engulfed the forested land of the bay and formed islands such as **Mont Saint-Michel** and the Îles Chaussey, Granville – once far inland – became a coastal town. The tip of the cape, 700m from the church, is called the Pointe du Roc (48.8341, -1.6139; Parking 48.8343, -1.6125, 100m) and has expansive views of the bay and the Îles Chaussey 10km away.
48.8364, -1.6055

20 Avranches

The imposing Basilique Saint-Gervais-et-Saint-Protais (St Gervais and St Proteus' Basilica) houses the skull of St Aubert, Bishop of Avranches in the early 700s. Not only did St Aubert establish the sanctuary on Mont **Saint-Michel**, but he is also said to have delivered the townspeople of Avranches from a dragon. The beast kept emerging from the sea to feed on their herds, but St Aubert tamed it by throwing his stole around its neck, then commanded the dragon to go back into the sea and never return. On display in its own reliquary in the basilica is St Aubert's pierced skull.
48.6864, -1.3583; Parking 48.6868, -1.3581, 90m

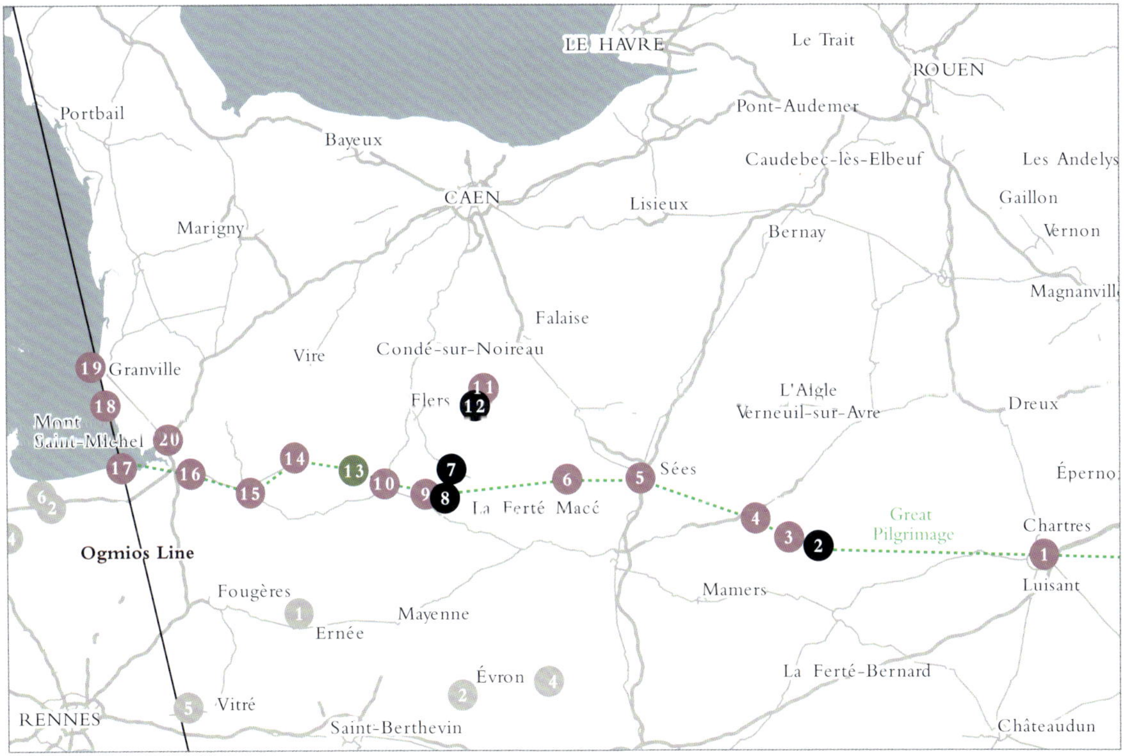

THE APOLLO LINE

The Apollo line is a long-distance alignment of sacred sites that runs all the way from Skellig Michael off the west coast of Ireland to Mount Carmel in Israel. The line passes through France from Mont Saint-Michel on the Normandy coast to the Susa Valley in the Alps.

The alignment was initially discovered in the 1960s by the respected French academic Jean Richer who realised that sites in ancient Greece sacred to the god Apollo fell on a straight line that centred on the oracle at Delphi. His brother Lucien then found that when the 'Apollo line' was extended westwards, it passed through major sanctuaries and shrines dedicated to the Archangel Michael. Starting at Monte Sant'Angelo on the slopes of Monte Gargano in Italy, the line then passed through Sacra di San Michele in the Italian Alps, Mont Saint-Michel in Normandy and St Michael's Mount in Cornwall to end at Skellig Michael off the coast of Ireland. These Michael sites had once been sacred to pagan gods and were re-dedicated when they were Christianised.

In all, the alignment covers over 4,000 km and is oriented 60 degrees west of north. In ancient times it formed a sacred way, a pilgrimage between sanctuaries, which was then adopted by Christian pilgrims when the way became known as the Sword of St Michael – a slash across the landscape made by Michael's sword. In Christian maps such as one displayed in Sacra di San Michele, the eastern end of the alignment has been moved from Mount Carmel to Jerusalem, 100km further south, turning it into a pilgrimage to the Holy City.

In 2000, two dowsers, Paul Broadhurst and Hamish Miller, discovered earth energies along the Apollo alignment. Flowing serpent-like through the land, these were reminiscent of currents the Druids called wouivre, and there were two of them, one male and one female, weaving around the straight line of the alignment. They named the male current Apollo and the female Athena, and found that when these flowed out into the landscape, they passed through many other sacred sites such as medieval cathedrals and megaliths. Where the two currents cross they form powerful 'nodes', which in France are located at Mont Saint-Michel, Bourges and Cluny.

Significantly, both Apollo and the Archangel are said to have conquered dragons or serpents: Apollo overcame the serpent Python, guardian of Delphi, while Michael famously defeated Satan in the form of a dragon or serpent. French scholar of mythology, Henri Dontenville, highlighted yet another unexpected connection between St Michael, Apollo and the giant Gargantua, who is associated with megalithic sites and prominent rock features throughout France. Gargantua can be viewed as an embodiment of earth energies as well as being associated, like Apollo, with the path of the sun. The giant's legends also connect him with the Archangel's sites, such as Mont Saint-Michel and the significantly named Monte Gargano.

17

APOLLO & ATHENA: TO THE SACRED CENTRE

The Apollo and Athena currents that came together at Mont Saint-Michel run through this part of France from northwest to southeast. They cross Mayenne and Sarthe in the northern Loire region before entering France's Centre region. Mayenne and Sarthe cover what was once the important medieval province of Maine, with its capital at Le Mans. The male Apollo line runs to the north and the female Athena line to the south until they reunite at the cathedral of Bourges – a powerful energy point.

Bourges is now regarded as the geographical centre of France, while Romorantin, another town on the line, almost became the nation's capital and sacred centre around 500 years ago. The landscape through which the line passes is generally flat with some ranges of low hills, the countryside varying between forests, farmland and moors. Its most outstanding natural feature is the Loire Valley, carrying France's longest river from northeast to southwest, with many tributaries flowing into it.

The energy currents run through megalithic sites, springs and castles, but their path is predominantly marked by places of worship founded in the Middle Ages or earlier – including churches, chapels and magnificent cathedrals. Many were built on ancient pagan sites that previously marked the course of the energy currents and they often contain sculptures and other decorations displaying symbolism relating to the serpentine *wouivre* currents. One of the most powerful sites, in Issoudun, was built in the 1800s, yet many of its features are evocative of the energy currents that flow through it. The Apollo line runs through some major towns and cities, while Athena's path takes it through more isolated sites and smaller towns and villages, just skimming the outskirts of the city of Tours.

MAYENNE

1 Dolmen de La Contrie, Ernée

Once known as the Cave au Diable, the Dolmen de La Contrie is one of several megalithic sites the Athena current runs through after leaving **Mont Saint-Michel** 50km away. Made up of great slabs of stone resembling the scales of an enormous lizard, the ancient burial chamber is set in a magical location amid woodland that surrounds a gently trickling stream. The womb-like structure is 7m long with three massive capstones supported by 12 upright slabs.

A similar megalithic site of about the same size, the Allée Couverte de La Tardivière (48.3289, -0.9142) is visible in a field 2km to the east.

48.3272, -0.9346; Parking: 48.3269, -0.9316, 270m

2 Notre-Dame de l'Épine, Évron

This grand basilica, through which the Athena current passes, was the church of a Benedictine abbey at the heart of Évron. There's been an abbey on the site since the 7th century, founded by St Hadoin, Bishop of **Le Mans**, although the church we see today dates from 300 years later. It was built on an ancient megalithic site, as was revealed when two menhirs were uncovered during renovation work. One, standing 2m high, is now in a flowerbed by the southern wall. The second, which is slightly smaller, was placed outside Évron's mairie (town hall, 48.1564, -0.4006).

The abbey's foundation legend is depicted in a stained-glass window as well as on sculpted reliefs. According to this, a pilgrim was passing through the area on his way back from the Holy Land with a prized relic, a phial containing some of the Virgin's breast milk. He fell asleep beneath a thorn tree (épine), hanging the bag containing the relic on a branch. When he awoke the tree had grown to an enormous height and the bag was now out of his reach. St Hadoin, who was passing by, prayed to the Virgin and the branch bent allowing him to retrieve the bag. Hadoin took this as a

sign that she desired an abbey in her name to be built there. The reliquary containing the milk can still be seen in the Chapelle Saint-Crépin (St Crispin's Chapel, 48.1565, -0.4025), which is adjacent to the basilica.
48.1567, -0.4033

3 Cave à Margot, Saulges

One of the caves of the Grottes de Saulges was home to the fairy queen Margot who was said to have hidden treasure under rocks and megaliths around the area. An ancient cult revered her, and as recently as the mid-19th century the people of the valley would sacrifice black animals, especially hens, to Margot in the belief that her magic would bring them good fortune. It's thought that these local beliefs blended traditional fairy lore with the memory of ancient goddess worship.

Found within a deep valley, the caves were prehistoric habitations and are now famous for their cave art. A cleft in the cliff leads to a vast winding complex of chambers and galleries, one known as the Palais de Margot, featuring wall paintings and engravings, some dating back 25,000 years. They depict human figures, horses, cattle, birds and long-extinct animals such as the woolly rhinoceros.

The Grottes de Saulges are open May–November, giving access to **Margot's Cave** and several others in this remarkable site.
47.9928, -0.4008, €€; Parking: 47.9938, -0.3990, 150m

SARTHE

4 Sillé-le-Guillaume

The course of the Apollo line leads to this delightful small town in the Pays de la Loire region, which is dominated by the four towers of the medieval **Château de Sillé-le-Guillaume** (48.1850, -0.1261, open July-September, €) and the spire of the Église Notre-Dame (48.1844, -0.1267). They are beside each other on a hill at the heart of the town, giving the castle a commanding view of the surrounding countryside. The Apollo line flows first through the oldest part of the church, which was originally the castle's chapel, before passing through the castle itself.

An older and more mysterious castle lies in the forest just north of town beside a lake called the Grand Étang. Known as the Château des Deffays (48.2118, 0.1284, parking

2

3

4

48.2133, -0.1296, 250m), it was already in ruins when first mentioned in a document of 1405 so its origin is a mystery. Only the foundations now remain, surrounded by a moat. According to a curious local legend that perhaps hints at ancient pagan rites, if someone goes into the ruins on the night of a full moon and shouts "I am here!" three times, the Devil will rise from the lake.

5

Today, however, the Grand Étang is a leisure attraction with a beach and water sports.

Parking: 48.1852, -0.1252

5 Le Mans Cathedral

On reaching one of the most historic cities in northern France, the Apollo line leads directly to **Le Mans Cathedral**, dominating the skyline with its 64m-high tower. The colossal Romanesque structure with its spectacular flying buttresses dates back to 1060 and is dedicated to St Julian, the first Bishop of Le Mans. Carvings above the doorway, through which the Apollo line enters, can be seen as symbols of the wouivre, such as a dragon with a forked, coiling tail and a centaur whose tail, also curling, bizarrely ends in a head. The symbolism of winding foliage and fantastical beasts with serpentine tails is found throughout the interior too, at the tops of the columns and arches. The interior is a vast space with a vaulted roof 30m high, the medieval stained-glass windows bathing it in multicoloured light.

Outside the cathedral, a towering **menhir** rests in an angle in the wall by the main entrance. There are several local names for it, including the Caillou (Pebble) de Gargantua and Pierre Saint-Julien but it's most commonly called the Pierre au Lait (Milk Stone). The 4.5m menhir of pale pink sandstone, which looks as if it has been poured and then congealed into its present shape, was originally part of a dolmen that was destroyed. It was moved to its current spot in 1778. There's a small cup mark in the menhir, and the local custom was for women who wanted to become pregnant to rub it with their finger, polishing the stone around it over time.

Another significant medieval building in the old city is the **Église Notre-Dame de la Couture** (Cultivated Land, 48.0022, 0.2000), the only surviving part of an important abbey founded around the year 600 by St Bernard, Bishop of Le Mans. According to legend, the precise spot was chosen by the Archangel Michael, who descended from the sky to show Bernard where it was to be built. Le Mans also has some of the best-preserved Roman walls in Europe and over a third of the city enclosure survives with its distinctive multicoloured bands and patterns.

48.0092, 0.1989; Parking: 48.0107, 0.1971, 250m

6 La Fontaine-Saint-Martin

This village takes its name from the healing spring of St Martin set in pleasant grounds behind the 12th-century Église Saint-Mar-

5

tin (47.7910, 0.0512). Known for healing ailments of the eyes, the spring became a place of pilgrimage in the Middle Ages. The Athena line passes through both the church and the spring.

St Martin of Tours is said to have come to the area in the 4th century to convert the inhabitants who were worshipping Jupiter and Isis. Needing water to baptise them, Martin struck a rock with his staff and the spring burst forth. It's now set in a well shrine that houses a statue of the saint and the water flows into a basin shaped like a horse's hoofprint. The imperious Lord of Champagne is said to have brought his horse to drink the holy water but its hoof became stuck to the rock until he begged pardon for his sacrilege.

In a woodland glade 5km from **La Fontaine-Saint-Martin** are the **Menhirs de la Mere et la Fille** (Mother and Daughter, 47.7833, 0.0900; roadside parking 47.7837, 0.0901, 30m). The 'mother' stone is 4.5m tall, the 'daughter' about half that size. The Athena line, running northeast–southwest, passes through both. They are the only remaining stones from a longer alignment of some 20 menhirs oriented to sunrise on the summer solstice, which was still visible in the 19th century. The alignment may have included the very striking **Pierre Potelée** (Plump Stone, 47.7809, 0.0945), 400m away, one face of which is pockmarked with cavities.

47.7910, 0.0515; Parking: 47.7910, 0.0500, 140m

Menhirs de la Mere et la Fille

6

INDRE-ET-LOIRE

7 Abbaye de la Clarté-Dieu, Saint-Paterne

The Athena current goes straight through the gates of this 13th-century Cistercian monastery, running across its grounds and then on towards Tours. Like many monasteries, the abbey was closed down during the French Revolution and became a farm. Fortunately, this prevented buildings constructed from the Middle Ages to the 17th century from being demolished, and only the abbey's church was completely lost. As a result, the site has been remarkably well preserved, giving something of the feel of what life was like for the monks, and it's now an open-air museum. The nearby Fontaine Saint-Clair, known for curing eye ailments, is one of several healing springs in the land around the abbey.

47.6014, 0.4564, €

7

8 Dolmen de la Grotte aux Fées, Saint-Antoine-du-Rocher

In a ring of trees amid farmland, this impressive burial chamber is 11m long and made up of 12 large chunky stones – the middle one of its three capstones being truly enormous. Other large stones lie around the site. The dolmen is oriented west–east and the Athena current runs through it at right angles.

A notice tells of pagan ceremonies at the dolmen until St Anthony of Touraine Christianised the area in the 6th century. However, the dolmen remained at the centre of the community until the 18th

6

8

8

Tour & Abbaye Saint-Paul, Cormery
9

Loches
9

century, and was the place where legal disputes were settled. According to local lore, which claims that three young women built the dolmen in a single night, if a stone is removed it will be back the next morning, and anybody who attempts to destroy the structure will die within a year. It's also said that fairies live within the dolmen, hence its name. Like many megaliths, it was believed to aid fertility.

In the village of Saint-Antoine-du-Rocher 4km to the north is the **Source de Saint-Antoine** (47.4962, 0.6315), a spring reputed to cure skin diseases that is set beside a cave in which Anthony is believed to have become a hermit. It's said that he forbade women from coming to the spring as he thought their presence would impair its healing powers.

A few kilometres away lies the historic town of Tours with its cathedral and medieval castle. Although the Athena line leads to the town, rather than continuing to the centre it flows to the western edge and runs through the site of the old Abbaye de Marmoutier (47.4031, 0.7172), now occupied by a college but open to the public. The abbey was founded in 372 by the celebrated St Martin of Tours and was one of the region's best-known abbeys in the Middle Ages. It was dissolved during the French Revolution and its buildings demolished, only some towers and walls surviving. However it was revived in the 19th century by the Sisters of the Sacred Heart who had a new chapel built. The Athena current flows through the

Église Notre-Dame-de-Fougeray

old abbey grounds to a rock face penetrated by caves that were once used by hermits.

47.4629, 0.6504; Parking: 47.4634, 0.6508, 50m

9 Cormery

In the town of Cormery, the Athena current passes through two medieval towers less than half a kilometre apart. First is the Tour Saint-Paul (47.2689, 0.8361), the gateway to a Benedictine abbey founded in 791 and closed down at the French Revolution, though extensive and atmospheric ruins remain. A road now goes through the gateway, the town having grown up within the ruins. The second tower is that of the **Église Notre-Dame-de-Fougeray** (47.2683, 0.8408) on the eastern edge of Cormery, built in the 12th century but added to over the centuries. Cormery is on the Indre, one of the tributaries of the Loire that gives the département its name, and from there the Athena line follows the river, 3km upstream running through the village of **Courçay** where the Église Saint-Urbain (47.2500, 0.8767, parking 47.2498, 0.8764, 50m) was founded around 1000.

Further along the river Indre is the historic town of **Loches** (Parking 47.1287, 0.9949). The Cité Royale has many buildings from the Middle Ages and Renaissance, including the towering 36m-high keep of the Château de Loches (47.1247, 0.9969, €€).

Parking 47.2688, 0.8371

LOIR-ET-CHER

10 Chapelle Saint-Gilles, Montoire-sur-le-Loir

The Apollo current runs directly down the axis of this curious 11th-century Romanesque chapel beside the river Loir, passing under the domed ceiling which has wonderful medieval frescoes, including an enigmatic one of Christ crowning two knights. Originally the chapel of a priory said to have been founded by Charlemagne, it now stands amid the priory's ruins – a site made all the more scenic by the backdrop of the remains of the medieval castle (47.7497, 0.8572). The chapel is privately owned but the keys can be borrowed for a small fee from the Café de la Paix (47.7525, 0.8617) in the Place Clemenceau, 300m away. Further east, some 15km from Montoire-sur-le-Loir, the Apollo current flows through the apse of the Église Notre-Dame (47.7172, 1.0589) in **Nourray**. Outside the church is the Polissoir du Petit Fontenail (Polishing Stone), a massive flat Neolithic stone, 4.5m long and 2.3m wide, broken into two pieces and marked with grooves and basins. The stone's name refers to the belief it was used to sharpen stone axes.

47.7516, 0.8583, €

11 Dolmen de la Pierre Levée, La Chapelle-Vendômoise

The Apollo current runs directly through this remarkable burial chamber, its stones gnarled by millennia of exposure to the elements. Also known as the Table du Diable, its two capstones are balanced on large megaliths. It sits amid a small grove of trees in a field just outside the village of La Chapelle-Vendômoise, where local tradition says that the

Chapelle Saint-Gilles

dolmen was built by the fairies and that their music can still be heard coming from it at night. Another tale is that the giant Gargantua shook the stones out from his shoe.

47.6610, 1.2580; Parking: 47.6612, 1.2575, 40m

12 **Blois**

Reaching the historic city of Blois, the Apollo current runs through the **Château Royal de Blois** (47.5856, 1.3311, €€). For 150 years the castle was the court of the Kings of France, after Louis XII established his base there in 1498. The current avoids Blois' splendid Renaissance Cathédrale Saint-Louis (47.5883, 1.3361) and instead passes through the tower of the older **Église Saint-Nicolas** (47.5842, 1.3314), which was originally the church of a 12th century abbey. It's an impressive building with three 70m-high towers and a vast cathedral-like interior.

The centre of Blois has many medieval buildings, including half-timbered houses that date from the 15th century. An especially fun one is the **Maison des Acrobates** (Acrobats, 47.5881, 1.3350) opposite the cathedral. It was built in the 1470s and on its timbers are carved figures who are climbing and frolicking. The town is a major stop on the Via Turonensis, one of the pilgrim trails of the Camino de Santiago (Way of St James) that runs from **Paris** to **Saint-Jean-Pied-de-Port** and then on into Spain.

From St Nicholas' Church, the Apollo line heads for the **Église Saint-Saturnin** (47.5819, 1.3378) on the south bank of the Loire. Originally a modest church, its fame grew after boatmen found a wooden statue of the Virgin in the river. Believing that Mary would help those who prayed to her, local people named the statue the Bonne Dame des Aydes (Good Lady of Relief) and the church became a place of pilgrimage. Its popularity led to the construction, in around 1500, of a new building in the flamboyant Gothic style with large cloisters. Pilgrims on the Camino, who crossed the Loire by a nearby bridge, also came to pray to the Bonne Dame. The original statue was destroyed during the French Revolution but a replacement was made in 1860. She is credited with saving Blois-Vienne across the Loire from being engulfed in a great flood in 1866, an event commemorated in a stained-glass window in the church. St Saturnin's also houses a statue of Archangel Michael and the Dragon.

In 1126 Henri of Blois, son of the Count of Blois, became the Abbot of Glastonbury Abbey, which is famously associated with King Arthur and the Grail. Henri was also the uncle of Henri of Champagne, whose wife Marie was the patron of Chrétien de Troyes – the author of the first Grail romance.

Leaving Blois, the Apollo line runs through

the 12th-century tower of the **Église Saint-Gervais-et-Saint-Protais** (St Gervais and St Proteus, 47.5705, 1.3556) in the suburb of Saint-Gervais-la-Forêt, on the road to Romorantin. Midway to Romorantin the Apollo line flows through the centre of the village of **Fontaines-en-Sologne**, passing through the half-timbered houses dating from the 15th–17th centuries and the Église Notre-Dame (47.5093, 1.5500). Built in the 12th century, the church is huge for such a small place. The village's name comes from the many springs in the surrounding area, which feed several pools and lakes.

Parking €: 47.5884, 1.3355

13

13 Romorantin

Located 60km to the southwest of **Bourges**, Romorantin was once considered not just the kingdom's geographical centre but also its magical heart and it very nearly became France's capital. At the turn of the 16th century, Romorantin's castle was in the possession of the powerful Louise of Savoy, mother of Francis I, the future French king. She was patroness of some of the greatest magicians and astrologers of her day, employing their talents to ensure that her son, then an outside contender for the crown, would one day become France's greatest king. In expectation, mother and son planned to build a magnificent new capital city in Romorantin. A year after he was crowned king, Francis and Louise invited Leonardo da Vinci himself over from Italy to design their capital and oversee its construction. Da Vinci's concept was for a completely new city filled with architectural wonders and a magnificent palace. Replacing the castle, this new palace would be at the centre of a network of canals extending throughout France. Although building work started, it was abandoned because of Leonardo's untimely death in 1519. However Francis used elements of the design in his new palace at **Chambord** (47.6161, 1.5172), 30km away, which is full of magical symbolism. Although considered one of the masterpieces of Renaissance architecture, Chambord is a pale reflection of Leonardo's vision for Romorantin. Today Romorantin is a quiet town on the river Sauldre. The Apollo current passes through the Château de Romorantin, of which only two towers remain (neither open to the public) along with some of the walls that can be seen either side of the Rue de la Fossé aux Lions (47.3581, 1.7422). The line then runs on to the graceful Église Saint-Etienne (St Stephen, 47.3566, 1.7444) which was founded in the 11th century. Around 7km south of Romorantin, at **Villefranche-sur-Cher** the Apollo line runs through the Église Sainte-Marie-Madeleine (St Mary Magdalene, 47.2933, 1.7725) with its central octagonal tower. It was built in the 12th century as part of a commandery of the Knights Hospitaller and contains pagan imagery atop the inner columns, including a green man and a sheela na gig. The interior of the church also features horned, demon-like figures with wings and curling tails instead of legs; one is holding two snakes, symbols of the *wouivre* energy lines. The tower marks a change in the Apollo current's orientation from north–south to its more usual northwest–southeast direction.

Parking: 47.3581, 1.7411

INDRE

14 Levroux

The Athena current runs through Levroux's grand **Église Saint-Sylvain** (St Silvanus, 46.9797, 1.6142), dedicated to an early saint who, according to legend, brought Christianity to the area. Known as the 'little cathedral' because of its size, it's constructed of yellow stone with a tower 50m high. The Porte de Champagne (46.9785, 1.6139) is one of several vestiges of the medieval fortified town and the last remaining of its seven gateways. Part of the castle, now an

12 Fontaines-En-Sologne

13 Église Sainte-Marie-Madeleine

13 Mary Magdelene

14

empty shell, can be seen on a rise just north of the town (46.9873, 1.6106).

On the northern outskirts, the healing **Fontaine Sainte-Rodène** (46.9819, 1.6072, parking 46.9820, 1.6085, 150m) is at the end of a short tree-lined path. The spring was a pagan sacred place dedicated to Rodene, a goddess or spirit of flowing waters. When St Martin of Tours came to Levroux, he kept the dedication but transformed Rodène into a Christian saint, making her a disciple of St Silvanus. The spring's waters are believed to cure headaches.

Parking: 46.9789, 1.6118

15 Issoudun

A bustling town with many historic sites and tranquil spots beside the river Théols, Issoudun is a place of pilgrimages both ancient and modern. It lies on the Via Lemovicensis, the Camino de Santiago pilgrimage route that begins in **Vézelay**. The Athena current visits the **Tour Blanche** (46.9478, 1.9897, open April-September, €) the 30m high keep of the medieval castle that was built by Richard the Lionheart. One of its towers, to which a clock was added in the 16th century, is the Porte de l'Horloge (Clock Gate, 46.9486, 1.9903) in Issoudun's main square. The line then flows through the town's parish church, the stately **Église Saint-Cyr** (St Cyricus 46.9483, 1.9922) built of bright white stone. It's on the site of an original church that according to tradition was founded by Charlemagne.

The Athena line also flows through the tower of a more modern religious edifice 400m to the north, the **Basilique Notre-Dame du Sacré-Coeur** (Basilica of Our

15

15

Lady of the Sacred Heart, 46.9519, 1.9942). At this place of pilgrimage, the current's energy becomes amplified and symbols of the *wouivre* abound. The very grandiose basilica is devoted to the Sacred Heart movement that grew up in the 1800s, based on the visions experienced by a 17th-century nun at **Paray-le-Monial**. It was built in the mid-19th century and soon attracted large numbers of pilgrims. There's an ambulatory around the choir where the pilgrims process in a circle, adding to the potent energy of the place.

Parking: 46.9490, 1.9869

CHER

16 Église Saint-Michel, Chârost

Following the Via Lemovicensis pilgrimage route, the Athena current next visits the Église Saint-Michel in Chârost. This eye-catching 12th-century church sits opposite one of the medieval town gates and is constructed of red and white sandstone. The tops of the columns along the church's aisle are decorated with carvings of animals, birds and fantastical creatures – including two winged female figures, usually described as harpies. Behind the very opulent altar is a stained-glass window of the Archangel Michael. Every year on Candlemas (1 February, the pagan Imbolc), the tapestry of Michael in the church is paraded around Chârost to invoke the Archangel's blessing for the year's crops, especially the vineyards.

46.9947, 2.1175

17 Bourges Cathedral

Bourges' location is generally considered to mark the very centre of France, but its position on the Apollo and Athena lines reveals there's more to this than just geography. It's here that the two currents cross for the first time since **Mont Saint-Michel** 340km away, forming a powerful node within the cathedral.

The Cathédrale Saint-Étienne in Bourges is an extraordinary towering, cavernous Gothic structure that is equal in stature to those of Paris and Chartres. Among the multitude of carvings on the exterior are many grotesque and fantastic creatures, including dragons and curly-tailed gryphons – symbols of the *wouivre* energy. One of the scenes over the main entrance shows Archangel Michael smiling rather enigmatically and weighing the souls of the departed. You can climb up the steps (almost 400) of the north tower to get a stunning view over the city.

The Apollo current enters the western end and runs parallel to the cathedral's famous gnomon (sundial). This narrow brass strip, set into the floor in 1757, is oriented north–south, parallel to the Paris Meridian (or Rose Line) (see **Paris Observatory**) which itself passes 4.6km west of the cathedral.

A beam of sunlight that shines through a hole in a stained-glass window 20m above passes across the line at noon each day, and

17

17

17

17

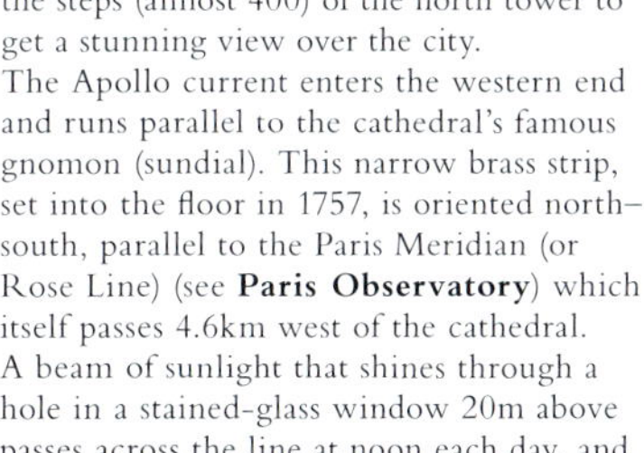

16

on midsummer day (the summer solstice), it exactly fills a circle marked out on the gnomon. The Athena current comes in through the buttressed tower at the western end and meets the Apollo current in the centre of the floor, about 6m from the main entrance. Bourges, the Roman Avaricum, also has some amazingly well-preserved Gallo-Roman walls and Avaricum also features in the story of the warrior Riothamus. This legendary King of the Britons ruled in the mid-5th century and some take him to be an inspiration for the 'King Arthur' story. Gregory of Tours, writing about a hundred years later, tells of a great and lengthy battle between Riothamus' forces and the Visigoths at Bourges that ended in defeat for Riothamus. The King retreated to Burgundy, where he was killed at a final battle near **Avallon**, 120km away. The story pre-dates later Arthurian legends of the mortally wounded Arthur being taken to the island of Avalon after his final battle with Mordred.

From Bourges Cathedral, the two lines again take separate courses with Athena now running to the north and Apollo to the south, until their next crossing point at **Cluny**, 190km to the southeast. The Apollo current follows the Grand Chemin Royal (Great Royal Way) to **Lyon** and beyond into Italy. This route was used by traders and pilgrims on their way to and from Rome and was very well travelled.

47.0822, 2.3992; Parking €: 47.0808, 2.3986, 250m

18 Église Saint-Martin, Plaimpied

The Apollo current passes directly through the tower of this fascinating abbey church. The capitals at the top of the pillars supporting its high arches depict many mythical and fantastical creatures, including giants, green men, sirens, cats, and pelicans with intertwining necks. One shows the Temptation of Christ, who sits with his feet on two dragons. As with many of the churches and chapels on the Apollo current, much of the imagery is unexpectedly pagan

19

18

18

19

19

and seems to represent the earthly current of the *wouivre*. Even the commune's official website states that the church was built on an important telluric energy spot!
The church's crypt is light, high and spacious, its white-painted ceilings decorated with red flowers. The crypt is dedicated to St John the Baptist and is oriented to sunrise on the summer solstice, which at the time it was built fell on his feast day of 24 June. It was used as an ambulatory, around which pilgrims would progress in a circle between four monoliths that stand at the points of the compass.
46.9983, 2.4553

19 Église Saint-Etienne, Dun-sur-Auron

Huge in size for such a small town, this church sits on the Grand Chemin Royal and therefore needed to accommodate those on pilgrimage to Rome. The Apollo current comes directly through the entrance and crosses at right angles to its axis. Founded in 1019, the church has some intriguing decoration, including several carvings of dragons and other fantastical beasts. There's a mural of St Margaret of Antioch on top of a serpentine dragon, depicting the legend in which the Devil in the form of a dragon tried unsuccessfully to swallow her. A stained-glass window shows St George on horseback battling another dragon, while a sculpture on one of the pillars is of a siren whose hair, curling around her, resembles tentacles.
There are vestiges of the medieval town, most strikingly a castle known as the Salle-le-Roi/Palais Royal (46.8846, 2.5709) in the town centre. It originally dated from the 12th century and was surrounded by fortifications of which a gate tower, now a clock tower, remains. There are also well-preserved ramparts (46.8827, 2.5687).
A further 18km to the southeast, the Apollo current passes diagonally through the tower of the Église Saint-Roch (46.7994, 2.7836), built in the mid-1100s in the small village of **Neuilly-en-Dun**.
46.8867, 2.5744

NIÈVRE

20 Nevers Cathedral

Located on top of a small hill, **Nevers Cathedral** was founded in the 10th century on the site of a Gallo-Roman temple to the god Janus. Unusually it's oriented towards the west so the choir and altar sit exactly over the site of the pagan temple. The cathedral's tower is covered in carvings of figures and has many gargoyles and grotesques jutting out from it like spines.
The legend of the cathedral's founding is depicted in a relief above one of the arches of the nave. One night, the Emperor Charlemagne dreamed he was being hunted through the forest by a wild boar. When he prayed for help, a naked boy appeared promising rescue if the emperor gave him clothes, which he duly did. Once dressed, the boy mounted the boar's back and rode off. Charlemagne asked his advisors what

20

21

the dream meant and Jerome, Bishop of Nevers, interpreted the child as St Cyricus, who was martyred as an infant with his mother St Julitta at Tarsus in Turkey. Charlemagne was advised to restore the cathedral at Nevers, which had fallen into disrepair, and dedicate it to the pair as the Cathédrale Saint-Cyr-et-Sainte-Julitte. In the 10th century, the relics of the two saints were united in the cathedral.

The Athena current passes through the very oldest, Gothic parts of the cathedral, including an ancient baptistry that was rediscovered after the Second World War. The line then continues to the majestic Romanesque Église Saint-Étienne (46.9919, 3.1642) 750m further on. Built in the late 11th century, it sits on the site of a convent founded by the Irish monk and missionary St Columbanus 400 years earlier.

Nevers is a very historic town filled with churches, chapels and convents. It's on the Via Lemovicensis, one of the main trails of the Camino de Santiago from **Vézelay**. Around 750m from the cathedral is the **Espace Bernadette-Soubirous-Nevers** (46.9922, 3.1522), a pilgrimage centre in honour of St Bernadette of **Lourdes**. After her visions of the Virgin in her home town Bernadette entered a convent in Nevers and in 1925, 46 years after her death, her body was exhumed for the third time and found to be uncorrupted. It's now displayed in the Espace Bernadette, the main chapel of the sanctuary, which also has a replica of the grotto of Lourdes.

46.9872, 3.1572; Parking €: 46.9877, 3.1582, 180m

20

21 **Bibracte**

An extraordinary site covering one of the highest summits in the Morvan mountain range, Bibracte was an oppidum (fortified town) and the capital of the Gallic tribe of the Aedui. It was a trading and manufacturing hub described by Julius Caesar as 'the grandest and richest town of the Aedui', as well as a Druidic centre with a nemeton (sacred grove) at the most elevated point. Lost to time for millennia, it's now possible to view and walk around to get an idea of the town's former scale and grandeur. The foundations of Bibracte's walls and buildings are spread over the crown of the 820m high Mont Beuvray – an area of open ground above heavily forested slopes that offers panoramic views to the south and west.

Bibracte is on an alignment of key Gallic centres that runs across France from the southwest into Luxembourg. Some 75km northeast of Bibracte, the line passes through the sacred centre of **Alésia** where the great Gallic hero and warrior-king, Vercingetorix, fought the Roman army led by Julius Caesar. After the Gallic defeat in 52 BC, Bibracte was abandoned and over time its location completely forgotten, its existence known only from Caesar's account. When the site was rediscovered by archaeologists in the middle of the 19th century and found to cover an area of 1.5 square kilometres, the foundations of villas, workshops and metalworking forges were unearthed. Some of the massive defensive structures have been completely reconstructed, most notably the main gate to the site, the Porte de Rebout (46.9305, 4.0417).

Bibracte's most unique construction is the **Bassin Monumentale** (46.9278, 4.0371), a 12m-long pool sculpted from pink granite. While its perfect condition makes it appear like a modern replica, this is the original pool, carefully uncovered by archeological digs, and the best-preserved Celtic stone monument ever found. Its exact function is unknown but the pool clearly had a mystical aspect given it was designed according to a complex sacred geometry based on two circles intersecting with a Pythagorean triangle. In addition, the structure is oriented to the summer and winter solstices with a staggering degree of accuracy. The similarity of its shape to a birth canal has also been noted. The basin isn't fed from a water source, and it's been speculated that it wasn't filled with water but a sacred liquid, perhaps mead. There are several water sources on the mountaintop, one now known as the **Fontaine Saint-Pierre** (46.9224, 4.0340) was once a sacred site as revealed by the coins and devotional offerings found during excavation. The original square pools and the walls have been reconstructed.

A chapel was built on the remains of Bibracte's temple in 376 by St Martin of Tours during his mission to convert the people of the region. The chapel and a succession of replacements fell into ruin but a new **Chapelle Saint-Martin** (46.9211, 4.0367) was erected on the spot in 1876 to mark the 1,500th anniversary.

On one of Mont Beuvray's three peaks is a natural feature known as the **Pierre de la Wivre** (46.9320, 4.0355), a 4m-high and 12m-long ridge-shaped outcrop of grey rock that has weathered, giving it a scaly appearance. In the lore of this part of France, the 'wivre' is a supernatural creature in the form of a woman with dragon's wings and a serpent's tail, and it's said she hid her treasure beneath the rock. In appearance, the wivre is very much like depictions of the fairy Melusine found in the Western Lowlands

(see **Melusine's Tower**), and the name also clearly relates to the Druids' serpentine *wouivre* currents of Earth energy. Vercingetorix is said to have addressed his army from this stone before leading them into battle at Alésia.

There's a museum at the foot of Mont Beuvray (46.9323, 4.0479, €€, open mid-March to mid-November; parking 46.9326, 4.0488, 50m) displaying artefacts unearthed at Bibracte and giving more information about this unique site.

46.9244, 4.0350; Parking: 46.9230, 4.0365

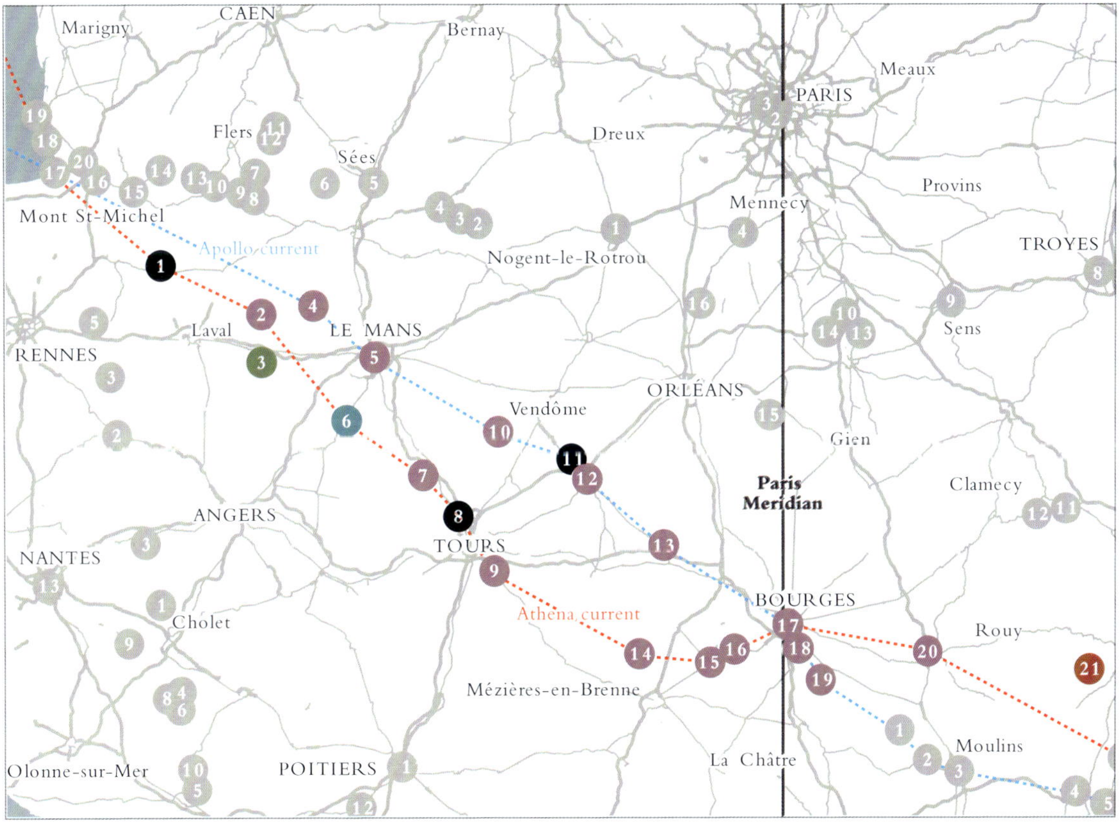

APOLLO & ATHENA: CLUNY TO THE ALPS

The interweaving male and female currents of Apollo and Athena continue their course from the country's centre to the abbey at Cluny where they cross and form a node before continuing onwards to the Alps. As they traverse the mountains and pass into Italy they converge again at the next node, the great shrine to Archangel Michael at Sacra di San Michele.

On their way up to the Alps the currents mainly travel through a rural landscape, with quiet villages amid farmland and vineyards, although they also pass through two of France's most historic cities of Gallo-Roman heritage, Lyon and Vienne. The low-lying agricultural landscape steadily rises to the Alps where it becomes a world of snow-capped mountains, beautiful alpine lakes and narrow passes.

Most of the sites through which the energy streams pass are places of worship that were built in the Middle Ages. They range from quaint village churches to grander places of worship that were once part of important abbeys, such as Belleville-en-Beaujoulais, and from isolated chapels such as the dramatic mountaintop Chapelle Saint-Michel to magnificent city cathedrals. Many of these religious buildings were constructed on sites that were sacred in pre-Christian times. Recurring symbols of the *wouivre* energy are found carved into the stonework, especially the tops of columns, and include fantastical creatures with curling, serpentine tails. Especially significant is the location of Cluny Abbey, whose power and influence in the Middle Ages rivalled that of Rome itself.

Two major sanctuaries built in the 19th century lie on the route of the female Athena current. They are the Basilica of Ars, France's most important pilgrimage centre after Lourdes, and Lyon's Basilica of Notre-Dame de Fourvière, which is imbued with a dynamic female energy. Designed by the same architect, both great churches contain imagery seemingly inspired by that in ancient pagan temples.

ALLIER

1 Église Saint-Aignan, Pouzy-Mésangy

The Apollo current passes directly beneath the tower of this quaint 12th-century church on the outskirts of the village of Pouzy-Mésangy. It lies within the enclosure of a medieval castle with part of the moat still visible beside the road. The tops of the columns in the cavern-like interior are decorated with sculpted patterns of twisting foliage and circles in the form of flowers, wheels and spirals that can be seen as symbolic of the *wouivre* and the sun energy of Apollo.

46.7103, 3.0047; Parking: 46.7086, 3.0041, 300m

2 Église Notre-Dame, Agonges

The Apollo current passes diagonally through the imposing tower of Agonges' 12th-century parish church, a stately red and white stone building. There are hunting scenes sculpted into the tower's stones and, inside, the tops of columns are decorated with roughly-carved figures and faces, some with grotesque expressions.

A local legend tells how the priest replaced the church's medieval wooden statue of the Virgin, Notre-Dame de la Ronde (Our Lady of the Round), with a new image, but next morning found the old one back in its original spot and the replacement unceremoniously knocked to the floor. The old statue was then locked in a cupboard, which was found empty the following day. When plague struck the village soon afterwards, it was seen as the Virgin's punishment. Some time later, Notre-Dame de la Ronde was found in a thorn thicket over 30km away near the village of Chazeuil, and a chapel (46.3282, 3.3900) was built there for her. The people of Agonges regularly made the long journey there as penitence for having cast her out.

46.6063, 3.1571

3 Moulins Cathedral

Fittingly for a major site on the Apollo current, solar imagery is found throughout Moulins Cathedral. It was customary in the Middle Ages to burn a wheel made of wax before its famous Black Madonna, Notre-Dame de Moulins, a ritual that can be seen as symbolising the sun's regenerative powers. In an elegant shrine above the altar of her own chapel, the Madonna sits on a throne with the Child on her lap, holding a closed book. Carved from very dark wood, the image is believed to be at least a thousand years old and was brought back from a Crusade to the Holy Land in the 12th century. There's a life-size marble statue of Joan of Arc praying to the Black Madonna, commemorating the time when the real Joan prayed here before leading the French army against occupying English forces in 1429.

The church in which Joan of Arc venerated Notre-Dame de Moulins was replaced by the current 15th- century cathedral, dedicated to Notre-Dame de l'Assomption (Assumption). Inside are housed many celebrated works of art, and the very white stonework intensifies the light from its many stained-glass windows. When in 1655 Moulins was ravaged by a fire that threatened the cathedral, one of the townsfolk threw the cloak adorning Notre-Dame de Moulins into the flames, at which point the conflagration was said to have been extinguished.

In Moulins' centre and close to the cathedral are other buildings from the Middle Ages, including vestiges of the castle of the Dukes of Bourbon with its conspicuous 45m-high Tour Mal-Coiffée (Poorly Capped Tower, 46.5664, 3.3308).

A tunnel once linked the Bourbons' castle to the crypt of the parish church of **Saint-Pierre** (St Peter, 46.5667, 3.3547; Parking €) in **Yzeure**, less than 2km exactly due east, to which the Apollo current also runs. A legendary winged dragon once had its lair in this tunnel, emerging at night in search of prey. In return for defeating the dragon, the Duke of Bourbon promised to pardon a condemned prisoner, supplying him with armour, a lance and a pack of hounds. After a long and fierce battle the prisoner killed the beast, ending the menace and winning his freedom. The church in Yzeure is 12th century but the crypt is that of an earlier church and some believe the Black Madonna was originally displayed there. The columns either side of the entrance are adorned with sculptures of fantastical beasts, with more on the pillars inside. The interior also features the twisting and spiralling patterns found in churches all along the Apollo-Athena line, which echo the serpentine currents that flow along it.

46.5667, 3.3317; Parking €: 46.5658, 3.3304, 150m

5

Notre-Dame de Romay

5

SAÔNE-ET-LOIRE

4 Église Saint-Saturnin, La Motte-Saint-Jean

Built on the site of an earlier church, the 19th century Église Saint-Saturnin (St Saturninus) is visited by the Apollo current and sits on a small hill of unknown origin above the river Loire. The most eye-catching feature of the interior is a shrine to the Virgin in the form of an artificial grotto, and from the exterior there is a delightful view across the valley.

46.4946, 3.9638

5 Basilica of the Sacred Heart, Paray-le-Monial

When this grand basilica became the focus of a worldwide Roman Catholic cult, the small town of Paray-le-Monial became the second most important pilgrimage site in France after **Lourdes**. There's been a church on the spot beside the river Bourbince since 977, but today's magnificent building was raised in the 19th century and incorporates parts of earlier churches. The interior of this famous holy site is filled with light from its many windows, giving it a powerful intensity. Like **Cluny Abbey**, which it closely resembles but on a smaller scale, the basilica lies on the Apollo current, which here flows through the front and runs all the way along its centre. Carvings on columns preserved from an earlier church depict fabulous creatures, including mermaids and

5

5

4

mermen with two curling fish tails in place of legs – an image found in many churches on the Apollo-Athena line.

Paray-le-Monial became famous in the 1670s when a nun, Marguerite-Marie Alacoque, experienced visions in her convent's Chapelle de la Visitation (46.4511, 4.1222). However, the cult of the Sacred Heart (Sacré Coeur) really took off in the mid-19th century when the Roman Catholic Church began to promote the pilgrimage, leading to the town's church being raised to the status of a basilica in 1875. Marguerite-Marie Alacoque was declared a saint in 1920, and her body is now displayed in the chapel. The rise of the Sacred Heart led to other chapels and churches dedicating themselves to the cult, such as at **Issoudun**, and in particular the iconic Basilica of **Sacré-Coeur** in Montmartre, Paris.

Just 1.5km due east is the 11th-century **Chapelle Notre-Dame de Romay** (46.4490, 4.1420), which precisely aligns with the Basilica of the Sacred Heart and the next Apollo site, the **Butte de Suin**. The current flows powerfully through the chapel. Beside it is a fountain known for relieving eye ailments, which in the past made the chapel a place of pilgrimage in its own right. There's a shrine in the form of a grotto in the grounds outside which is fed with water from the healing spring.

46.4497, 4.1214; Parking: 46.4503, 4.1204, 100m

6 Butte de Suin, Suin

The Apollo current, now flowing directly east, reaches this spectacular location 25km on from **Paray-le-Monial**. The landscape becomes more rugged as the ground steadily rises, and the area around the village of Suin takes on an otherworldly quality, with extraordinary rock outcrops and large stones scattered seemingly randomly across the landscape. Some show signs of having been shaped by hand, although when and by whom is lost to time.

The Apollo current heads for the area's most dramatic feature, the isolated hilltop known as the Butte de Suin, but first it

6

6

flows diagonally through the tower of Suin's 11th-century Église de la Vierge (Virgin, 46.4336, 4.4747) before passing directly between its two altars. The church lies at the foot of the Butte, which was the site of a temple to Mercury in Roman times, and later a medieval castle of which little remains. The jumble of enormous rocks at the summit is topped with a huge statue of the crowned Virgin Mary that can be seen from miles around. She looks westward back along the Apollo current and at her feet a serpent swallowing its own tail forms a circular ouroboros. From the observation point at the top of the Butte there are views in all directions and on a clear day as far as Mont Blanc in the Alps, 180km away.

In the **Bois de Morphée** (Morpheus' Wood, 46.4431, 4.4647) just over a kilometre north of the village are rock spurs and piles of boulders, some as high as 10m. The wood's eerie name recalls a local tale that this wood was once shrouded in complete silence, with no sounds of birds or insects – as if nature within was in a deep sleep. On the edge of the wood is the Pierre Qui Croule (Crumbling Stone, 46.4429, 4.4660), a 70–80 tonne boulder balanced on another that can be moved merely by pressure from a foot. The most mysterious monoliths are just outside the village in the area known as Le Parioloup (46.4352, 4.4732). One, the Pierre des Blancs (White Stone), is shaped

into a chair or throne and faces the rising sun. Another is named the Dolmen from its appearance, although some think it's a natural rock formation.

46.4333, 4.4753; Parking: 46.4342, 4.4746, 150m

7 Église Saint-Pierre-et-Saint-Benoit, Perrecy-les-Forges

The Athena current runs to the distinctive octagonal tower in the centre of Perrecy-les-Forges' church and the master altar directly beneath it. Built around 1020, the church was originally part of a priory, which accounts for its grand size in such a small town. The interior is rather austere but, like many churches on the Apollo and Athena currents, the capitals at the tops of the columns are adorned with a variety of supernatural and otherworldly beings that seem to symbolise the energies and forces flowing past them. One shows Archangel Michael taming the dragon and there are mermaids with splayed double tails that are characteristic of sites on the alignment. An especially intriguing sculpture depicts a woman suckling two serpents.

46.6125, 4.2150; Parking: 46.6127, 4.2162, 130m

8 Cluny Abbey

The Apollo and Athena currents meet and cross to form a powerful node at this site, formerly one of Europe's most significant spiritual centres. It was founded as a Benedictine abbey in 910 and became the centre of a renewal of monasticism that made Cluny the most influential and richest religious hub after Rome itself. The abbey established many priories in France, as well as in England and Scotland. Naturally, as its power grew the abbey itself became larger and grander, and by 1200 it was the largest religious building in Christendom. It held this position for almost 400 years until surpassed by St Peter's in Rome. The abbey housed the most famous and extensive library in Europe.

Cluny Abbey was almost totally destroyed in the wake of the French Revolution and its stone was carted off for building material. Of its original eight towers, only one octagonal bell tower survives intact, along with the remains of two others. There are also buildings and cloisters that were built in the 17th and 18th centuries, which now house a college. Here, the Apollo

8 Chapelle des Moines, Berze-la-Ville

8 Eglise Saint-Marcel

8 Chapelle des Moines, Berze-la-Ville

8 Cluny Abbey

8 Eglise de la Conversion-de-Saint-Paul

and Athena currents come together at an unremarkable spot on the lawn amid the cloisters. Nothing marks it, although given the destruction the abbey has suffered, who knows what may once have been there?
Around the centre of Cluny there are ramparts, towers and gates from the medieval fortifications. Especially eye-catching are the Tour Fabri (46.4366, 4.6592) in the Abbey Park and the tall, thin tower called the Zaronde (46.4355, 4.6627).
The confluence of the two earth currents is neatly symbolised in imagery on the **Fontaine des Serpents** (46.4348, 4.6566), 200m from the Abbey in the Rue Mercière, which was built in the 18th century for pilgrims on their way to join the Camino de Santiago (Way of St James) to Spain. In a niche beneath a scallop shell is a carving of an urn with two golden serpents.
The Athena current flows out of the town of Cluny through the octagonal and sharply pointed tower of the medieval **Église Saint-Marcel** (46.4311, 4.6619), whose hall-like interior has surprisingly little decoration. From Cluny it takes a southerly course, parallel to the river Saône, with which it gradually converges.
The bell tower and remaining parts of Cluny Abbey are open to visitors, the entrance fee including admission to the adjacent Museum of Art and Archaeology. A joint ticket is available that also gives entry to another famous religious building that lies on the Athena current 8.5 km from Cluny, the **Chapelle des Moines** (46.3636, 4.7006, €; parking 46.3640, 4.7013, 60m) at **Berzé-la-Ville**. This Monks' Chapel was the property of the abbey and is renowned for the majestic 12th-century frescoes that cover its walls, offering a glimpse of what the interior of Cluny Abbey might have looked like in its heyday. The Athena current runs through the oldest part of the priory that houses the chapel, built on a rock spur that gives an expansive view across the countryside.
At a distance of just 2 km from the Chapelle des Moines, the Athena current passes through the axis of the quaint 12th–14th century **Église de la Conversion-de-Saint-Paul** (Conversion of St Paul, 46.3386, 4.7011) in the village of **Bussières**. It contains a statue of the Virgin with a serpent at her feet – a composition found in many religious sites on the Apollo and Athena currents.
46.4344, 4.6592, €€; Parking €: 46.4340, 4.6633, 400m

9 Roche de Solutré, Solutré-Pouilly

The Athena current runs across the lower slopes of the stunning Roche de Solutré that rises from flat land covered in vineyards. There's a winding trail to the peak that gives a sensational view over the plain of the Saône and, looking east, to the Alps. The rocky hill is an important prehistoric site, settled in the Palaeolithic Age and giving its name to the Solutrean culture of flint toolmakers. The first finds were made here by archaeologists in the 1860s and there's information about the discoveries in the museum of prehistory (46.2980, 4.7189, €), housed within the hill itself.
Continuing its course almost directly south, the Athena current runs through the very grand **Église Saint-Pierre** (46.1898, 4.7361) in the village of **Romanèche-Thorins**. Today's church was built in the 1860s but there's been one on the site since the 11th century.
46.2986, 4.7181; Parking: 46.2972, 4.7156, 1200m

AIN

10 Cité Médiévale de Pérouges, Pérouges

Entering the old medieval hilltop town just outside the town of Pérouges and seeing its half-timbered houses, cobbled streets and ancient archways gives a real sense of travelling back in time. It's no surprise that it's often used as a movie and TV location.
The Apollo current flows through the **Église Saint Marie-Madeleine** (45.9036, 5.1783), built in the 15th century and fortified with battlements and arrow-slits. Inside, the Apollo line runs directly through a statue of St.George subduing a dragon.
Significantly, the name Pérouges is the French form of Perugia in Italy, which also lies on the Apollo current. People have speculated that the town was originally founded by colonists from Perugia, although nobody knows for sure. A further sign of the close connection between the two towns is that Pérouges' coat of arms, featuring a gold dragon with a serpentine tail, is identical to Perugia's except that the Italian city's dragon is silver.
45.9033, 5.1792; Parking €: 45.9052, 5.1767, 300m

11 Église Notre-Dame de l'Assomption, Lhuis

The medieval church in this charming village in the foothills of the Jura retains the imprint of a Gallo-Roman sacred sanctuary that once stood on the spot, as the ancient shrine's white stone was used in its construction. One bears an inscription to the Matrae Sacrae, the Mother Goddesses. Outside stands a stele engraved with a solar disc representing the sun god Taranis, a fitting symbol as this site lies on the Apollo current.
Lhuis is 2.5km from the very scenic **Défilé de Malarage** (45.7417, 5.5008), a gorge where the river Rhône is forced through narrow rock walls. On a forested peak just before the northern entrance to the gorge are the fire-blackened remains of the walls of the Abbaye Saint-Alban (45.7443, 5.4966). According to a local legend, the monks would cross the river to a convent, where they and the nuns would engage in debauched revelries. As punishment for breaking their holy vows, one day fire rained down from heaven and destroyed both buildings.
45.7461, 5.5347

12 Basilica of Ars, Ars-sur-Formans

Although it has a population of only around 1,500, the village of Ars-sur-Formans on the Athena current is a major Catholic sanctuary that attracts half a million pilgrims and visitors every year. The draw is the celebrated 'Curé d'Ars', the parish priest

11

11

12

Jean-Marie Vianney, who ministered to the villagers in the mid-19th century. Vianney was renowned for his piety, miracles and good works, especially the setting up of free schools. He was declared a saint in 1925, but it was the Curé's healing powers that brought people flocking to Ars while he was alive. The crutches of the lame and disabled people he restored to health are still displayed in one of the side chapels.

This very grand and opulent basilica was built in honour of Vianney, whose body is displayed in an ornate shrine, his face covered by a wax mask. It was constructed around the original 10th-century parish church, and is unusual in that its architecture blends Eastern Orthodox and Classical styles. Some of the interior decor and imagery resembles that of ancient temples, such as winged lions at the bottom of columns. After running through the presbytery, the Athena current flows to the altar, directly beneath the central tower.

Adjacent to the basilica's northern side, the Curé's presbytery has been preserved with Vianney's original furniture. The Chapelle du Coeur (45.9928, 4.8231) was built in 1930 to house Vianney's heart (coeur), which is kept in a bronze reliquary.

45.9925, 4.8231; Parking: 45.9934, 4.8207, 200m

RHÔNE

13 Abbatiale de l'Assomption, Belleville-en-Beaujolais

A symbol encountered all along the Apollo and Athena alignment, a mermaid holding her splayed double fishtail, is much in evidence in this imposing church that is also known as Notre-Dame de Belleville. Its grand scale and prodigious 17m-high tower reveal its origins as the church of a large abbey of which it is the only surviving part. The first stone, placed on a gold coin, was

13

13

laid in 1168, and work was finished six years later. Inside, carved into the tops of columns, are more mystic images including snakes spewing from the mouths of human heads. 46.1075, 4.7506

14 **Notre-Dame de Fourvière, Lyon**

From the hill of Fourvière in the historic quarter of Vieux Lyon, the Basilica of Our Lady dominates this city and has been described as a 'modern temple to the Goddess'. The basilica is home not only to conventional images of the Virgin Mary but also to two Black Madonnas, and even a statue of the goddess of wisdom.

Fourvière was the site of the forum of the Gallo-Roman city of Lugdunum, named for the Celtic god Lug, whose name derives from 'light' and who the Romans equated with Mercury. The hill later became a sanctuary to the martyr Thomas Becket, St Thomas of Canterbury. The architect of the basilica, built at the end of the 19th century, was Pierre Bossan who also designed the **Basilica of Ars**, another important Athena site with many elements unexpected in a modern Christian place of worship. The basilica is rectangular in shape with a tower at each corner representing the four cardinal virtues of ancient Greece. There's a dome above the main altar at the eastern end, on the top of which is a statue of Archangel Michael who, standing on the subdued dragon with its twisting tail, looks down on Vieux Lyon below. It's a replica of the statue atop the Église Saint-Michel at **Saint-Michel-Mont-Mercure** in the Vendée. Above the basilica's entrance are winged lions, which also feature in the Ars basilica. Angels and other winged creatures, some with serpentine tails, are all around the sumptuous and soaring interior. Perhaps most remarkable of all is a double-winged statue of Sapientia, the goddess of wisdom, which sits at the top of the grand stairway from the crypt to the upper church.

The Athena current runs through the basilica to a tower containing its oldest part, the Chapelle Saint-Thomas (45.7619, 4.8225) or Chapelle de la Vierge (Virgin). On the top of the 19th-century tower stands a magnificent gold statue of the Virgin Mary but the Black Madonna that gives the basilica its name, Notre-Dame de Fourvière, has pride of place on the chapel's altar. The deep black figure, a replica of the ancient original destroyed in the 16th century Wars of Religion, is considered Lyon's protective talisman. A second Black Madonna, Notre-Dame de Bon Conseil (Good Counsel) was installed in the 1750s in one of the side chapels, and has since been coloured a lighter shade. The basilica's crypt houses a collection of images of the Virgin from all over the world, including copies of several other Black Madonnas.

There's a wealth of sights in Vieux Lyon from every age of its long history. Just 400m from the basilica is the Théâtre Antique de Lugdunum (45.7597, 4.8197), a Roman theatre still used by performers. Below the Fourvière hill, overlooked by the basilica, stands the medieval Cathedral of St John the Baptist (45.7608, 4.8272) and 300m away is the extraordinary Tour Rose (45.7628, 4.8269), a tall thin tower housing the spiral staircase of a lavish Renaissance residence, now an upmarket hotel.

Lyon has long been regarded as a city of magic and it was through the city that new Renaissance ideas from Italy made their way into France. This 'rebirth' of the arts and sciences also challenged religious

14

14

14

14

15

15

thinking, and ideas that were inspired and driven by magical philosophies led to the growth of esoteric societies and orders. At that time, Lyon's flourishing literary scene included Rabelais, whose works popularised the giant Gargantua, and from those same circles in the 1530s emerged an anonymous and mysterious work, the *Great and Inestimable Chronicles of the Great and Enormous Giant Gargantua*. Encoded within the giant's journey was the ancient pilgrimage trail from the east of France, via **Chartres Cathedral** to **Mont Saint-Michel**. Lyon's reputation for magic, sorcery and occultism continued to the present day, with many key figures in the French magical revival of the 19th and 20th centuries basing themselves in the city.

45.7625, 4.8225; Parking €: 45.7606, 4.8285, 900m to the basilica via an uphill path or 300m to the funicular railway (45.7600, 4.8264) that runs to the top of the Fourvière hill.

ISÈRE

15 Vienne

In Vienne the Athena current flows through the tower of what is thought to be one of the oldest churches in France. Dedicated to St Peter, it has occupied the site since the 5th century although the building we see today is largely medieval. No longer a church, it now houses the **Musée Archéologique Saint-Pierre** (45.5230, 4.8709, parking 45.5234, 4.8711, €) which is filled with art and artefacts from Gallo-Roman Vienne, many depicting gods and goddesses such as Mercury, Diana and Bacchus. Also displayed are capitals of columns from the sanctuary of Apollo that depict curling, scaly serpents, just as in many churches on the Apollo and Athena currents. The city of Vienne, which stretches along the banks of the Rhône, is steeped in history, with many buildings and monuments surviving from the Gallo-Roman era. One of the most impressive is the **Temple of Augustus and Livia** (45.5256, 4.8742) dedicated to the Roman Emperor who was considered a god, along with his wife. After the fall of the Roman Empire it became a Christian church dedicated to the Virgin Mary then, during the French Revolution, a Temple of Reason. It's now a historic monument in one of the town's squares. The Egyptian-style obelisk known as the Vienne Pyramid (45.5164, 4.8678) once stood at the centre of a Roman Circus but is now on a roundabout. According to legend it marked the tomb of Pontius Pilate, the Roman governor who condemned Jesus, was exiled to Gaul and is thought to have died in Vienne. The Roman Théâtre Antique (45.5247, 4.8789) is still used for concerts.

There's also much of Vienne's medieval heritage to be seen. The ruins of Château de la Bâtie (45.5308, 4.8764, private) stand high on Mont Salomon overlooking the town. At the Gothic Vienne Cathedral (45.5242, 4.8731), the Church Council of 1312, presided over by Pope Clement V, ordered the disbanding of the Knights Templar.

Parking 45.5256, 4.8753, €

16 Église Saint-Martin, Montseveroux

The Athena current passes through the oldest part of Montseveroux's Église Saint-Martin, built at the end of the 1200s. The small village has a number of Renaissance houses and a medieval castle, now the mairie (45.4287, 4.9707), which can be visited.

45.4294, 4.9711; Parking: 45.4289, 4.9700, 150m

15

16

17 Les Trois Pucelles, Saint-Nizier-du-Moucherotte

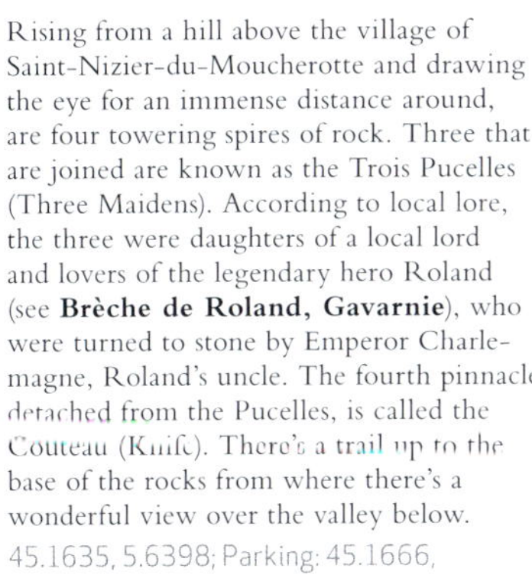

Rising from a hill above the village of Saint-Nizier-du-Moucherotte and drawing the eye for an immense distance around, are four towering spires of rock. Three that are joined are known as the Trois Pucelles (Three Maidens). According to local lore, the three were daughters of a local lord and lovers of the legendary hero Roland (see **Brèche de Roland, Gavarnie**), who were turned to stone by Emperor Charlemagne, Roland's uncle. The fourth pinnacle, detached from the Pucelles, is called the Couteau (Knife). There's a trail up to the base of the rocks from where there's a wonderful view over the valley below.

45.1635, 5.6398; Parking: 45.1666, 5.6400, 700m

SAVOIE

18 Notre-Dame de l'Assomption, Yenne

Passing into the increasingly mountainous territory of the old Duchy of Savoy, the Apollo current reaches the attractive small town of Yenne that overlooks the river Rhône. It passes through the medieval parish church's tower, which is in an unusual position at the side of the building. The interior of the church, though high and spacious, is dark and has a cave-like feel.

45.7047, 5.7575

19 Chapelle Mont-Saint-Michel, Curienne

After passing through the historic city of Chambéry, once capital of the powerful Duchy of Savoy, the Apollo current flows over Mont Saint-Michel, namesake of

the monumental island at the start of the Apollo-Athena alignment in France. On this mountain's summit is an octagonal chapel dedicated to the Archangel. It was built in 1879 but replaced a much more ancient chapel whose exact origins are lost in the mists of time, although it's known that it was on the site of a Roman temple to the sun god Apollo. The original chapel's foundations as well as its altar, can be seen 50m away (45.5513, 6.0019) and the Apollo current runs directly through them.

The mount is 900m above sea level and it's an uphill hike along a trail through the forest to the chapel with its 360-degree views. Chambéry lies to the west and to the south is the valley of the Trouée des Marches where the Athena current flows through the **Sanctuaire de Notre-Dame-de-Myans**. To the east is the smaller valley of the Combe de Savoie looking across to the Alps. Every evening the chapel is illuminated and from below it appears to be hovering in the night sky.

One of several hiking trails through the forest surrounding Mont Saint-Michel leads to the Grotte des Fées (45.5552, 5.9999), around 600m from the chapel. With a tunnel-like opening, the narrow cave is believed to be the abode of the fairy folk and crystals in the rock make it sparkle in torchlight. The trail to the cave is hard going in places.

45.5510, 6.0012; Parking: 45.5572, 6.0097, 1.1km

20 Notre-Dame-de-Tout-Pouvoir, Bozel

The small town of Bozel lies in the valley of the river Doron, over 800m above sea level with peaks topping 2000m on either side. The Apollo current runs through a chapel built to house the statue of Notre-Dame-de-Tout-Pouvoir (All-Powerful) which is immediately behind the Église Saint-François-de-Sales with its very ornate and prominent tower. The statue was originally in a niche on the outside of a previous church, where it gained a reputation for healing those who prayed to it. The current chapel was built in the 1740s soon after St Francis' church, to house the statue and was constructed in the extravagantly opulent baroque style of the period. The main façade has paintings of scenes from Mary's life and above the entrance is a statue of the Virgin standing over a serpentine dragon.

Like so many, the original Notre-Dame-de-Tout-Pouvoir was destroyed during the French Revolution and the current chapel is a 19th century replacement. However, it continues to attract pilgrims and is still known for its miracle cures.

45.4434, 6.6473; Parking: 45.4424, 6.6470, 150m

21 Chapelle Saint-Antoine, Bessans

The village of Bessans, 1750m up in the wide valley of the Haute-Maurienne and surrounded by mountains and glaciers is covered in deep snow from autumn onwards. A little unexpectedly, the Apollo current doesn't flow through the parish church on the edge of the village but to the simple chapel beside it. The exterior features murals and the interior walls are covered in painted panels thought to be from the early 1500s. A local legend, a variation of one found throughout France, is attached to the old bridge over the river Arc in the village. After a flood had washed the bridge away, the

23

townsfolk employed a builder to construct a new one. However, when he realised that he wouldn't be able to do the work by the deadline he made a deal with a stranger who agreed to finish the job in return for all the worldly goods belonging to the first to cross the bridge. When it was completed, and with the stranger waiting to claim his fee, the first to approach was a goatherd, driving his flock ahead of him. The first goat onto the bridge, recognising the waiting stranger as evil, charged and pierced him with its horns. At this point, horns sprung from the stranger's head, revealing him to be a demon. He fled empty handed.

45.3200, 6.9951; Parking: 45.3199, 6.9958, 70m

22 Lac d'Aiguebelette

This glorious Alpine lake surrounded by forest-covered mountains is visited by the Athena current and lies on the ancient road through the Col Saint-Michel – the pass that leads to the valley now occupied by the city of Chambéry. A local legend explains the origin of the two islands at the lake's southern end. Where the lake is now there was once a plain with a town at its centre, which was infamous for its vices and immorality. One day Jesus came there in the guise of a beggar, asking for food and shelter. The only person who offered him some bread was a poor widow. The 'beggar' asked her if there was anyone else in town as kind and charitable as her, to which she replied that the only other was her daughter. That night the plain was flooded and the town submerged, only the two women's houses remaining above water on the newly-formed islands.

45.5578, 5.8014; Parking: 45.5443, 5.8154

23 Notre-Dame-de-Myans

This important Black Madonna site is thought to be the first centre of pilgrimage established in France, and it still attracts around 100,000 pilgrims a year. Above the church is a great bronze-gilt statue of the Virgin Mary and Child, 5.5m high, which was erected in 1855 on the remains of the clock tower.

Myans' church lies in the wide valley of the Trouée des Marches, surrounded by mountains, with a view to the **Chapelle Saint-Michel** 4km to the north where the Apollo current flows. The Athena current passes directly through the sanctuary's magnificent marble and gilt crypt that houses the Black Madonna. Sometimes referred to as the Queen of Savoy, Notre-Dame de Myans was carved from ebony in the 12th century. She and her Child are now crowned and dressed in golden cloaks.

A fresco in the nave depicts the cataclysmic event that established the sanctuary as a place of miracles. In 1248, one face of the massive Mont Granier (45.4647, 5.9253), 7km away, collapsed in what is thought to be the greatest landslide ever experienced in Europe, leaving a sheer 1900m-high white cliff. The rocks swept down the valley, devastating the town of Saint-André at the mountain's base as well as several villages, killing thousands. However, the rockslide halted just before the Black Madonna's chapel. According to the legend, the catastrophe was the work of demons, and those sheltering inside the chapel could hear the fiends further back urging their comrades at the front to finish their task and destroy the chapel, but getting the response "*Nous ne pouvons, la Noire nous en empêche*" ("We cannot, the Black One prevents us") – the words now inscribed above the fresco.

45.5143, 5.9876; Parking: 45.5118, 5.9874, 300m

22

23

24

24 Saint-Pierre d'Extravache, Val-Cenis

The last Athena site in France is this isolated 11th century church, standing alone amid a breathtaking landscape of towering snow-capped mountains. It lies on the route leading to the Col du Mont-Cenis, the pass that crosses the Alps into Italy. It's said to be on the site of the very first Christian building in France, a chapel built by two disciples of St Paul on a pagan sacred site. There are remnants of murals inside, which are now hard to make out.

45.2172, 6.8031; Parking: 45.2163, 6.8043, 125m

25 Sacra di San Michele

The Apollo-Athena alignment that started its journey at **Mont Saint-Michel** in Normandy now crosses the border into Italy and ends at one of Europe's major sanctuaries dedicated to Archangel Michael, the Sacra di San Michele. The Apollo-Athena currents unite again at this commanding, fortress-like shrine, which embraces the summit of Monte Pirchiriano at the southern entrance to the Susa Valley. The complex of buildings is constructed on several levels around the mountain's peak and where the rock itself becomes part of the sanctuary's walls, the natural and manmade are fused organically into one powerful site.

Like Mont Saint-Michel, the site is said to have been chosen by the Archangel himself. Legend tells how he appeared to a hermit, Giovanni Vincenzo, who was living on Monte Caprasio on the other side of the valley and commanded the holy man to build a chapel in his name. Vincenzo, who later became Bishop of Ravenna, gathered the timber to build it on his mountain but Michael carried it across the valley to Monte Pirchiriano.

The chapel evolved over the centuries, especially when it became a stop on the pilgrims' trail that passed through the Susa Valley, the Via Francigena (Way of France) from Canterbury, England, to Rome. After the Crusades, the trail was extended to the Italian coast and across the sea to Jerusalem, passing the other major Italian sanctuary of the Archangel at Monte Gargano. Most of the shrine's edifice we see today was built in the 12th century although the earliest parts, including the crypt, are from the late 900s.

Standing guard at the shrine's main entrance is a 5m-high modern statue of the Archangel, then once through the imposing 40m high façade, you enter the main church via the Scalone dei Morti. This 'Stairway of the Dead' was so named because the skeletons of deceased monks were once displayed in the niches on either side. At the top of the stairway is the Porta dello Zodiaco (Zodiac Portal), a masterpiece of medieval sculpture depicting the signs of the zodiac and constellations.

Beyond the portal, the soaring interior of the church, on the site of the original chapel, is filled with a potent energy. Oriented towards sunrise on Archangel Michael's Feast Day of 29 September, the church sits on the very top of Monte Pirchiriano, its tip visible beneath the

25

first pillar on the left of the nave. At the tops of the columns supporting the arches are carvings of fabulous creatures, including images characteristic of many other sites along the Apollo-Athena alignment: mermen with curling double tails and women suckling serpents. A map within the sanctuary shows the alignment of Michael sites that begins at Skellig Michael in Ireland and runs through France from Mont Saint-Michel to Sacra di San Michele and Monte Gargano in Italy, exactly following the Apollo line. Its inclusion and display show that the Church recognises the line, even if interpreting it differently and extending the line to Christianity's holiest place, Jerusalem, rather than its actual alignment to Mount Carmel.

Before it arrives at the sanctuary, the Athena current flows from Briançon (ancient Brigantium, 44.8964, 6.6356) 40km to the southwest and follows the course of the ancient Via Heraklea (Heraklion Way). This 1,600km straight track, oriented to sunrise on the summer solstice, begins in Portugal at the Sacred Promontory (modern Cape St Vincent) crossing Spain and southern France before travelling directly up the Col de Montgenèvre (Montgenèvre Pass) into Italy. In ancient times this was known as the **Matrona Pass** and dedicated to Matrona, the triple-aspect Mother Goddess of the Celts. The Athena current then meets the Apollo current, which has travelled directly across the mountains from **Bessans**, and the two cross, forming a node just outside Sacra di San Michele at the ruins of a chapel on a mound beside the road to the main entrance. Known as the **Monk's Sepulchre** (45.0962, 7.3421), the chapel is thought to have been one of the earliest parts of Sacra di San Michele and was built to the same plan as the Holy Sepulchre in Jerusalem.

On the very edge of the mountain are the ruins of an old abandoned monastery, with the five-story Torre della Bell'Alda (Tower of the Beautiful Alda, 45.0983, 7.3430) overlooking the valley from the top of a cliff. The tower takes its name from the tale of a peasant girl, Alda, who ran up it when fleeing from enemy soldiers. Trapped, she threw herself from the top, praying to Archangel Michael to save her and landed safely at the bottom of the cliff. However, when she tried to repeat the miracle for local people who doubted her story, Alda fell to her death. There's now a terrace in the monastery ruins that gives a terrific panoramic view over the valley.

45.0981, 7.3436, €€; Parking €: 45.0933, 7.3392, 500m

25

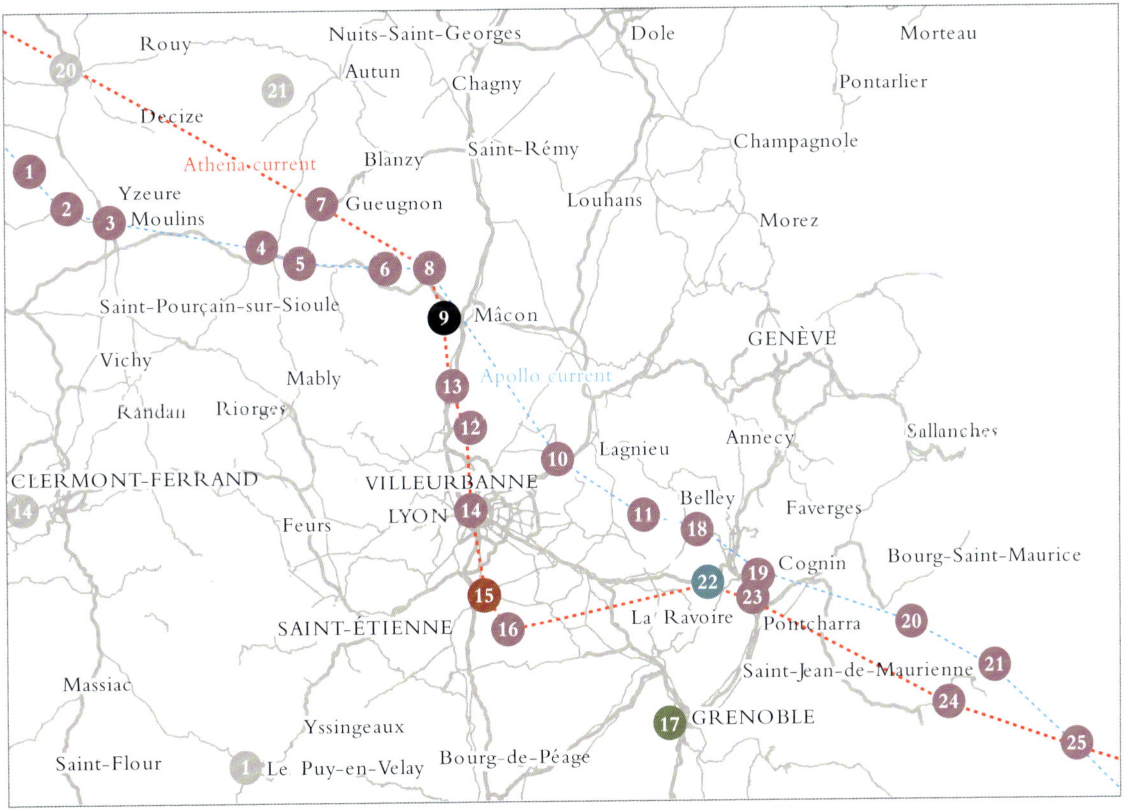

Rouy
Nuits-Saint-Georges
Dole
Morteau
20
Autun
21
Chagny
Pontarlier
Decize
Champagnole
1
Athena current
Blanzy
Saint-Rémy
Yzeure
7
Gueugnon
Louhans
2
3
Moulins
Morez
4
5
6
8
Saint-Pourçain-sur-Sioule
9
Mâcon
GENÈVE
Vichy
Mably
13
Apollo current
Randan
Riorges
12
Annecy
Sallanches
10
Lagnieu
CLERMONT-FERRAND
VILLEURBANNE
14
LYON
14
11
Belley
Faverges
Feurs
18
Cognin
Bourg-Saint-Maurice
22
19
23
15
SAINT-ÉTIENNE
16
La Ravoire
Pontcharra
20
Saint-Jean-de-Maurienne
21
Massiac
24
17
GRENOBLE
25
Yssingeaux
Saint-Flour
1
Le Puy-en-Velay
Bourg-de-Péage

WESTERN LOWLANDS AND THE FAIRY MELUSINE

Rarely rising above 250m, this region is relatively low-lying compared to most of France, but the diversity of landscapes is enriched by the change in climate from north to south. A long-distance alignment of sacred sites known as the Ogmios line can be traced through the region. Originating far to the north at the Callanish stone circle in the Outer Hebrides of Scotland, the line travels through Glastonbury Tor in England and Mont Saint-Michel in Normandy before entering the region from the north where it then passes by many castles, churches, abbeys and megalithic sites. Dolmens, in particular, are believed to be the work of 'fées bâtisseuses' (fairy builders) who carry the boulders down from the hills. Goblin-like lutins or korrigans, here called 'farfadets' are also present, but the region also has its own cast of supernatural characters, such as 'lascifs' – tiny men who if they meet a human at dusk force them to dance until exhausted. Shapeshifters loom large in local traditions, including the 'garache', a werewolf-like creature that also possesses magic powers, and the 'ganipote' which can take on many animal forms. There are also many legends of dragons or serpents, such as the Grand Goule of Poitiers.

Pride of place in the region's lore goes to Melusine, the half-woman, half-serpent being from the fairy realm. Her legend is found throughout France and beyond, but has its origin here, for it was in the forest around Lusignan that the knight Raymondin of Poitiers met the fairy Melusine by an enchanted spring. The two fell in love and married, and Melusine took on fully human form, though every Saturday she was secretly cursed to be a serpent from the waist down. She made Raymondin swear that he would never seek her out on that day. By her magic Melusine built the castle of Lusignan as their home, and the couple had ten sons, all but the last two bearing a fairy mark. Their descendants became the powerful House of Lusignan, and Melusine is said to have raised their castles at Vouvent, Mervent, Tiffauge, Châteaumur and Pouzauges, each in a single night of the full moon, working between midnight and cockcrow. She's also credited with creating many other structures including several churches. One day, however, Raymondin spied on her while she was bathing on a Saturday. Heartbroken, she later transformed into a winged serpent and flew off, abandoning her husband – but her presence has never left the region.

MAINE-ET-LOIRE

1 Bellefontaine Abbey, Bégrolles-en-Mauges

Located near the Ogmios alignment, the Cistercian Abbaye de Bellefontaine was founded in the early 1100s, probably on the site of an earlier hermitage. A peaceful place of meditation and contemplation, it's still a working monastery with a farm and orchards. As the name, meaning 'beautiful spring' implies, there's a natural spring said to flow with healing water, especially for the eyes. The spring is by the Chapelle Notre-Dame de Bon Secours (Good Help, 47.1535, -0.9375), a separate building within the abbey grounds.

47.1519, -0.9386; Parking: 47.1505, -0.9379

2 Pouancé Castle

The scale of the Château de Pouancé compared to its small-town setting reveals its historical importance as a strategic fortification on the frontier with Brittany. The castle, which dates from the 12th–15th centuries, once had six towers including the Tour de la Dame Blanche, and was surrounded by a deep moat. Today the walls and four of the towers remain, the court within being a garden walk that's open all year round, but the moat has been filled in. It's one of several castles near the Ogmios alignment that passes through the region. In the town of Pouancé one of the medieval gateways, the Porte Angevine (47.7408, -1.1761), survives and could have come from the pages of a storybook. The church is dedicated to Mary Magdalene (47.7397, -1.1769) and was built in the 1800s, replacing an earlier one established back in the 11th century.

Just south of the town is the imposing **Menhir de Pierre Frite** (47.7003, -1.1604). An unexpected discovery in a quiet rural area, it stands over 5m tall and towers over a tree-lined farm track a short way off the D6, signposted from the main road. Wildflowers grow around the menhir's base and a small niche carved into its eastern face once held a statue of the Virgin Mary, presumably in an attempt to Christianise it. There's a local legend that the stone marks a buried treasure trove. The Pierre Frite is also near the Ogmios alignment, as well as on an alignment of megaliths that runs right across France from Haute-Savoie on the border with Switzerland to the Brittany coast. The enchanting Ruisseau des Nymphes (Nymphs' Stream) with wooded banks runs through the area, crossing the D6 2km south of the menhir.

47.7419, -1.1783; Parking €: 47.7409, -1.1777

3 Saint-Florent-le-Vieil Abbey, Mauges-sur-Loire

The Ogmios alignment passes by a number of religious sites in the region, and Saint-Florent-le-Vieil Abbey on a promontory overlooking the Loire is one of the most impressive. It's named after St Florent of Anjou, a 4th-century Roman soldier who converted to Christianity and established a hermitage on what was then a remote spot. Some 400 years later an abbey was built on the site on the orders of Charlemagne, who dedicated to it a vessel that some believe was the Holy Grail: the cup used at the Last Supper. When the Vikings invaded the region in the 9th century the monks fled,

taking the relic with them, after which it was lost to history. Today the abbey is a cultural centre and art gallery.

47.3641, -1.0193; Parking: 47.3629, -1.0204, 170m

VENDÉE

4 Châteaumur Keep

The only surviving part of one of the medieval castles said to have been built by the fairy Melusine in a single night, the Donjon (Keep) of Châteaumur still has a commanding presence even in its partly ruined state. The keep is in an unusual setting, in the middle of a circle of houses at the centre of the village where the streets follow the outline of the vanished castle. Like all the 'Melusine' castles, it was associated with the fairy's reputed descendants, the House of **Lusignan,** and is near the Ogmios alignment.

46.8461, -0.8325; Parking: 46.8456, -0.8323, 50m

5 Vieux Château, Mervent

This castle plays an important part in Melusine's story, as it was here that Raymondin discovered his wife was half-serpent. His subsequent harsh words to Melusine caused her to abandon him, her foot leaving an imprint in the stone sill as she launched herself from the window. Taking on her serpentine form, she flew screeching to **Lusignan** and circled the castle three times. Melusine then departed for the sacred mountain of Montserrat in Spain, where she was seen for the last time and where Raymondin was eventually buried. Mervent's Vieux Château stands on a high point overlooking the valleys of the Vendée and Mère and is surrounded by an immense forest that extends north to **Vouvant**. It was built on the site of an Iron Age hillfort and is known as the Old Castle to distinguish it from the later Renaissance château built outside Mervent. Only its outer walls now remain, surrounding a public park. Like the other castles in the Melusine tale it was said

to have been built using Melusine's magic. Historically it's associated with Geoffrey I of Lusignan, Lord of Vouvant and Mervent, who appears in the legend as Geoffrey Grand'Dent (Great-Tooth), the most famous of the ten sons of Melusine and Raymondin. Like nearby Vouvant, the castle lies near the Ogmios alignment.
46.5239, -0.7567

6 Pouzauges Castle

Legend tells that the townsfolk of Pouzauges, astounded at finding the Château de Pouzauges more complete every morning even though no workers were to be seen, wanted to know how it was being done. One man hid in the Bois de la Folie (46.7888, -0.8423) on the hill that overlooks the town to keep watch. At midnight the fairy Melusine appeared but sensed that she was being spied on. Enraged, she cried out that she would remove a stone from each of her five castles every year

until there was nothing left of them, which explains why Pouzauges and all the others she built are now ruins. Like **Mervent** and **Vouvant** castles, it also lies near the Ogmios alignment. The castle belonged to the Viscounts of Thouars, the leading nobles of Vendée who were closely related to the House of **Lusignan**, and who also owned **Châteaumur Keep**. In the 15th century, Pouzauges was the residence of Catherine de Thouars, wife of the notorious Gilles de Rais (see **Tiffauges Castle**). She retreated there with their daughter when her husband's crimes were exposed.

Although the château is now in ruins, its keep and parts of the walls and towers can still be seen in the centre of the town. The grounds are open all year round, and the keep can be visited on certain days in July and August.

46.7849, -0.8392; Parking: 46.7852, -0.8382, 100m

7 Saint-Michel-en-l'Herm Abbey

Once a remote and isolated spot on a wild coast, Saint-Michel-en-l'Herm grew into a town as land was reclaimed from the sea over the centuries, and the shoreline is now some 6km away. It was Saint-Michel's former isolation that brought monks here from Ireland in the early Christian period to found an abbey. It's also likely that it was once a pagan sacred site, explaining the dedication to St Michael, the archangel who fought against Satan. On the edge of the town, the **Fontaine de Saint-Martin** (46.3541, -1.2589) was also considered sacred in pre-Christian times then subsequently re-dedicated to a Christian saint. The abbey flourished as the area's population grew with the recovery of land for farming, becoming one of the most famous in France and being redeveloped many times. In 1516 it became the **Royal Abbey of Saint-Michel-en-l'Herm** (46.3530, -1.2503, €) when the Pope gave French kings the authority to appoint its abbots. It's now privately owned but open to the public. Another legend hinting at the area's pagan past tells how it was terrorised by giant serpents that inhabited the **Île de la Dive** (46.3042, -1.2467), then a small island off the coast. When St Hilary of Poitiers visited the Abbey in the 4th century, the monks asked for his help in ridding them of the menace, and at his command the serpents fled into the sea. It's been suggested that this refers to the presence of a pre-Christian cult site on the isle alongside the first monasteries. The land around the island has now been reclaimed from the sea and still rises from the flat farmland, bordered by cliffs. There are houses on the former island, and caves including the Grotte de l'Ermite (Hermit).

Parking: 46.3531, -1.2515

8 Saint-Michel-Mont-Mercure

Sited on the highest point in this region of France, the church of Saint-Michel-Mont-Mercure is a significant site on the Ogmios

9

alignment that runs south from **Mont Saint-Michel** in Normandy. The hill was once dedicated to the Celtic god Lugus and then to Mercury (Mercure) by the Romans. When the region was Christianised, the church was re-dedicated to Archangel Michael as Mercury's equivalent – both being messengers of their respective gods. Michael's legendary slaying of the dragon, here representing paganism, probably also played a part. During the French Revolution, which aimed to shift power away from the Church and de-Christianise France, the name of this church was changed back to Mont-Mercure, and subsequently to its present name combining the two. The Église Saint-Michel is topped by a golden sculpture, nearly 10m high, of Archangel Michael defeating the dragon. A replica stands on the dome of the Basilica of **Notre-Dame de Fourvière** in Lyon, built in the 19th century. There's been a church dedicated to St Michael on this spot since the Middle Ages, the original modest-sized one having been demolished in 1877 to make way for the new, much more triumphant edifice.

46.8317, -0.8830; Parking: 46.8294, -0.8838, 260m

9

9 Tiffauges Castle

Overlooking the wide river Crûme, the Château de Tiffauges is one of the five castles said to have been raised by Melusine's magic. Like all the castles attributed to her, it has a connection to the Lusignan dynasty: the Viscount of Thouars for whom it was built was married to one of the family. The castle has another, darker reason for its place in history. It is known as 'Bluebeard's Castle' owing to one particular resident, the notorious Gilles des Rais, a 15th-century war hero and military companion of Joan of Arc who was one of history's first recorded serial killers. It's now a picturesque ruin with reconstructions of medieval siege towers and trebuchets bringing the era to life. Medieval re-enactments are held there in the summer.

47.0164, -1.1147; Parking: 47.0152, -1.1152, 150m; Open April-September, €€

10 Melusine's Tower, Vouvant

The town of Vouvant glories in its connection with the fairy Melusine: a museum dedicated to her legend sits in the Office de Tourisme (46.6731, -0.7707) just outside the castle grounds. The famous cylindrical watchtower, the Tour Mélusine, is topped with a weathervane in the form of a silhouette of the half-serpent fairy woman and is all that remains of Vouvant Castle, said to have been built by Melusine in a single night and originally boasting seven towers. Her tower is open to visitors, with nar-

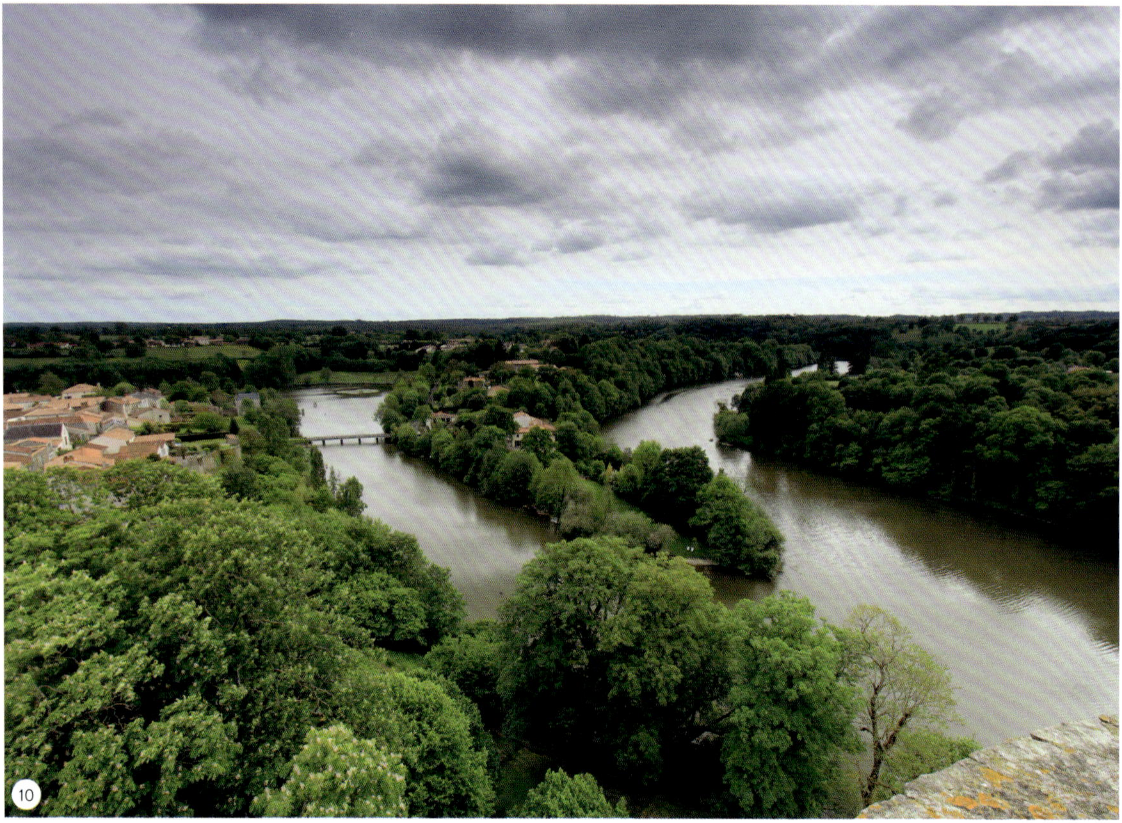

10

10

10

Notre-Dame de l'Assomption

10

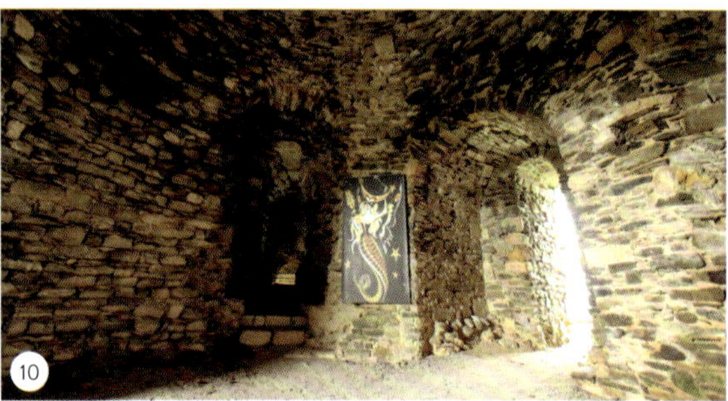

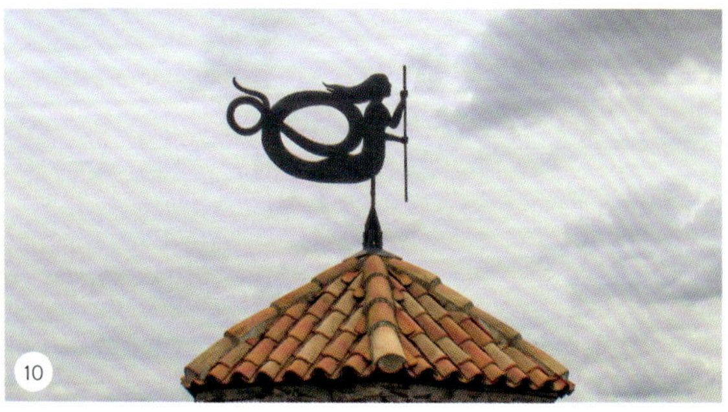

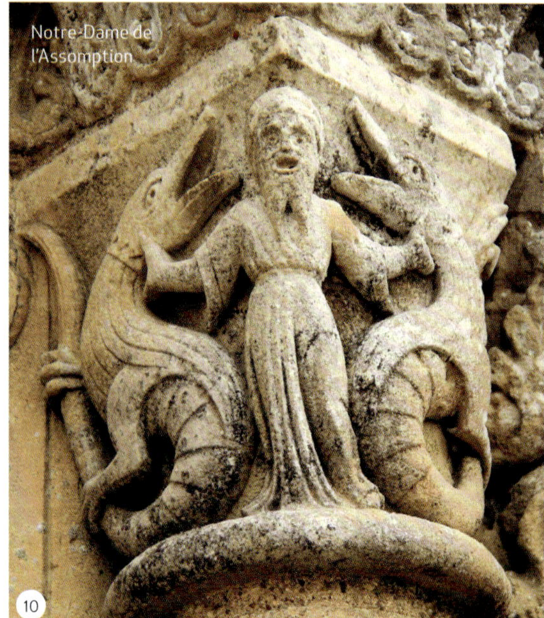

row, steep steps to the top where there's a panoramic view over the river Mère and the surrounding landscape. The Tour Mélusine lies near the Ogmios alignment, between her castles at **Pouzauges** and **Mervent**.
Vouvant castle was founded at the start of the 11th century on a promontory on a bend in the Mère, and in the mid-1100s passed by marriage into the Lusignan family who had the large fortress constructed with the aid of Melusine's magic. According to one story, Melusine was chased from the castle by St Louis (King Louis IX) and escaped by opening the earth with a kick of her heel, disappearing below ground and emerging at Jazeneuil, some 65km away near **Lusignan**.
The King gave thanks for his triumph over the fairy at the **Église Notre-Dame de l'Assomption** (46.5720, -0.7697), a grand edifice built when Vouvant was first founded but added to and restored over the centuries. The ancient crypt, only rediscovered in the 1850s, contains the remains of sculptures and a Merovingian sarcophagus. As well as building the castle, in the early 13th century the Lusignan family also had Vouvant encircled with fortifications, including 30 towers. Much of the fortifications are still standing, making Vouvant the only remaining walled town in the Vendée.

46.5736, -0.7717; Parking: 46.5730, -0.7711, 70m

VIENNE

11 Notre-Dame-la-Grande, Poitiers

One of the key places in the unfolding tale of Melusine and her husband Raymondin is this church. According to legend, Raymondin was the nephew of the Count of Poitiers, Aymar, who he accidentally killed during a wild-boar hunt. Guilt-stricken, Raymondin fled into the forest around **Lusignan**, where he encountered Melusine. She promised that if he married her, she would not only use her magic to stop him being suspected of having deliberately killed Aymar but would also make him a powerful lord. The Count's funeral, at which Raymondin was one of the mourners, was held in the church of Notre-Dame-le-Grande in Poitiers.
The interior of the church is painted in a variety of geometric patterns and colours, creating a more energised atmosphere than normally found in a medieval church. The statue of Notre-Dame-la-Grande is famed locally for the 'Miracle des Clefs' (Miracle of the Keys), which saved Poitiers when it was besieged by an English army in 1202. It's said that the English bribed one of the mayor's officials to hand over the keys to the town's gates, but when the official went to steal them he found they'd disappeared from their usual place. They turned up in the hand of the statue of the Virgin Mary in the church and that night the Virgin, along with the town's two patron saints, St Radegonde and St Hilaire, appeared to the English. Terrified by the town's holy protection, the English army hastily withdrew.
St Radegonde is a strong female presence in Poitiers' traditions and folklore. She was a 6th-century Queen of the Franks, the wife of the Merovingian King Clotaire I, and was renowned for her holiness, charity and kindness, as well as her abilities as a healer. One of history's first recorded vegans, Radegonde was said to have the power to tame wild animals, even wolves. After leaving her brutal husband, she founded the Abbaye Sainte-Croix (Holy Cross) to care for the sick, ministering to them personally. There are several legends about her exploits, such as her vanquishing of the Grand Goule. This fearsome dragon lived in the river Clain and roamed in caves beneath Poitiers, including those under the abbey, emerging to prey on the nuns. Radegonde defeated the monster with holy water. A wooden sculpture of the dragon used to be paraded in the town on St Radegonde's day, 13 August, but it's now preserved in the Musée Sainte-Croix (46.5792, 0.3478).

11

11

Radegonde's major shrine and a place of pilgrimage in the Middle Ages is the **Église Sainte-Radegonde** (46.5797, 0.3519; Parking 46.5798, 0.3529, 150m), where her tomb lies in the crypt.

Poitiers' **Église Saint-Hilaire le Grand** (46.5775, 0.3325) is dedicated to St Hilaire, the first bishop of the city in the 4th century. The crypt contains his relics and the church was also a pilgrimage centre. The current building dates from the 10th century and is on the site of Hilaire's original church from where witnesses reputedly saw balls of light emerge before the Battle of Vouillé in 507. This phenomenon was taken as a portent that the Merovingian King Clovis would be victorious over the Visigoths, a tipping point in European history. Another fascinating religious building, claimed as the oldest surviving Christian site in Europe, is the **Baptistère Saint-Jean** (46.5794, 0.3486, €), which some think was adapted from a pagan temple. The baptistery is now a museum of antiquities, especially noted for its collection of Merovingian sarcophagi.

At the turn of the 12th century, the **Palais des Comtes** (46.5828, 0.3425) was the court of the powerful Eleanor, Duchess of Aquitaine, who became Queen of France and then England through her marriages to their respective kings, Louis VII and Henry II. Eleanor's court in Poitiers was entertained by the troubadours who promoted the concept of courtly love that was famously played out there. The troubadours believed that true love was only attainable by admiring from afar and bestowing favours, a precursor to the chivalry of the Arthurian romances. Eleanor later had a great hall built in the palace that was one of the largest in medieval Europe and which still amazes by its size. While residing at **Domfront** in Normandy, she was patroness of the poet Wace, who popularised the Arthurian romances. She was often visited there by her daughter Marie of Champagne, accompanied by Chrétien de Troyes who wrote the first Grail story.

The fairy-woman Melusine is said to have dug, by kicking, a tunnel from **Lusignan Castle** to Poitiers, which emerged among the ruins of the Roman amphitheatre. Only a few remnants of the amphitheatre can be seen today in the Rue Bourcani in the city centre (46.5786, 0.3394), but its original shape and size are preserved in the road layout. In the Quartier des Dunes in Poitiers' eastern suburbs is the **Pierre Levée** (46.5746, 0.3620), a dolmen with

an enormous limestone capstone, 6m long and 3m wide, now collapsed on one side. There are competing legends concerning its origins. One tells that the Devil tried to kill St Radegonde on it, but she was miraculously saved. In another version, Radegonde herself erected the dolmen while other legends attribute it to Melusine.

46.5833, 0.3439; Underground parking €: 46.5840, 0.3452

12 **Lusignan**

This small town in Vienne has had a big impact not just on history but also on folklore and myth, being inseparable from the legend of the fairy Melusine, whose spirit fills its streets. According to legend, it was here that she first took on human form and tried to live as a mortal, and it was also the first of many places she was said to have built using her magic. Today she is an important part of the town's heritage, with shops and restaurants bearing her name and her half-human and half-serpent image adorning buildings of every kind. Lusignan is Melusine's town, even its inhabitants are sometimes known as 'mélusins'.

It was near here that at midnight during a full moon, Raymondin of **Poitiers** encountered Melusine and her two fairy sisters by an enchanted spring, the Fontaine de Soif (Spring of Thirst), after accidentally killing his uncle, the Count of Poitiers, in a hunting accident. The spring lies deep within the Forest of Coulombiers, which then covered the whole landscape around Lusignan, although today only isolated patches of woodland remain amid the farmland. Some think that the name comes from colum barium, an ancient sacred site dedicated to the cult of serpent-women.

Raymondin and Melusine fell in love and were married. She adopted a fully human form and kept her true nature secret from her husband, until the fateful day at **Mervent Old Castle** when Raymondin saw her serpent's tail and she fled. However, Melusine and Raymondin already had ten sons, and their descendants formed the House of Lusignan, one of the most important in European history. The family rose from being Lords of Poitou to become Kings of Cyprus and even Kings of Jerusalem, a title they continued to claim even after the Holy Land was lost to Christendom. After her departure, Melusine continued to haunt the town. She was said to fly around the towers and wail, banshee-like, to herald the death of one of the Lusignan family. Her appearances before the deaths of Kings Henri IV and Louis XIII were even recorded by Lusignan's officials.

A striking stone carving of Melusine can be seen on the Maison de Tourisme. It's only 100m from the Parc de Blossac, a spacious landscaped park laid out among the ruins of the **Château de Lusignan** (46.4372, 0.1278), one of the most famous castles of medieval France. The château was destroyed after a siege in 1575, which was preceded by an appearance of Melusine. Only scant ruins now remain, including those of the crumbling Tour Mélusine (46.4379, 0.1282). Rising over the town on a rock outcrop

15

14

16

is the thousand-year-old **Église Notre-Dame-et-Saint-Junien** (46.4361, 0.1231). It's also said to have been founded and built by Melusine. On the north portal are carvings of dragons along with many other weird, wonderful and demonic creatures. Pride of place is, of course, given to Melusine, who is depicted with wings unfurled. There are more paintings and statues of her inside, where the high and light interior creates a strong spiritual energy.

The Via Turonensis, one of the major pilgrimage routes on the Camino de Santiago runs through **Poitiers** and Lusignan. It also passes through the small village of Coulombiers, 7km northeast of Lusignan along the D611, whose name preserves that of the ancient forest nearby where Raymondin and Melusine first met. The village's 'lavoir' (washhouse), fed by the Ruisseau le Palais, has a charming **Mosaic of Melusine** (46.4861, 0.1864; Parking: 46.4856, 0.1849, 150m) depicting her bathing in the stream while combing her hair. This recently built structure confirms that Melusine still holds a special place in the hearts of the local people.

Parking: 46.4368, 0.1266
(Maison de Tourisme)

CHARENTE

13 Barbezieux Castle

One of a number of castles that are near the Ogmios alignment, the Château de Barbezieux was once a much larger fortification but still retains the entrance gate and 'granges' (barns) of the original structure. The celebrated troubadour Rigaut de Barbezieux, one of the early writers on the Holy Grail, came from the family that ruled the castle. Through marriage, the lordship of Barbezieux passed to the House of Rochefoucauld, an important family said to be descended from Melusine. Although a castle has stood on the site since the 11th century, a more imposing structure was built in the 1480s on the orders of Marguerite de Rochefoucauld, Dame de Barbezieux, to provide work for the local people during a time of hardship. It's also tempting to imagine that a desire to emulate the building work of her fairy ancestor also played a part. Today, the château is a cultural centre with a theatre and concert hall.

45.4731, -0.1575; Parking: 45.4726, -0.1567, 50m

14 Segonzac Spring

The Ogmios alignment passes this water source that rises in the middle of the quiet town of Segonzac. It's located behind the Église Saint-Pierre, the earliest parts of which are medieval. Water from the spring feeds a basin and then runs into a channel that carries it alongside the church. It's likely this was once a sacred spring.

45.6172, -0.2173

15 Dolmen de Garde-Épée, Saint-Brice

This majestic ancient structure, just outside the village of Saint-Brice on the outskirts of Cognac, is near the Ogmios alignment. It is one of the most outstanding of the many megaliths in this part of the country. The largest of the two stones forming its table is 6m by 3m and originally enclosed a rectangular burial chamber.

45.6900, -0.2514; Roadside parking: 45.6903, -0.2511, 50m

DORDOGNE

16 La Fontaine des Fées, Montcaret

Situated in a magical location near the Ogmios alignment, La Fontaine des Fées lies just off a country lane a little under a kilometre north of the village of Montcaret. Water gushes out of a stone culvert from an unknown origin deep within a mysterious tunnel-like cavern in the ivy-covered rocks, barely big enough to crawl inside but easy enough for a korrigan to run down! The spring has long been regarded as sacred: it was once known as the 'Fon Druidorum' or 'Source of the Druids'. It's the most important of several springs in the area that were venerated by the Romans and Gauls.

44.8652, 0.0685; Roadside parking: 44.8656, 0.0691, 50m

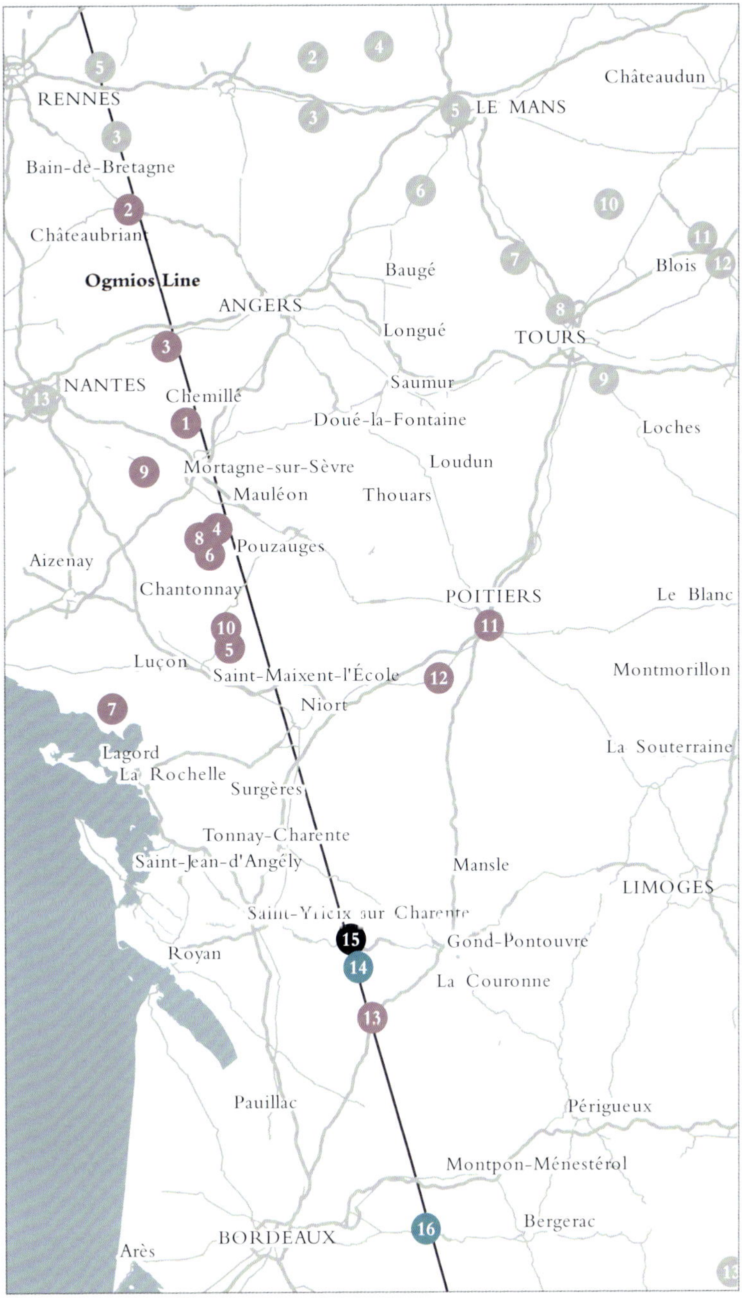

THE CAMINO DE SANTIAGO: LE PUY-EN-VELAY TO ROCAMADOUR

The Via Podiensis (Le Puy Way) that begins in Le Puy-en-Vélay is the most ancient and well-documented of the three main routes of the Camino de Santiago (Way of St James) that have taken pilgrims from throughout France to the shrine of St James the Apostle at Santiago de Compostela, Spain, since the Middle Ages. It's still the most popular for today's French pilgrims who undertake the journey of almost 1,600 kilometres. The trail comes together with the Via Turonensis (Tours Way) from Paris and Via Lemovicensis (Limoges Way) from Vézelay, at Saint-Jean-Pied-de-Port at the foot of the Pyrenees, before crossing the mountains into Spain. The trail is classified by UNESCO as a world heritage site and bronze or iron scallop shells are set into the road at various sites along the way to mark its route.

The Le Puy Way is made up of many stages with stops in towns and villages, where shelter and food were once provided by religious orders and where there are still hostels today. The winding trail passes through a variety of landscapes and spectacular scenery, from the mountains and valleys of the Haute-Loire to the plateau of Aubrac, taking in fields, dense forests and wide rivers. Along the way there are many fascinating reminders of the medieval pilgrimage route to discover. They include ancient churches and chapels, shrines to St Jacques (St James) and St Roch, the patron of pilgrims, along with many other saints, as well as medieval dwellings and old pilgrim bridges.

Many of the towns and villages, such as Saint-Côme-d'Olt and the incredible Conques, seem not to have changed since the Middle Ages. Some, such as Gourdon and Le Puy itself, are holy sites that were centres of pilgrimage even before the Camino was established, and where pilgrims on the Via Podiensis would stop to venerate the relics and icons of their saints. These travellers could also take detours from the main trail to other famous pilgrimage sites, such as Rocamadour.

Black Madonnas watch over both ends of this trail. The starting point, the Cathédrale Notre-Dame in Le-Puy-en-Vélay, houses two of these mysterious icons, and at the end is the shrine to perhaps the most famous of them all, Notre-Dame de Rocamadour. Along the way there are several others, less well known and the focus of local veneration, such as those at Saugues and Monistrol d'Allier. They add to the feeling that there is something very ancient and sacred about this route.

1 Église St. Michel d'Aiguilhe

HAUTE-LOIRE

1 Le Puy-en-Velay Cathedral

At 7 o'clock every morning, pilgrims gather around the statue of St James in the Cathédrale Notre-Dame to be blessed by the Bishop of Velay before setting off on the first stage of their long trek to Santiago de Compostela. The Romanesque cathedral is in an elevated position on the lower part of the Rocher Corneille (Crow Rock), one of two volcanic spurs that dominate Le Puy. The Rocher Corneille is the higher of the two at 130m, and on its summit is the 25m-tall statue of Notre-Dame de France (45.0472, 3.8853).

As one of the earliest centres of the Cult of Our Lady, the cathedral radiates a very strong feminine energy. This was deliberate on the part of the builders who fashioned the entrance as a symbolic return to the mother's womb. The cobbled street from the centre of the town rises to the yawning western portal and after passing through it, the visitor ascends the 134 steps of the 'escalier de ventre' ('stairway of the womb') to emerge in the centre of the cathedral. Given its hillside position, the interior is on several levels, which is unusual for a cathedral, and there's a powerful spiritual energy within. This is particularly strong behind the high altar and immediately below the spire owing to their location above a healing spring, which was incorporated into the cathedral's design. The edifice stands on an extraordinary alignment of Gothic cathedrals stretching across France from **Chartres** to **Arles**.

Le Puy-en-Velay has been a pilgrimage centre in its own right since ancient times. Although now a sanctuary to the Virgin Mary, the site blends Christian and pagan visions of the sacred feminine. The first known monument there was a Neolithic dolmen that stood on the summit of Mont Anis, the ancient name for the Rocher Corneille. Anis is reminiscent of the ancient Celtic Mother Goddess Anu and Black Anis from English folklore. According to the cathedral's foundation story, in 430 a

Église St. Michel d'Aiguilhe

1

woman named Villa fell gravely ill with a fever and in a dream was told by the Virgin Mary to climb Mont Anis and lie down on the dolmen. When she did so she had a vision of 'a multitude of angels and saints, and above them, a woman of royal dignity and majesty; her face, her clothes, everything about her was of extraordinary beauty'. Villa was miraculously cured and was told by Mary that, in return for being healed, she should build a chapel on this spot. Villa convinced the local bishop to climb the hill, which he found mysteriously covered in deep snow even though it was the middle of July, and he watched transfixed as a wild deer trotted around the summit tracing the outline of a chapel. Convinced by these miracles, he had the chapel built with the magical dolmen still standing inside, where it became known as the 'Throne of Mary'.

Notre-Dame Cathedral was subsequently visited many times by French kings including the Emperor Charlemagne. The chapel was later replaced by a church and then, in the 11th century, by the present cathedral. Stones from a nearby ruined Gallo-Roman temple were used in its construction, some bearing sculptures and inscriptions to the Emperor Augustus and the local Celtic god Adido, which are still visible on the exterior walls.

By the time of the cathedral's construction, the dolmen from Mont Anis was no longer standing but one of its stones was set into the cathedral floor. Known as both the Pierre des Apparitions and the Pierre des Fièvres (Visions/Fever Stone), it is now in the Chapelle du Saint-Crucifix and those hoping for cures or visions lie upon it, which over the centuries has given it a polished surface.

Visions/Fever Stone

1

Notre Dame-du-Puy's history and legends hint at the site being sacred to the Mother Goddess, and further evidence can be found in the Black Madonna statues. The original statue, of Middle Eastern origin and thought to be the most ancient of France's Black Madonnas, was donated to the cathedral by St Louis (Louis IX) when he returned from leading a Crusade in Egypt. It was carved from cedar wood and depicted the Madonna, dressed in Eastern-style robes and wearing a curious helmet-like headdress of gilded copper, with the Child on her lap – both with faces painted black. Some have suggested it was a statue of Isis and Horus that was adapted into a Madonna and Child, and others that it came originally from Ethiopia. Unfortunately the statue was destroyed during the French Revolution, but recently an exact replica, based on precise engravings made just a few years before it was burned, was

1

1

1

2

installed in the cathedral's Chapelle du Saint-Sacrement (Holy Sacrament). Sixty years after the destruction of the original, a second Black Madonna, dating from the 17th century and brought from the nearby Chapelle de la Visitation (45.0442, 3.8856), was enthroned on the high altar and crowned by Pope Pius IX. It's carried in a procession through the town on 15 August, the Feast of the Assumption.

The Black Madonna and the Visions/ Fever Stone made Le Puy one of the most important centres of pilgrimage in France, even before the Camino de Santiago was established. It then became a key gathering place for pilgrims on that trail. Le Puy's Bishop Godescalc is said to have been the first to make the pilgrimage to Santiago de Compostela around the year 950. The Hôtel-Dieu (45.0460, 3.8844) beside the cathedral was built for pilgrims around 1140 and today it still carries out that function.

Half a kilometre from the cathedral is Le Puy-en-Velay's other powerful energy centre, the ancient **Église Saint-Michel d'Aiguilhe** (45.0500, 3.8825). Dramatically perched 80m high atop a volcanic spur known as the Rocher d'Aiguilhe (Needle Rock) it is reached by climbing 270 steps. There's been a chapel on the site since the mid-10th century, which was enlarged into a church two centuries later. Some historians believe that it replaced a temple to the god Mercury, which fits with other equally lofty sacred sites that were later dedicated to Archangel Michael. Over the entrance are carvings of a mermaid and a half-serpent woman reminiscent of the fairy Melusine. With its ancient stone columns carved from the living rock, the interior has a cave-like feel. There are medieval paintings of what look like Grail knights embarking on their mysterious quest, as well as a statue of St Michael slaying the dragon on the altar.

At the foot of the Rocher d'Aiguilhe, where a Temple of Diana stood in pagan times, is the small octagonal Chapelle Saint-Clair (45.0490, 3.8831), originally the chapel of a hospital for pilgrims. Both it and the Chapelle Saint-Michel show the influence of Islamic architecture, probably picked up by pilgrims in Spain.

At night between May and October, Le Puy-en-Velay holds a spectacular light show that illuminates its historic monuments, particularly the cathedral and the Église Saint-Michel d'Aiguilhe incuding its rock – the latter including a volcanic eruption and the Archangel Michael battling a fiery dragon. This seems a fitting visual representation of the site's Earth energies being subdued by heavenly forces. Not to be missed!

Parking: 45.0479, 3.8838, 300m from Notre-Dame Cathedral, 200m from the Église Saint-Michel d'Aiguilhe

2

2 Chapelle Saint-Roch, Montbonnet

This enchanting chapel is one of the first stops on the Via Podiensis from **Le Puy-en-Velay**. Like several other chapels and churches on the trail, it's dedicated to the patron saint of pilgrims, St Roch. According to a local legend, when the townsfolk of Bains tried to take the statue of St Roch for their own chapel, making off with it on a cart pulled by an ox and donkey, the two animals refused to move. They dug their hooves into a stone so heavily that imprints were left, showing that the statue of the saint wanted to stay exactly where he was.

44.9858, 3.7488; Roadside parking

3 Monistrol-d'Allier

An important stop on the trail, Monistrol d'Allier sits in a striking location in the gorge cut by the river Allier. The trail

drops down to the village from the 12th-century **Chapelle Saint-Jacques** (44.9855, 3.6472), built on the ruins of a pagan sanctuary on the 950m hilltop overlooking the valley. Crossing the river was hazardous in medieval times but today there's an iron bridge, built in the 19th century by Gustave Eiffel, famed for the tower in Paris. Marking the pilgrim's trail, behind the medieval Église Saint-Pierre (44.9686, 3.6425), there's a Gothic stone cross, erected in the 15th century.

Leaving Monistrol d'Allier the trail climbs the Mont de la Madeleine, and just before reaching the tiny hamlet of Escluzels about a kilometre away, it passes by the **Chapelle**

Chapelle Sainte-Madeleine

Sainte-Madeleine (44.9733, 3.6392, roadside parking 44.9734, 3.6397, 60m). The chapel is in a grotto and has been there since at least 1300. A stone façade was built to enclose it in the 17th century. It's thought that the chapel was the work of pilgrims returning from the **Cave of Mary Magdalene** in Provence, who were inspired by that holy site.

A little off the pilgrim's way, 6km from Monistrol d'Allier, is the Chapelle **Notre-Dame d'Estours** (45.0042, 3.5897), which

4

takes its name from a château that once existed nearby. The chapel was built to house a Black Madonna, also called Notre-Dame d'Estours, which is very similar in appearance to the one in **Saugues** (see next entry). It marks the spot where the wooden statue was found after the Virgin Mary appeared to two shepherd boys.

Parking: 44.9672, 3.6443

4 Saugues

The **Église Saint-Médard** (St Medardus, 44.9605, 3.5471) contains a Black Madonna statue, Notre-Dame de Saugues, which is the twin of the one in the Chapelle Notre-Dame d'Estours near **Monistrol d'Allier**. It dates from the mid-1100s and shows signs of Middle Eastern origin. Since the statue was first photographed in the 19th century, the faces of the Madonna and Child have been repainted to tone down their dark skin.

The town's major landmark is the tower at its centre, the Tour des Anglais (44.9600, 3.5472), so named for once being occupied by English soldiers. It's all that remains of the 13th-century castle, though the streets of the town centre retain the outlines of the castle walls.

Close by the tower is the **Musée Fantastique de la Bête de Gévaudan** (Fantastical Museum of the Beast of Gévaudan, 44.9602, 3.5471, €, open mid-June to mid-September), which is devoted to Saugue's main claim to fame – a historical mystery that has entered into the area's folklore. The Beast of Gévaudan was a fearsome creature that terrorised the area in the 1760s, claiming many victims and becoming the talk of the whole of France. While many took it to be a supernatural visitation, perhaps a werewolf or a demon, for the more sceptically-minded the most likely candidate for the mystery beast was one of the wolves that were then found throughout France. The size and ferocity of the beast, however, suggest there was more to it. The attacks stopped in 1767 after a hunter killed an animal like a wolf but much larger than most. This happened shortly after a great procession of the population to **Notre-Dame d'Estours**, the Black Madonna at Monistrol d'Allier, to pray for her help in ridding the land of the terror. To find the museum follow the pawprints painted on the streets!

Parking: 44.9587, 3.5462

4

LOZÈRE

5 Saint-Alban-sur-Limagnole

The picturesque Église Saint-Alban at the centre of this town on the pilgrims' way dates back to the 1100s, though it's been much added to over the centuries. The tops of the columns inside are decorated with mythical creatures such as mermaids, gryphons and centaurs. There's also a colourful statue of St James, holding his pilgrim's staff and wearing his signature hat decorated with a scallop shell. Clinging to the iron cross atop the bell tower is an image of the Beast of Gévaudan that terrorised the area in the 18th century (see **Saugues**). Saint-Alban-sur-Limagnole was one of the places where hunting parties for the beast gathered.

44.7811, 3.3875

5

6 Nasbinals

In the charming village of Nasbinals is the 11th-century Romanesque Église Sainte-Marie (44.6625, 3.0464), and a scallop shell set into the pavement outside signifies that it is on the route of the Camino. Set on a 1,200m-high volcanic plateau within the Aubrac Regional Nature Park, the village and surrounding land were the property of the **Abbaye Saint Victor** in Marseilles during the Middle Ages. The Lac de Saint-Andéol (44.6187, 3.0814), 7km to the southwest, was a pagan cult centre that was suppressed during the Christianisation of the region in the 5th–6th century. It's marked by a cross on a mound on the lakeside, although there's evidence that the worship secretly survived in the area for several centuries.

Parking: 44.6621, 3.0463

6

6

AVEYRON

7 Aubrac

Made up of just a few buildings amid the flat rural landscape of the Plateau d'Aubrac 1,300m above sea level, the village grew up around a monastery and hospital. These gave shelter and care to pilgrims and were founded by the Abbey of Sainte Foy (St Faith) at **Conques**. Only parts of the original establishment survive, along with the 12th-century **Église Notre-Dame-des-Pauvres** (Our Lady of the Poor, 44.6223, 2.9873). Its bell, known as the 'cloche des perdus' ('bell of the lost'), was used to guide pilgrims to the village dur-

6

5

7

ing bad weather. The village's 14th-century tower, the Tour des Anglais (44.6222, 2.9870) is also still standing.

A further 6.5km on, after descending from the plateau into the valley of the river Boralde and passing through the village of Saint-Chély-d'Aubrac, the Camino crosses the **Pont des Pèlerins** (Pilgrims' Bridge, 44.5889, 2.9217). Built in the Middle Ages, the bridge features a tall stone cross with a crude carving of a pilgrim at its base.

Parking: 44.6205, 2.9868

8 Saint-Côme-d'Olt

As with many towns on the Via Podiensis from **Le Puy-en-Velay**, entering Saint-Côme-d'Olt feels like stepping back in time. In the fortified citadel at its heart are houses and buildings from the 1400s and 1500s, and parts of the medieval ramparts still stand. These include two of the gates: the Porte Neuve (New Gate, 44.5155, 2.8155) and Porte Théron (44.5152, 2.8143). The Hôtel de Ville (Town Hall, 44.5153, 2.8147) is modified from the medieval castle.

At the town's very centre is the **Église Saint-Côme-et-Saint-Damien** (St Cosimo and St Damian, 44.5150, 2.81530), which has a twisted steeple over 40m high. Among the figures carved into its great oak doors is a soldier riding a llama, made by a pilgrim who had been to South America.

A statue of St Michael and the Dragon once stood above the entrance but, very worn and damaged, it's now in the town's museum housed in what was the original parish church, the Église Saint-Pierre (44.5167, 2.8156), also known as the Chapel of the Penitents. The trail exits the town by a picturesque 16th century bridge over the river Lot.

Parking: 44.5155, 2.8141

9 Espalion

Located by the wide river Lot, Espalion is another timeless town with many medieval buildings, particularly on the river's south bank. The trail enters by the **Église Saint-Hilarian-Sainte-Foy de Perse** (44.5178, 2.7711, Parking), Perse being the old name for the town. The church is built on the spot where Hilarian, confessor to the Emperor Charlemagne, was beheaded by Moorish raiders in 730. According to legend, the holy man carried his head to the nearby spring, the Source de Fontsanges, to wash it before taking it to his mother for burial. The spring, which is now lost but commemorated in the name of the area close to the church, had previously been sacred to the pagans. A monastery was built there in the 11th century, originally dedicated to Sainte Foy (St Faith), who was especially venerated in **Conques.** Hilarian's dedication was made later and pilgrims on the trail would stop to venerate the saint's relics. The monastery later became the parish church.

In Espalion there are a number of chapels and churches built to support the pilgrims in the Middle Ages. There was also a commandery of the Knights Templar, who owned a large amount of land in the surrounding area. The Pont-Vieux (Old Bridge, 44.5228, 2.7632) across the Lot was built in the 11th century.

The chapel of Espalion's hospital and medical centre (44.5270, 2.7615) houses a Black Madonna, Notre-Dame La Négrette, carved in black wood, crowned and robed. It's said to have been brought back from the Crusades by one of the lords of the Château Calmont d'Olt (44.5181, 2.7527, Open April-November, €€), the ruins of which overlook the town. The statue was originally installed in the castle's Chapelle Saint-Michel but when the castle fell into disuse it was moved to the pilgrims' hostel and eventually into the hospital's chapel. The Madonna is the protectress of Espalion's children as well as the sick. Her statue is said to weep and if repainted she returns to her original colour.

Parking: 44.5208, 2.7651

10 Estaing

Overshadowed by the imposing Château d'Estaing (44.5539, 2.6728, open to the public on certain weekdays April to October, €), the town was founded in the 11th century and added to substantially over the centuries. Key sites within the town are the Gothic Pont d'Estaing (44.5531, 2.6719) spanning the river Lot, and the 15th-century Église Saint-Fleuret (44.5543, 2.6725) housing the relics of the town's patron saint, St Fleuret. Another site dedicated to him, just north of the town, is the Chapelle Saint-Fleuret (44.5573, 2.6707, Parking), now a hostel for pilgrims. Opposite is the spring, the Fontaine Saint-Fleuret, topped with a statue of the saint. The spring is facing the chapel on the other side of the road, so be careful when visiting as there's no footway.

Parking: 44.5534, 2.6724

11 Conques

A highlight on the Via Podiensis is the completely preserved medieval town of Conques, hidden in an idyllic wooded valley of the river Dourdou. Its many medieval buildings are strung out along the hillside, including a medieval abbey church, holy wells, sacred shrines and chapels. Much of the medieval walls survive, too, along with their gateways. The town's centrepiece, rising above the houses, is the **Église Abbatiale Sainte-Foy** (Abbey Church of St Faith, 44.5992, 2.3981), famous for its stone carvings and art from the Carolingian period.

In the Middle Ages, Conques was an extremely important pilgrimage site and one of the first to have its own pilgrims' trail. In many ways this was the model for the Camino de Santiago. Conques' fame rested on its possession of the relics of Sainte Foy, a 3rd-century virgin martyr who died at Agen (Lot-et-Garonne), some 150km away. She was a favourite saint of the Merovingian Frankish kings who considered her their intermediary with Christ. An abbey dedicated to her was founded in Conques by Clovis, and re-established by Charlemagne after it was destroyed by the Moors. Around 870, Sainte Foy's relics were stolen from Agen by a monk from Conques – a surprisingly common practice at the time, with a successful theft being taken as a sign of the saint's blessing. Many miraculous cures were attributed to the relics, leading to the abbey becoming a place of pilgrimage and the founding of the Abbey Church in the 11th century. Foy's skull is enclosed in a reliquary known as 'La Majesté de Sainte Foy' covered in gold and precious stones, which is kept in the Treasury – a separate building within the Abbey grounds. On the saint's feast day of 6 October, the reliquary is carried around the town.

Another standout feature of Conques is the **Chapelle de Saint-Roch** (45.5976, 2.3934), one of several chapels in and around the town. Dedicated to the patron

Chapelle Sainte-Foy

Chapelle de Saint-Roch

saint of pilgrims, it was built in the 15th century and dramatically sited on a rock spur below the town. There's a footpath down to it from the Rue Charlemagne, part of the trail that passes through one of the town's medieval gates, the Porte du Barry. The footpath passes the Fontaine du Barry (44.5989, 2.3958), one of several springs in and around the town where pilgrims could quench their thirst.

About 70m after passing the path off to the chapel, the Rue Charlemagne arrives at the narrow pink sandstone **Pont des Pèlerins** (Pilgrims' Bridge, 44.5983, 2.3925), which takes the Via Podiensis across the river Dourdou.

In the forest a kilometre along the trail from Conques is the small **Chapelle Sainte-Foy** (44.5961, 2.3871). It's built on a healing spring, especially known for curing diseases of the eyes. A notice by the chapel tells the legend of the spring's origins. The monk who stole St Foy's relics, exhausted from the journey back to Conques, fell asleep at the spot. He dreamed that the saint appeared and asked him, "Do you want wine for a day, or water forever?" When he awoke, and having decided he would go for the water, he struck the rock with his staff and the spring burst forth.

Parking: 44.5987, 2.3939

LOT

12 Rocamadour

The highlight of the trail that began in **Le Puy-en-Velay** is Rocamadour, one of the most famous holy sites in France, where a castle perched on the edge of the deep canyon of the river Alzou towers over religious

12

12

12

buildings and medieval streets below. Rocamadour became famous in the 12th century with the discovery of the body of St Amadour, the hermit who created the first sanctuary in a cave in the cliff face. He was found buried beneath the threshold of his cave in 1166. However, the site is more famous for its much-venerated shrine to the Black Madonna, Notre-Dame de Rocamadour, visited by pilgrims who come to pray to the statue from far and wide. Climbing up the ancient steps into the Cité Sainte (Holy Citadel, 44.7994, 1.6178) you are walking in the footsteps of the thousands of pilgrims who have come before you to worship at her shrine.

Records show that Rocamadour has been a place of pilgrimage since 1105, when Pope Pascal II spoke of it as one of the four holy places of Christianity, along with Santiago de Compostela, Rome and Jerusalem itself. Renowned for its miracle cures, it became even more famous when St Amadour's body was found.

The Cité Sainte is reached by the 216 steps of the Grand Escalier (Great Stairway) that climbs to the archway of the Porte Sainte (Holy Gate) giving entry to the main square of the sanctuary, which is surrounded by churches and chapels. There you can find the medieval Basilica Saint-Sauveur (Holy Saviour) with the crypt of St Amadour beneath, as well as six chapels dedicated to various saints and the **Chapelle Notre-Dame de Rocamadour** (44.7994, 1.6175), the home of the Black Madonna.

Carved from black wood, Notre-Dame de Rocamadour sits, eyes closed, with the Child on her knee; both are crowned. The Black Madonna was already so famous for the miracles she performed for those who prayed to her that in 1172 a book, the *Livre des Miracles de Notre-Dame de Rocamadour,* was written. It included the miracle of Princess Sancha of Navarre at **Sauveterre-de-Béarn** in the Pyrenees, who was saved from an accusation of witchcraft thanks to the intercession of the Black Madonna. In gratitude, the princess donated a richly adorned mantle for the Madonna's statue in Rocamadour.

Notre-Dame de Rocamadour was especially regarded as the protectress of those who went out to sea, with the many models of sailing vessels hanging in the chapel standing as testimony. A magical bell in the ceiling of the chapel is said to ring whenever the Black Madonna saves a sailor.

Thrust into the rockface outside the chapel is a sword known as Durandel, the magical weapon that the Frankish hero Roland used to defeat the invading Moors. Legend tells how, when Roland was killed at the **Brèche de Roland** (Roland's Breach) some 300km away in the Pyrenees, the sword was carried by Archangel Michael to Rocamadour and buried itself in the rock.

From the car park in the Alzou valley it's a 200m walk up to the Grand Escalier, where there is also a lift going up. Alternatively park at the top (44.8003, 1.6163) and take an inclined lift down.

Parking: 44.8003, 1.6186

13

13 Gourdon

Surrounded by forested hills, Gourdon lies on the trail beyond **Rocamadour**, before it rejoins the main Via Podiensis towards **Saint-Jean-Pied-de-Port** and Spain. At the centre of the medieval town with its narrow streets are the ruins of the **Château de Gourdon** (44.7378, 1.3825), with the fortified Église Saint-Pierre (44.7371, 1.3822) below.

Just outside Gourdon is a site that was a place of pilgrimage in its own right, the **Chapelle Notre-Dame-des-Neiges** (Our Lady of the Snows, 44.7328, 1.3922), which was built next to a healing spring.

Around 4km southwest of Gourdon is the **Château de Costeraste** (44.7080, 1.3517), constructed in 1218 by the Baron of Gourdon, a supporter of the Cathars at the time of the Crusade against them (see **Montségur**, Languedoc). When the pilgrimage to Rocamadour developed, Costeraste was ideally situated for pilgrims coming from northern Europe, who travelled from the Atlantic coast along the river Dordogne. Nearby is the Dolmen de Costeraste (44.7061, 1.3433), its 40-tonne capstone supported by a single upright stone.

Parking: 44.7372, 1.3830

PUY-DE-DÔME

14 Puy de Dôme, Clermont-Ferrand

At almost 1,500m, the Puy de Dôme is the highest peak in the range of volcanic mountains known as the Chaîne des Puys. Standing on this high point, while gazing at the spectacular panoramic views, is a stirring and unforgettable experience. The mountain was created by fire, formed from the lava of a volcanic eruption, and has long been held as a sacred place. It has been described as France's Mount Olympus, the abode of the gods.

To the Gauls, the mountain was sacred to the god Dumias, the origin of 'Dôme'. When the Romans came they merged him with their equivalent deity Mercury, building a great temple on a series of terraces just below the peak. It was a wonder of its day: the 1st-century Roman writer Pliny the Elder

14

described its huge bronze statue of Mercury, but no trace of it now remains. The Temple of Mercury has been partially reconstructed but is fenced off, so is not directly accessible. Just above it, on the highest point, there's now a meteorological station.

In the 15th and 16th centuries the mountain gained a reputation as a place where witches, called 'fatsillères', held their Sabbats, during which they were said to conjure the Devil in the form of a goat. Driving up to the summit is no longer permitted but it can be accessed by a small tourist railway from the valley below (€€€, Parking 45.7706, 2.9857). There's also a steep and winding 2km walking trail, the Chemin des Muletiers (Mule Drivers' Track, Parking 45.7638, 2.9568). As the Puy de Dôme is so high it's cold at the top even in summer and from September to March the peak is usually covered in snow, so come prepared.

45.7725, 2.9642

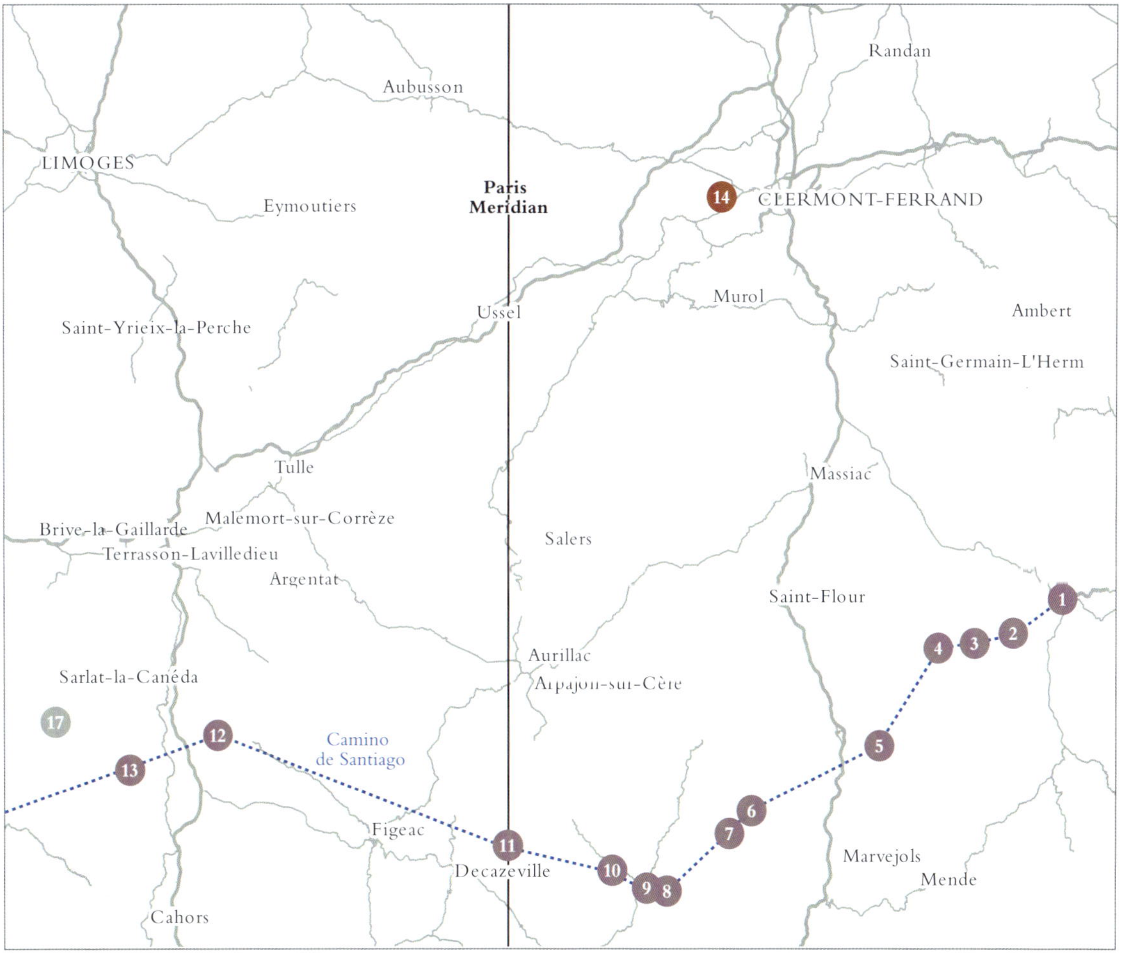

Randan
Aubusson
LIMOGES
Paris Meridian
14
CLERMONT-FERRAND
Eymoutiers
Murol
Ussel
Ambert
Saint-Yrieix-la-Perche
Saint-Germain-L'Herm
Tulle
Massiac
Brive-la-Gaillarde
Malemort-sur-Corrèze
Salers
Terrasson-Lavilledieu
Argentat
Saint-Flour
1
2
3
4
Aurillac
Sarlat-la-Canéda
Arpajon-sur-Cère
17
12
Camino de Santiago
5
13
6
7
Figeac
11
Marvejols
10
Decazeville
9
8
Mende
Cahors

WESTERN PYRENEES AND BASQUE COUNTRY

Running from the Atlantic coast along the Pyrenees – the immense range that forms the border between France and Spain – this region takes in parts of today's Nouvelle-Aquitaine and Occitanie. Although flatter land lies to the north, the most magical sites are in the mountains and valleys that become higher and steeper the further south one ventures. Tales of 'fées' (fairies) and other nature spirits are everywhere to be found, attached particularly to water sources and caves. Most of the isolated valleys are forested, containing many rivers and streams that flow down from the Pyrenees, as well as feeding hot mineral sources such as the Fontaine Chaude at Dax. Dotted through the region are many scenic and historic towns and villages, most notably the medieval Sauveterre-de-Béarn.

The region combines a long Christian heritage with much older beliefs, often blending them seamlessly, and the age-old rituals at traditional sacred sites have been re-dedicated to Christian saints. This blending is even evident at Lourdes, where the visions of the peasant girl Bernadette transformed it into one of the world's most celebrated Christian sanctuaries. Pilgrimage routes run throughout the region, the main trails of the Camino de Santiago coming together at Saint-Jean-Pied-de-Port at the foot of the Pyrenees.

The west of the region is part of the Basque Country that straddles the French and Spanish sides of the Pyrenees. The Basques are a distinct people with their own identity, culture, history and a language unrelated to any other European tongue. They have their own folklore and beliefs, centering on natural places such as the sacred mountain of La Rhune. Their priests and priestesses, known as *sorginak*, performed rites that were magical and shamanic. They were devoted to the mother goddess Mari, who is believed to live within various Pyrenean mountains with her consort Sugaar, the god of thunderstorms who takes the form of a serpent or dragon. The Basque call their fairy folk who live in caves near springs and streams *laminak*. These beings are seen as elf-like in the eastern part of the Basque Country, while towards the Atlantic coast they are young women with long hair and the feet of animals. Basque lore also includes wild men and women called *basajaunac*.

LANDES

1 Fontaine Chaude, Dax

Located in the centre of a town square, the Fontaine Chaude or Roman Hot Spring is a place of calm in the busy town of Dax. It is also known as the Source de La Nèhe, after the Nehae, the Celtic goddesses of rivers and springs. The water, which is at a constant 64° C and rich in mineral salts, has been used for healing skin ailments and rheumatism since Roman times; according to legend, a Roman legionnaire realised his sick dog had recovered after wallowing in the spring's mud. Water from the source flows into a pool surrounded by a stone enclosure. While it's no longer possible to bathe in the water, it pours into basins on the outside through spouts in the form of lions' heads. The water and mud are used in a number of healing establishments in the town. Another sign of Dax's Roman origins is located 150m from the Hot Springs in the narrow Rue Cazade. It is the crypt of a Gallo-Roman temple (43.7098, -1.0524, €), discovered during building work and where some of the archaeological finds are displayed. The Cathedral of Notre-Dame de Dax (43.7083, -1.0531; Parking €: 43.7094, -1.0569, 300m) is on the site of another Roman temple. Dax is on the Via Turonensis, the branch of the Camino de Santiago pilgrimage route that begins in Paris.

43.7108, -1.0528; Parking €: 43.7121, -1.0534, 150m.

1

PYRÉNÉES-ATLANTIQUES

2 La Rhune, Sare

The 900m-high peak of La Rhune (*Larrun* in Basque) is the sacred mountain of the Basques, and is steeped in magic and sorcery. The border between France and Spain runs through its summit, which was reputed to be the ritual meeting place of Basque magicians called *sorganik* who were devotees of the mother goddess Mari. There are

2

many legends and folktales about La Rhune, the signature one telling of Herensuge, a serpent or dragon with seven tails, who lives in caverns deep within the mountain. Herensuge is said to have spat out molten gold, silver and other metals that burned away the forests on the slopes and were then carried away by streams – a story that explains why the upper slopes of La Rhune, unusually for the region, are largely free of trees. There are, though, ancient forests and springs on the lower parts of the mountain that are haunts of the elf-like *laminak*.

La Rhune's grass and fern covered slopes are for the most part gentle and inhabited by wild ponies called 'pottocks'. From the summit, which has a restaurant and gift shop, there's an expansive view over the Basque Country on both sides of the border and to the Atlantic coast. A charming tourist train, the Petit Train de La Rhune, runs up there from a station on the Col de Saint-Ignace, a pass on the D4 between Ascain and Sale (43.3250, -1.6009, €). There's also a road up for cars from the Spanish side. Otherwise the summit can be reached by several well-signposted hiking trails of varying lengths. Most are easy going and the closest starts from Sare (parking 43.3116, -1.5842, 5km), recognised as one of the most beautiful villages in France. Witness to the mountain's sacred past are the many ancient dolmens, cromlechs, standing stones and remains of stone circles that can be seen on the slopes. Most are collapsed, but the Dolmen Altzaran (43.3142, -1.6096) and Gastenbakarre Menhir (43.3139, -1.6005), both just off the main trail from Sare, are worth checking out.

La Rhune gives its name to the larger range making up this part of the Pyrenees, which has many caverns deep within it. The vast cave system, the **Grottes de Sare** (43.2683,

2

1

-1.5714, €€), about 6km south of the village, shows signs of habitation from over 40,000 years ago and is open to visitors (closed over Christmas and during January), its strange serpentine rock formations enhanced by a sound and light show. In Basque folklore, one of the caverns named Leiza is said to be the lair of a malevolent deity known as Etsai. 43.3092, -1.6356

3 Saint-Jean-Pied-de-Port

Founded in the Middle Ages around a castle on the river Nive de Béhérobie, Saint-Jean-Pied-de-Port is where the main pilgrimage trails of the **Camino de Santiago** come together before climbing through the Col de Roncevaux – the pass that crosses the Pyrenees into Spain. On their way into town, pilgrims once passed the chapel of the Magdalene, its former site now marked by a cross, the Croix de la Madeleine (43.1663, -1.2172), just off the D933 1.5km east of Saint-Jean. Pilgrims then entered the town through the Porte Saint-Jacques (St James Gate, 43.1636, -1.2344). Within the medieval high town is the Gothic church dedicated to Notre Dame de l'Assomption and also known as Notre Dame du Bout du Pont (43.1624, -1.2371), where pilgrims can stop and pray before attempting to cross the pass. Parking: 43.1630, -1.2380

4 Sauveterre-de-Béarn

The medieval border town of Sauveterre-de-Béarn was built on a rocky escarpment above the wide river, the Gave d'Oloron, which acts as a natural moat. The 900-year-old Église Saint-André (St Andrew, 43.3986, -0.9394) is also fortified and beside it is an impregnable tower nearly 40m high, now known as the Tour Monréal (43.4006, -0.9386 €). The tower houses a historical museum, open April–November, with a model of the medieval town as its centrepiece.
Crossing the Oloron into the town is the **Pont de la Légende** (43.3969, -0.9408), now partly collapsed. It too was fortified and there was a hostel for pilgrims on one side. The legend that gives the bridge its

name is that of 'Queen Sancie' (Sancha of Navarre), a Spanish princess and widow of the Count of Béarn. Accused of witchcraft in 1170, she was thrown from the bridge into the deep river with her hands and feet bound, but her innocence was proved when she was carried safely to the bank. In thanks for her divine protection, she had a rich mantle made for the Black Madonna of **Rocamadour**. The wooded Île de la Glère (43.3966, -0.9395; Parking 43.3960, -0.9415) below the village, where Sancha came ashore, is now a nature reserve. There's a footbridge to the island from the car park.

Today Sauveterre-de-Béarn is a modest village in the western Pyrenees, the scale of its medieval buildings revealing its former significance. It is a stopping place on one of the main pilgrimage trails of the **Camino de Santiago**, the Via Lemovicensis that begins in **Vézelay**. Its name, meaning 'Safe Land of Béarn', signifies that it was once a place of sanctuary under the authority of the Church, and within its sacred ground fugitives could not be pursued. Sauveterre's lord in the 14th century was the celebrated Gaston Phoebus, Count of Foix, renowned as a wise ruler, fierce warrior and talented author. Many poems, songs and tales survive about his legendary exploits, real or imagined. Gaston took his nickname of Phoebus ('Shining') from one of the titles of the god Apollo.

Parking: 43.3994, -0.9391

3

5 Source de la Bidouze, Forêt des Arbailles

Deep within the Arbeilles Forest, the source of the river Bidouze has been the scene of many sightings of the elf-like *laminak* – nature spirits who are especially fond of rivers and springs. The stream flows out of a wide, deep grotto in the cliff face from an underground lake within the mountain. There's a 5km hiking trail to the cave, a gentle uphill walk that gets steeper towards the end and which runs alongside the Bidouze as it descends through a cascade of small waterfalls.

The wild Arbailles Forest, covering 45 square kilometres of mountains and valleys, lies just to the north of the Pyrenees. It is an enchanted place with many rivers and streams, as well as caves and chasms, some of which were once inhabited by Neanderthals. Called *Arballa* by the Basques, the forest is filled with fabulous creatures from their folklore and the deepest parts are the haunts of wild men and women, *basajaunak*. The forest is also where the seven-tailed dragon Herensugue, who lived within the

5

6

sacred mountain of **La Rhune**, met his end, poisoned by a hero from the town of Caro (Basque *Zaro*) near **Saint-Jean-Pied-de-Port**. As Herensugue flew to the sea to die, with his breath he burned down a large part of the forest.

On the far side of the mountain is another memorable site, the **Fontaine d'Ahusquy** (43.0965, -1.0199), a mineral spring known for its healing waters. Set high on an open mountainside, the spring offers breathtaking views over the valley and mountains. It is surrounded by impressive stonework that includes a carving of the lion rampant from the coat of arms of the Basque province of Soule, to which the area once belonged. Although only 4km directly south of the Source of the Bidouze, the spring is on the opposite side of the mountain so it's best reached by road: the route up is signposted from the Auberge d'Ahusquy on the D117. In the forest just off the road between the Auberge and the village of Aussurucq are two of the most accessible megalithic monuments in the Arbailles Forest, the **Dolmens d'Ithe** (43.1014, -0.9650; 43.1069, -0.9664). They are the only pair now visible from what was a much larger ancient burial site.

43.1324, -1.0216; Trailhead parking: 43.1642, -1.0291, 5km

HAUTE-PYRÉNÉES

6 Brèche de Roland, Gavarnie

Situated 2,800m up on the border between France and Spain, the Brèche de Roland (Roland's Breach) is an extraordinary sight. It is almost as if a huge rectangular section, 40m wide and 70m high, has been deliberately cut out of the highest point of the mountain crest. Adding to the sense of otherworldliness, the breach lies on the perimeter of a striking geological feature known as the Cirque de Gavarnie, a great bowl shaped depression carved out by glaciers over millions of years.

The breach takes its name from Roland, a celebrated 8th-century warrior and nephew of the Emperor Charlemagne. It is now almost impossible to separate the historical figure of Roland from the many myths and legends that have grown up around him, as most famously described in the 11th-century *Chanson de Roland* (*Song of Roland*). He is a folk hero throughout France, with legends about him attached to many sites, such as the **Trois Pucelles** in Isère. For the people of the Pyrenees, who took

6

him especially to their hearts, he was the heroic defender of their lands against the Moors and the Vascones, ancestors of the Basques. In the Pyrenean traditions, Roland became a giant who wielded the magical sword Durandel, forged by the blacksmith god Galan and given to Charlemagne by an angel for him to present in turn to his most eminent warrior. After many heroic exploits and adventures, Roland was betrayed and defeated at the Battle of Roncevaux in Spain in 778, making his last stand against the Vascones on the summit of the Pyrenees. Realising he was about to die and not wanting Durandel to fall into enemy hands, he tried to shatter his sword against the rock but instead its blade hewed a vast gap through the mountain, creating the Brèche. Roland then threw Durandel into the valley, where it miraculously flew to **Rocamadour**, nearly 300km away, embedding itself in the cliff of the Chapel of Our Lady of Rocamadour, where it can still be seen.

The Brèche de Roland can be reached from the village of Gavarnie, around 7km away down in the valley. There are several trails of varying length and difficulty that lead up to the Refuge de Sarradets (42.6861, -0.0333), a climbers' lodge that has a view of the Brèche, 0.5km away. A steep climb up the final slope leads to the gap itself. It's best to visit in the summer months; in winter snow transforms the area into a ski resort, and the hike definitely shouldn't be attempted in bad weather. The scenery on the climb is spectacular, including the Grand Cascade de Gavarnie (42.6934, -0.0045), at 420m the highest waterfall in France, which is visible from many points along the trail.

42.6908, -0.0336; Parking €: 42.7362, -0.0123, 7km

7 Eget, Aragnouet

The lovely village of Eget has scenic views over the forested valley of the river Aure to the Pyrenees rising above. Its small medieval church is famous for 10th-century wall paintings that were discovered during renovations in 2017. In the neighbouring village of Le Plan, 6km up the valley, is the **Chapelle Notre-Dame-de-l'Assomption** (42.7807, 0.1949), built in the 12th century by the Knights Hospitaller but often called the 'Chapel of the Templars'. It houses a 700-year-old Black Madonna statue known evocatively as the 'Trône de Sagesse' (Throne of Wisdom). Eget and Le Plan are on the **Camino de Santiago** pilgrimage route that passes through the valley.

42.7978, 0.2717

8 Lourdes

Situated at the end of the long valley of the Gave de Pau river that runs from the high Pyrenees, Lourdes is world famous as one of the major holy sites of Catholicism. In 1858 it was a small, poor agricultural town, when the visions of 14-year-old Bernadette Soubirous suddenly put it on the map. The first vision happened when she and some friends visited the Grotte de Massabielle (Old Rock), now the **Grotte de Lourdes** (43.0975, -0.0583), then located in a wild area outside the town on the far side of the Gave de Pau. Bernadette saw an apparition, a young girl dressed in white, and this was the first of many visions she had at the same spot over the next three months. As the story spread, Bernadette was accompanied by a growing number of townsfolk, although only she could see and hear the girl. She described the apparition as smaller than herself – and Bernadette was known to be unusually short for her age. During one encounter Bernadette, in a state of trance, dug with her hands in the cave floor and uncovered a spring, the water from which is now used for healing throughout the sanctuary. In local lore, fairies often took the form of small white ladies or girls, and some of the townsfolk interpreted Bernadette's vision as one of the 'fées'. Others took it to be the spirit of a local woman, respected for her piety and kindness, who had recently died. To begin with, Lourdes' authorities and clergy saw the excitement surrounding the teenager's claims as un-

Christian superstition and tried to put a stop to it, erecting a barrier across the cave where a makeshift shrine had been set up. The figure never named herself, Bernadette calling her simply *Aqueró* ('It' or 'That' in the local patois), or the 'white girl' or 'little girl'. However, towards the end of the series of visions, Aqueró declared "I am the Immaculate Conception", a term for a teaching about the Virgin Mary that the Pope had recently approved. Four years after the apparitions, the local bishop recognised them as genuine visions of the Virgin and so began Lourdes' rise to fame as a Marian shrine, and the town's rapid growth as a place of pilgrimage and healing. The **Basilica of the Immaculate Conception** (43.0974, -0.0583) was subsequently built above the cave where Bernadette had her visions. Later, the larger Basilica Notre-Dame du Rosaire (Rosary) was built lower down in front of it, and to mark the centenary of Bernadette's visions, in 1958 the vast underground **Basilica Saint-Pie-X** (St Pius X, 43.0972, -0.0536) was opened.

The numerous basilicas, churches, chapels and shrines are now known collectively as the Sanctuary of Our Lady of Lourdes. The presence of priests, nuns and monks serving the millions of visitors Lourdes receives each year, as well as the many sick and disabled in search of healing, creates a heightened atmosphere of intense devotion. The major sanctuaries are on the west side of the town, separated from the main town by the river. The town itself is packed with souvenir shops selling a huge assortment of religious statuettes and holy water bottles, as well as museums and other visitor attractions, mostly dedicated to Lourdes' Christian heritage. The imposing medieval castle (Château Fort de Lourdes, 43.0967, -0.0492 €€; Parking €: 43.0961, -0.0485) above the town now houses a museum of the history and culture of the Pyrenean region.

Traditional beliefs going back to more ancient times have also been kept alive in the area, especially those associated with natural features such as water sources and caves, of which there are many around and even beneath Lourdes. The most spectacular are the two large caverns now known as the **Grottes des Deux Maries** (Two Marys, 43.0961, -0.0603) within the Colline de Calvaire (Calvary Hill) that is part of the main sanctuary. The first, 50m wide and 10m high, houses a shrine to Mary Magdalene and beyond it is an even larger cave, 80m deep and 15m at its highest point, dedicated to Our Lady of Sorrows. The grottoes were inhabited in prehistory and included among the many archaeological finds is a treasure, the 'cheval de Lourdes' – a horse carved from a mammoth tusk 13,000 years ago. Another evocative natural site is the Grottes du Loup (Wolf Caves, 43.0964, -0.0678) in the 180m-high peak just a kilometre west of the sanctuary. Beside the main road out of Lourdes to the north is the **Peyre-Crabère** (Goat Stone, 43.1094, -0.0700), an ancient menhir said to be a woman who was turned to stone.

Parking: 43.0971, -0.0507

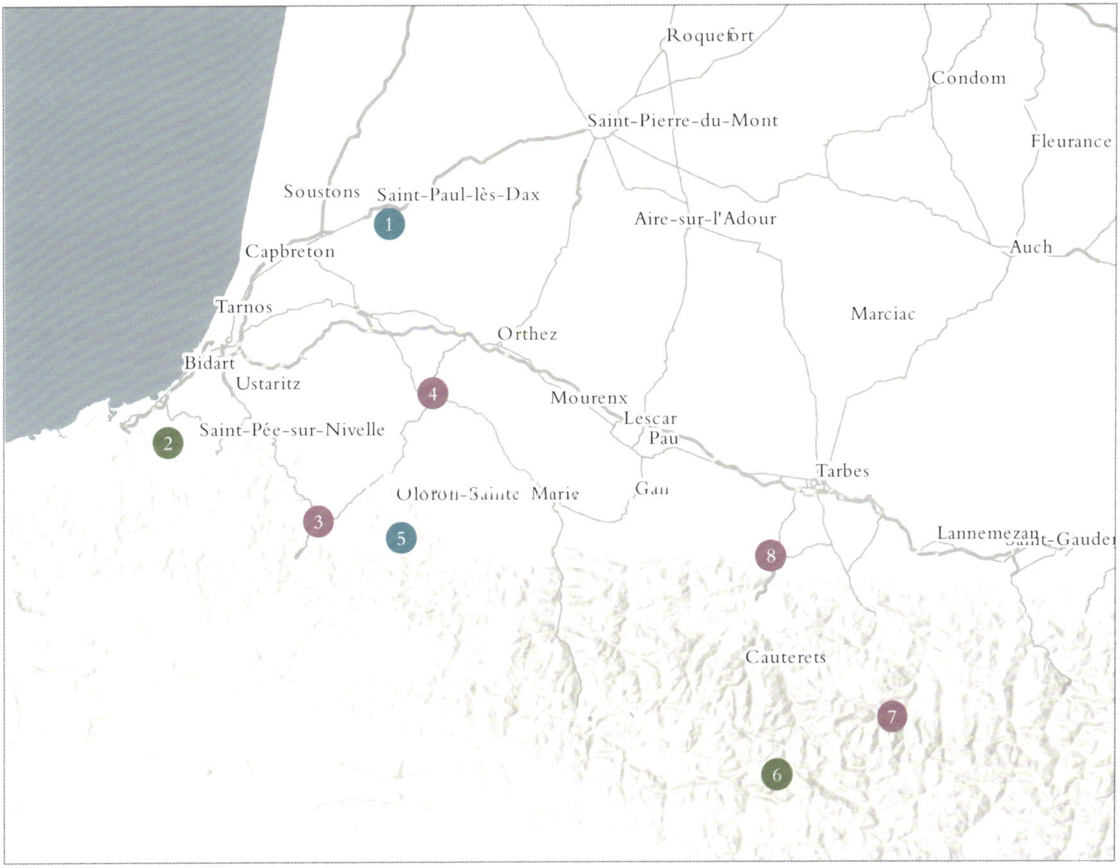

Roquefort
Condom
Saint-Pierre-du-Mont
Fleurance
Soustons
Saint-Paul-lès-Dax
1
Aire-sur-l'Adour
Capbreton
Auch
Tarnos
Marciac
Orthez
Bidart
Ustaritz
4
Mourenx
Lescar
2
Saint-Pée-sur-Nivelle
Pau
Tarbes
Oloron-Sainte Marie
Gan
3
5
Lannemezan
8
Cauterets
7
6

2

THE LANGUEDOC: CATHAR COUNTRY

Named for its native language, the 'Langue d'oc' or Occitan, the Languedoc lies between the Montagne Noire range to the north and the towering peaks of the Pyrenees in the south. To the east is the Mediterranean coast and to the west the Ariège. The low-lying plains of the river Aude with the historic city of Carcassonne make up the north, while the south is dominated by the Corbières, a limestone plateau from which rise imposing hills and mountains, the most prominent being the mysterious Mount Bugarach. Several rivers rise from these peaks, cutting deep gorges and ravines through the rock, and the many water sources include thermal and salt-water springs.

The Languedoc, once known as Occitania, is now part of the Occitanie region that includes Ariège and the Pyrénées-Orientales. It bears the imprint of the many peoples that have settled there – the Celts, Romans, Visigoths, Moors and Franks. In the Middle Ages it was an independent region ruled by the Counts of Toulouse, but that ended with the Crusade launched by the pope against the 'heretics' known as the Cathars, after which it came under the control of the King of France.

The Corbières was the heartland of Catharism, its alternative name being 'Pays Cathare' (Cathar Country). A long hiking route, the Sentier Cathare, runs from the Mediterranean to the Ariège, taking in many of the dramatically sited castles where the Cathars retreated during the brutal 13th-century Crusade against them, and including Montségur, the famous site of their last stand. The Languedoc was also a major centre for the Knights Templar, and the region was home to around one-third of all Templar land and property in Europe.

The presence of a deep but heretical devotion to Mary Magdalene pervades the province and the sense that folk memory carries some secret about her is so strong that several researchers have described her veneration there as an 'Underground Church'.

The aura of great secrets harboured within the Languedoc continues into the modern era, with the twin villages of Rennes-le-Château and Rennes-les-Bains at the heart of a web of interconnected mysteries. The most famous centres on the unexplained wealth and unconventional activities of Abbé Saunière, Rennes-le-Château's priest at the turn of the 20th century. The story has spawned numerous theories and bestselling books, none of which have yet satisfactorily solved the mystery.

ARIÈGE

1 Montségur Castle

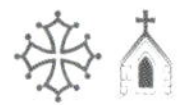  

The mountaintop location of the **Château de Montségur** is exhilarating and elemental, giving a sense of a place of power, yet the stones also exude the memory of the historic tragedy that occurred there. It is one of the most evocative sites in southern France, famous as the scene of the last stand of the Cathars. Although the Crusade to root out the last survivors continued for a few more years in places such as **Quéribus Castle**, the fall of Montségur marked the end both of the Cathars as a religious movement and the independence of the Languedoc region. When, in 1208, Pope Innocent III called the Crusade to wipe out Catharism, this pushed the Cathars further into the foothills of the Pyrenees. Montségur became the stronghold not only for their religious leaders but also for the banished nobles and knights who had been stripped of their lands because they were sympathisers. The fortifications had been built at the beginning of the 1200s on the site of an earlier ruined castle, on the orders of the Lord of Montségur, Raymond de Péreille, who clearly saw trouble coming. However, as they were oriented precisely to the solstices there seems to have been more to Montségur than a straightforward defensive structure: its layout incorporated sacred magical principles.

As the Cathars' headquarters, Montségur became the ultimate target of the Crusade. Blanche of Castile, the powerful mother of France's Louis IX, called it the 'head of the dragon' that had to be cut off. The fortress was besieged several times but stood firm until an all-out effort was made to capture it in 1243. After a ten-month siege the defenders surrendered, and two weeks later they came down from the mountain, the majority refusing to renounce their faith

and walking calmly to the great pyre that had been raised to burn them.
However during the ceasefire, according to the testimony of some of those who did recant, four Cathars escaped by being lowered down the mountain on ropes, taking with them something of great importance. This gave rise to the legend of the 'Cathar treasure', although theories differ on whether it consisted of objects of material value, sacred artefacts or holy texts. Some believed it was the Holy Grail, a theory that brought members of occult societies to the area in the 1930s in the belief that it was still hidden there. The idea was even taken seriously by some within the Nazi hierarchy, including the medievalist and SS Officer Otto Rahn who was sent to the Montségur area on a quest for the Grail. Some believe that the Grail castle of Montsalvat in Wolfram von Eschenbach's epic medieval poem, *Parzival*, was based on Montségur.
The castle's solstice alignments may hint at the survival of a solar cult in the area dating back to ancient times, which also lay behind a curious ritual centred on the **Pic de Saint-Barthélemy** (St Bartholomew's Peak, 42.8192, 1.7711), 8 km south of Montségur and now linked to it by a hiking trail. The mountain, which is 2,350m high, has long been regarded as sacred, and there are several megalithic monuments on its flanks as well as a lake named the Étang du Diable (Devil). The peak used to be named Mount Tabor, after the biblical scene of Jesus' Transfiguration, but was subsequently dedicated to St Bartholomew in the 17th century. Following an old custom, the inhabitants of the surrounding valleys would sleep on the summit on the night of 23rd August so they could witness the sunrise on 24 August, St Bartholomew's feast day. However, as the tradition dates to well before the peak's renaming, it seems that the Church picked a saint whose feast conveniently coincided with the ancient ceremony in order to claim it as Christian. Even more intriguingly, an alignment known as the 'Sunrise Line' links several sites around **Rennes-le-Château**, including Blanchefort Castle near **Rennes-les-Bains**. When extended, this line passes through the summit of the Pic de Saint-Barthélemy and is oriented precisely towards sunrise on 24 August.
Montségur Castle is open to the public all year apart from January. There's a steep climb up from the parking area at the base. **Montségur museum** (42.8717, 1.8335, €; parking 42.8709, 1.8326) in the village below the mountain, though small, is worth a visit.
42.8756, 1.8325, €€; Parking: 42.8740, 1.8269, 700m.

AUDE

2 Aguilar Castle, Tuchan

On a hill 100m above the plain of Tuchan, the **Château d'Aguilar** is one of many strongholds in the Languedoc that are today renowned for their association with the Cathars' struggle to preserve their 'heretic' religion. Unlike those that existed before the Crusade against them was launched, Aguilar Castle was specifically expanded and heavily fortified to defend against the Crusading army. After it was siezed, and its Cathar lord imprisoned at Carcassone, Aguilar was recaptured and became the gathering point for the rebel forces who unsuccessfully besieged **Carcassonne** in 1240. Aguilar Castle is the lowest and least well defended of the 'five sons of Carcassonne' – the Cathar fortifications that later protected the border between France and Spain. The other four castles are **Peyrepertuse**, **Puilaurens**, **Quéribus** and **Termes**. The castle can be visited between April and October.
42.8906, 2.7469, €; Parking: 42.8912, 2.7485, 200m

1

1

2

3 Le Bézu Castle

On the crest of a 750m-high ridge above the very small village of Le Bézu are the ruins of **Château du Bézu**, built by the enigmatic Knights Templar. Originally known as Albedunum (White Fortress), the site commands views over the whole of the plateau to the north and there are lines of sight to other fortresses, including **Peyrepertuse Castle** some 20km east. But there may be more to its location than strategic advantages: the castle features in several landscape alignments and geometries, for example forming a perfect triangle with **Rennes-le-Château** and Château Blanchefort above **Rennes-les-Bains**. Author and scriptwriter Henry Lincoln, who discovered this relationship in the 1990s, extended the geometry into a pentagram connecting five mountains in the area. Since then, even more complex patterns have been found in which Le Bézu is a key site, suggesting that the Templars were aware of an ancient system of landscape geometry.

The castle has its own mysteries and legends. In 1340, two knights were arrested by the king's men for illegally minting gold coins at the castle. Although forgeries in the sense that they hadn't been authorised by the King, the coins' gold content was purer than the official currency. Where the gold came from was never discovered. More eerily, locals tell of observing chains of lights, like those of torches carried in a procession, moving along the crest at night, which are taken to be the spirits of Templar knights. At the end of the single-track road that leads up from the village of Le Bézu, a trail climbs to the castle ruins.

42.8809, 2.3055; Parking: 42.8809, 2.3001, 600m

4 Carcassonne

  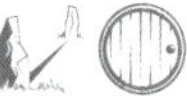

With its grand ramparts, towers and turrets the Cité (Citadel) of Carcassonne seems to have come straight out of a medieval fairy tale. Even with today's bustling tourist shops and attractions, the feeling of having slipped back in time remains as you walk the atmospheric narrow streets within the medieval city walls.

With this ancient hilltop citadel at its heart, today's sprawling city of **Carcassonne** developed over the centuries on the lower ground. By the 19th century, however, the citadel was largely abandoned and falling into decay until an intensive restoration project revived its former grandeur. It is now devoted entirely to tourism, with museums, exhibitions, gift shops, hotels, and only a handful of permanent residents. On account of the citadel's strategic position high above the river Aude and on major trade routes, the site has been occupied for millennia. After the Celts raised the first fortifications around 300 BC, it was occupied by the Romans, Visigoths, Franks, and even Arab invaders who held it for 40 years in the 8th century. The citadel was captured in 1209 during the Crusade against the Cathars and the entire population expelled. It became a base for the papal inquisition in their campaign to stamp out heresy in the region.

Carcassonne is on a major alignment, the 'Grand Meridian of Gaul', identified in the 1980s by Jean Richer, a professor of literature who was also a scholar of esotericism and sacred geography. The meridian runs through France from Dunkirk on the Channel coast through **Paris** and all the way south, passing through **Rennes-les-Bains**, and beyond into Spain.

The citadel is entered through the impressive **Porte Narbonnaise** (43.2066, 2.3659). At the entrance is a statue of Lady Carcas, a Muslim princess who took charge of the defence of the city during its long siege by the Christian Franks. Although Carcassonne's inhabitants were heavily outnumbered and supplies were running out, she won the day by subterfuge, such as placing straw dummies on the walls to give the impression of greater forces within. According to legend when the Franks withdrew and the victory bell was sounded the cry went up "Carcas sonne!" – "Carcas rings!" – giving the city its name.

4

Basilique Saint Nazaire

4

5

Within the walls are the 12th-century **Château Comtal** (43.2070, 2.3632, €€), built by the Counts of Trencavel and surrounded by a moat, and the imposing **St Nazaire Basilica** (43.2052, 2.3631), Carcassonne's original cathedral famous for its medieval stained-glass windows. Visitors often feel a strong spiritual energy within the basilica. Several legends centre on the **Grand Puits** (Great Well, 43.2074, 2.3642), 40m deep and the largest of several wells supplying the citadel with water. Its association with restless spirits and otherwordly beings indicates that for some reason the inhabitants felt uneasy about the well, which in Occitan is called *Lo Potz de las Fadas* ('The Fairies' Well'). 'The Devil's Lair', another local name, refers to the tale of seven blasphemous archers who were cast down it to Hell. Another legend is that the Visigoths hid the Jerusalem Temple treasure, which they had looted from Rome, in the Great Well.

The Cité de Carcassonne is a dream location for film and TV, most famously for *Robin Hood: Prince of Thieves* (1991), *Les Visiteurs* (1993) and the 2011 series based on Kate Mosse's novel *Labyrinth*.

43.2067, 2.3636; Parking €. 43.2063, 2.3678, 200m

5 Mount Bugarach

The harsh and brooding crags of the **Pech de Bugarach** (Mount Bugarach) give off a powerful but forbidding atmosphere. Standing alone and dominating the landscape, it is the highest point in the region at 1,230m. But it's not just Bugarach's size and isolation that draws the eye: it looks different from other mountains and seems somehow out of place. Even in an area steeped in mystery and magic, Bugarach stands out.

Pont Romain
5

The mountain is a geological wonder. Forces unleashed by the clash of tectonic plates that formed the Pyrenees 100 million years ago pushed the older rock layers above the younger ones, giving rise to Bugarach's name, the 'montagne inversée' ('upside-down mountain'). Others call it the 'sacred mountain' on account of its powerful aura. There is a network of caverns within and more than 50 cave entrances, many of which are unexplored. A century ago a local shepherd discovered a cave leading to an underground chapel, but was unable to find the entrance again.

There are legends of hidden treasure, including the Cathars' treasure smuggled out of **Montségur Castle**, and rumours that the Nazis searched for something on or in the mountain during the Second World War. Some even theorise that the Ark of the Covenant, brought from the Temple of Solomon in Jerusalem, is hidden within the caves. Those who go along with the theory argue that 'Bugarach' derives from 'Bourg de l'Arche' ('Town of the Ark'), as the village at the mountain's base is also called

Bugarach. Others take it even further, suggesting that Mount Bugarach is a gateway to an underground city or realm, perhaps the legendary Agartha at the earth's core. It's been claimed that Jules Verne got the inspiration for his classic *Journey to the Centre of the Earth* during a visit to the area and there is a character named Capitaine Bugarach in his 1896 novel *Clovis Dardentor*, a double allusion to the place as there's a farm called Les Capitaines just to the west of the village. This enigmatic book includes many cryptic references to sites in the region and individuals connected to its history and mysteries, particularly those relating to **Rennes-le-Château** and **Rennes-les-Bains**. Some consider the book as not only revealing Verne's awareness of these mysteries but also presenting their solution in coded form.

A more recent storyteller rumoured to have visited Bugarach is Steven Spielberg, and the site is said to have inspired key elements of his 1977 movie about extraterrestrial contact, *Close Encounters of the Third Kind*. Bugarach is certainly a hotspot for UFO sightings and activity, leading some to speculate that there is an alien base within or beneath the mountain, although 'earthlights' caused by energies generated by the peak's unique geology and seismic forces are another possibility. Magnetic disturbances, disorientation and even visionary experiences have also been reported by visitors. The forests around and on the lower slopes of Mount Bugarach are said to be inhabited by fairies and other elemental beings.

Mount Bugarach is part of a network of alignments between key sites in the area, such as **Pech Cardou**, and lies on the ancient Grand Meridian of Gaul, while the Paris Meridian (see **Paris Observatory**) passes close by. Bugarach also lies directly on the 1,600km-long Via Heraklea. This ancient Celtic alignment runs from the Sacred Promontory (today's Cape St Vincent in Portugal) to the Matrona (now Montgenèvre) Pass, named after the Celtic Mother Goddess, in the French Alps (see **Sacra di San Michele**).

All these mysteries and anomalies have made Bugarach a centre for 'spiritual tourism'. It caught the attention of the world's media in 2012, when those who subscribed to the global catastrophe predicted by interpreters of the Mayan calendar for 21 December 2012 believed the peak would be one of the few places on Earth to survive.

An eye-catching site nearby is the **Pont Romain** (42.8832, 2.3297), a Roman bridge arching over a ravine cut through the rocks by the river Blanque. The narrow bridge, which is by a waterfall, can be crossed on foot although some may find the lack of a parapet a little daunting. Park by the D14 from Rennes-les-Bains to Bugarach (42.8793, 2.3293, 1km), or for a longer trail continue on the D14 to park closer to Bugarach (42.8773, 2.3408, 2.5km).

There are two main trails to the summit of **Mount Bugarach**, where there are breathtaking views of the surrounding countryside as far as the Mediterranean to the east. The easier but longer and more circuitous track starts east of Bugarach, with parking at the Col du Linas by the D14 (42.8783, 2.3848, 3km). A steeper but shorter route, and more of a scramble in places, is even more dramatic. From just outside Bugarach, follow the D45 south towards Saint-Louis-et-Parahou and park after 2km along the road near the start of the signed trail (42.8560, 2.3672, 1.5km). This route passes rock formations that form eerie-looking shapes and figures, especially when the peak is shrouded in cloud, as it often is even in summer. It also passes 'La Fenêtre' ('The Window'), a spur pierced by a hole.

Summit 42.8636, 2.3792

6 Notre-Dame de Marceille, Limoux

In a tranquil spot just outside the town of Limoux, this enigmatic basilica gives off a curious atmosphere that blends conventional Catholicism and pagan nature worship. Elements in its history, particularly struggles for control by religious orders and individuals over the centuries, link it to some of the area's other mysteries, such as those of **Rennes-le-Château**, some 16km south. Some believe that this peaceful site holds a secret of great significance.

Built on the site of a pre-Christian sanctuary and replacing a 10th-century church dedicated to the Virgin Mary, Notre Dame de Marceille dates from the 14th century. In 1912 it was raised to the status of a basilica by Pope Pius X, an unusual honour for such an obscure and out-of-the-way church.

The basilica houses a mysterious Black Madonna, a statue of the Virgin and Child made of black wood and of uncertain date

– anywhere between the 6th and 12th centuries. Local legend tells that it was discovered by a farmer who, when herding his cows, found that they refused to go beyond a certain spot. Digging there, he uncovered the statue and took it home, but the next morning found that it had disappeared and was back in the ground where he'd found it. The third time it happened, the farmer realised this was a sign that a church had to be built on the site. The Black Madonna made Our Lady of Marceille a place of pilgrimage in the region, and is believed not only to have healed individuals but also to have protected Limoux from the plague on several occasions. In 2007 the statue's head was stolen but has since been replaced.

The site, which had a reputation for healing long before the statue's discovery, was a pagan sanctuary centred on a healing spring, the **Spring That Cures a Thousand Ailments** (43.0666, 2.2256). The Latin inscription on the shrine to the Virgin at the spring reads *Mille mali species virgo levavit aqua* ('The virgin has eased a thousand ailments with this water'). The water is thought to be especially beneficial for diseases of the eyes.

In the 1890s, the Bishop of **Carcassonne**, Félix-Arsène Billard, engaged in some distinctly shady dealings to gain sole control of Our Lady of Marceille, previously owned by several proprietors. Researchers into the Rennes-le-Château mystery believe that Billard acted as protector of its village priest, Abbé Saunière.

Our Lady of Marceille is singled out in the cryptic 1886 book by another priest, Abbé Boudet (see **Rennes-les-Bains)**. In the 1990s a Belgian researcher, Jos Berthaulet, claimed to have deciphered Boudet's code, and this led him to discover an underground vault, dating from the 3rd or 4th century, beneath a field between the basilica and the river Aude. The double-chambered vault, which is on private land, was explored and although empty, a tunnel within it was found to have been sealed off. However, Limoux's authorities blocked the entrance to the vault and it is hard to find given the field is now used for crops.

43.0672, 2.2261

6

6

Aphrodisiac Springs, Duilhac
7

7

7 Peyrepertuse Castle, Duilhac-sous-Peyrepertuse

One of several dramatic mountaintop fortresses in the Languedoc, the **Château de Peyrepertuse** is firmly associated with the Cathars and the Crusade to exterminate them. Now ruined, it sits atop an 800m limestone peak, commanding a panoramic view. At 300m in length it's the largest of the 'five sons of **Carcassonne**' (the other four castles are **Quéribus**, **Puilaurens**, **Termes** and **Aguilar**). It was also known as the 'celestial (or heavenly) Carcassonne'. Beneath the fortress are four cisterns and a vaulted passage leading to a spring, which enabled the inhabitants to withstand a long siege. There was a church dedicated to St Mary and a chapel of Sant Jòrdi (St George). During the Crusade, the Lord of Peyrepertuse sided with the Cathars, although the castle wasn't involved in any military action.

In the village of Duilhac-sous-Peyrepertuse is the **Fontaine des Amours de Duilhac** (Fountain of Love, 42.8639, 2.5657). Invigorating fresh water from the stream, the ruisseau La Fontaine, is piped into stone basins and is said to have aphrodisiac properties. Above the basins is a line from the 16th-century poet Pierre de Ronsard: 'Quiconque en boira qu'amoureux il devienne' meaning 'Whoever drinks will fall in love'. The Château de Peyrepertuse is a popular tourist attraction, open all year except Christmas and New Year. It's well signposted and about 2.5 km from Duilhac-sous-Peyrepertuse.

42.8708, 2.5553, €€; Parking: 42.8704, 2.5583, 500m

8 Puilaurens Castle, Lapradelle-Puilaurens

A spectacular mountaintop fortress on the Cathar Trail, the Château de Puilaurens sits at the western end of the rock spur of Mont Ardu. Its 700m elevation gives it a commanding field of view over the valley of the river Boulzane, which was known as the vallée Sainte-Croix (Holy Cross valley) in the Middle Ages. There are magnificent vistas southwards to the Pyrenees and, 10km to the north, to **Mount Bugarach**. The castle served as a refuge for Cathar men and women during the Crusade, although most of the fortifications seen today are from slightly later, when Puilaurens became a royal castle defending the French border with Spain. High ramparts follow the mountaintop's contours, and there are two towers, one rectangular and the other, the Tour de la Dame Blanche (White Lady), round. The name is said to commemorate the visit of Blanche de Bourbon in the mid-14th century but a local legend offers a different explanation. The White Lady is considered a spirit who appears shortly before a death occurs, when she can be seen walking the ramparts at night. Puilaurens Castle is in an area of great natural beauty, and there are several walking trails through forests and mountains. From Lapradelle-Puilarens, take the D22 towards the village of Puilaurens then follow the signposts to the château. From the village, there's also a walking route up through the forested slopes (42.8013, 2.3047, 1.5km). The castle is open to tourists from March to November.

42.8036, 2.2989, €€; Parking: 42.8038, 2.2957; 200m

9 **Quéribus Castle, Cucugnan**

The last stronghold of the Cathars after the fall of **Montségur** in 1244, the **Château de Quéribus** is in a particularly striking setting, perched on a 730m peak with a panoramic view from the Pyrenees to the Mediterranean. During the Crusade to eliminate their religion, the château sheltered Cathar leaders such as Benoît de Termes and was commanded by the renowned Occitan knight Chabert de Barbaira. It fell after a short siege in 1255, when Chabert was captured and forced to surrender Quéribus in return for his freedom. Like the other four 'sons of Carcassonne', Queribus then became part of France's frontier defences against Spain. After falling into ruin in the late 18th century, the site has been progressively restored over the last two decades and is one of the best preserved of the Cathar castles.

Like the other Cathar fortresses, it's popular with tourists and open all year round. From the village of Cucugnan, take the D123 towards Maury and park by the château sign (42.8373, 2.6084, 2km) or take the road up to the château and find the small car park (42.8392, 2.6208, 400m) at the bottom of the path.

42.8369, 2.6214, €€

9

10 **Rennes-le-Château**

Rennes-le-Château, the tiny 'village of mystery' and the subject of countless books and theories, attracts visitors from around the world. It sits on a hilltop 500m above sea level, overlooking the valleys of the rivers Aude and Sals, and shares the region's epic history of successive settlement by Celts, Romans, Visigoths, Cathars and Templars – all with their own stories of treasures and secrets. Some believe the village to be on the site of the lost Visigoth city of Rhedae.

Rennes-le-Château's fame rests on the mystery surrounding the Abbé Bérenger Saunière, the village's priest between 1885 and his death in 1917. It centres on the unknown source of the riches he lavished on building an elaborate 'domaine' (estate) and the complete renovation of his church, dedicated to St Mary Magdalene. Saunière's lifestyle and activities add to the mystery. There were frequent unexplained absences from his parish, when he is believed to have travelled to Paris and as far as Girona in Spain. In return, there were visits to his out-of-the-way village by prominent individuals, such as the internationally famed opera singer Emma Calvé and even a Hapsburg Archduke. Many of Saunière's visitors were involved in Paris' burgeoning esoteric scene. Reports of him digging in the graveyard at night with his faithful housekeeper and accomplice Marie Dénarnaud gave rise to further speculation, as did the curious, sometimes disturbing, symbolism in the statues and other images he commissioned for the church.

10

According to some, he had discovered a historical treasure or wealth hidden by Rennes-le-Château's noble family during the Revolution. Others believed the priest had found documents revealing a great secret, usually a sacred one – perhaps the location of a priceless artefact such as the Holy Grail or even the Ark of the Covenant. Another scenario is that Saunière was being paid by outsiders to search for something believed to be hidden in the area.

But none of the theories have been proven. Most begin with his discovery, early on, of hidden parchments during initial renovation work on the church. This certainly happened, although what the documents contained is unknown. The supposed parchments, bearing enigmatic codes, were published in the 1960s but many researchers believe these are modern fakes.

The most widely known theory is the one set out in the book that brought the Rennes-le-Château mystery to an international audience, 1982's *The Holy Blood and the Holy Grail* by Michael Baigent, Richard Leigh and Henry Lincoln. They argued that Jesus had been married to Mary Magdalene and, through their children, had founded a bloodline that not only survives to this day but is also protected by a secret society, the Prieuré de Sion (Priory of Sion). According to the three authors, Saunière

10

Tour Magdala

10

found documents proving the existence of the bloodline. The theory was taken up by Dan Brown for *The Da Vinci Code*, and he used Saunière's name for one of his characters. Brown's book and the subsequent feature film made the village even more famous and Rennes-le-Château now receives some 30,000 visitors a year. It is also a magnet for treasure hunters, spiritual seekers and those who simply love a mystery. There is a souvenir shop and esoteric bookshop as well as arts and crafts stalls during the tourist season, and two restaurants.

Saunière's domaine is open to the public between April and December, including entry to the Renaissance-style house, the **Villa Bethania** (42.9279, 2.2626, €), which he had built but strangely never lived in, using it only to entertain his many guests. The adjoining presbytery is now a museum housing key artefacts from the Saunière story. These include the 'Knight's Stone' raised from the church floor, revealing worn images on its underside – most strikingly a man, perhaps two, on horseback. You can also walk round the domaine's ornamental gardens and take in spectacular views from the terrace over the two river valleys.

The terrace ends at Rennes-le-Château's most iconic structure, the **Tour Magdala** (Magdala Tower, 42.9278, 2.2620, €), named after what is traditionally believed to be Mary Magdalene's place of origin; rather neatly, the word also means 'tower'. Saunière had it built as his library and study, although many see deeper significance in its architecture and positioning. It acts as a watchtower, a spiral stone stair giving access to the roof with its castle-like ramparts.

Entry to the **Église Sainte-Marie-Madeleine** (42.9280, 2.2627), the church at the heart of the mystery, is free. It was built in the 10th century as the private chapel of the Lords

10

10

Camp Grand

of Rennes but served as the village church after the original was destroyed by Spanish raiders. However, the main draw is the decoration that Saunière added, starting at the porch over which is inscribed the Latin phrase *Terribilis est locus iste* – literally 'This is a terrible place' in the sense of very serious, extreme or awe-inspiring. The visitor is then greeted by a large statue of a crouched demon, usually named as Asmodeus, bearing the holy water stoup on his back. The statue has been vandalised and then restored on several occasions. The traditional stations of the cross, which unusually run anti-clockwise around this church, include odd details that seem to be clues to *something*, and in which some researchers have discerned Masonic symbolism. A large bas-relief of the Sermon on the Mount on the western wall includes a small bag from which gold coins spill out through a rip. Naturally, a lot of attention has been devoted to the painting on the front of the altar, showing Mary Magdalene in prayer in a cave, to which the final touches were made by Saunière himself. It has been suggested that the landscape beyond the cave mouth points to a specific location somewhere in the Languedoc. It's another sign of the veneration of Mary Magdalene that pervades the region, hinting that the image holds a secret relating to this enigmatic and potent figure. Mystery also surrounds the whereabouts of the church's crypt, in which members of Rennes-le-Château's noble family, the Hautpouls, were entombed. Records as late as the 18th century refer to it, but the entrance is now lost. Outside, the church's graveyard holds Saunière's tomb, which Marie Dénarnaud – to whom the priest bequeathed his entire domaine – visited every night. She told villagers that she was often followed around the graveyard by 'feux-follets' (will-o'-the-wisps).

The mysteries aren't just confined to the village. Locations in the surrounding area, such as **Rennes-les-Bains** and **Notre-Dame de Marceille**, carry their own enigmas that may or may not be linked to the Saunière affair. To the north, on the opposite side of the Sals valley, is the village of Coustaussa (parking 42.9405, 2.2770), the scene of the unsolved brutal murder of one of Saunière's priest colleagues, the elderly Abbé Antoine Gélis, on 31 October 1897. Like Saunière, Gélis was found to have money far beyond his income or donations, with large amounts of cash in his church and presbytery. None of it had been taken when he was killed. Gélis' tomb can be seen in the village graveyard (42.9411, 2.2795). There are also the ruins of **Coustaussa Castle** (42.9401, 2.2768), destroyed during the Crusade against the Cathars. Above Coustaussa is a particularly mystifying site named **Camp Grand** (Great Camp, 42.9492, 2.2697), a large area covering the hilltop about 2.5 km from Rennes-le-Château. It features a huge concentration of several hundred strange stone buildings known as 'capitelles'. These are small dry-stone structures, mostly circular although some are square or rectangular, with domed roofs and a single entrance. Some have collapsed, others are intact. They tend to be described as shepherd's huts but there are good reasons to doubt this, not least on account of their sheer profusion, but also because some are completely solid with no interior space. Their original function is unknown, as is their age. Camp Grand also has massive dry-stone walls, three meters high in some places, enclosing small areas, and there are also stone ramparts around two meters thick. These 'fortifications' make no sense in terms of herding or agriculture. The first to draw attention to the site was Henry Lincoln, led there by his research into the area's landscape geometry, who revealed that a number of alignments from significant spots converged on the hilltop. He speculated the camp could be the remains of an ancient city, perhaps the lost Visigoth Rhedae. The terrain is difficult going, covered in thick scrub and other vegetation. Camp Grand is best reached on foot from Coustaussa (parking 42.9405, 2.2770, 1.5km) or by driving up the bumpy track.

Rennes-le-Château is on the winding D52, with car parks in and around the village.

Parking: 42.9280, 2.2650

Fontaine des Amours

11

Les Bains Doux, Hot Springs

11

Ritual at Chair of Isis

11

Source Salée

11

11 Rennes-les-Bains

This small spa village of around 200 inhabitants and swelled by tourists in the summer, is in many ways the counterpoint of its twin, **Rennes-le-Château**, which lies some 5km to the west. While the latter is on an exposed, arid hilltop, Rennes-les-Bains nestles in the deep valley of the River Sals and is surrounded by verdant forests. The two villages have a very different feel, yet they are bound together by mystery. **Rennes-les-Bains** has been renowned for its healing waters since at least the time of the Romans, who named it Aquae Calidae. Some believe that Mary Magdalene visited the town during this time. In the surrounding hills there are many caves as well as disused iron, copper and perhaps even gold mines. Several local legends speak of hidden treasure, such as the shepherd boy looking for a lost sheep who chanced on a cave filled with skeletons and gold coins but refused to reveal its location to the local lord. In another tale, a shepherdess came across the Devil himself, counting his own hoard of gold coins.

From the north, the entrance to the valley is guarded by two prominent peaks, each with its own story. To the east is the smooth dome of **Pech Cardou** (42.9399, 2.3237), its outline broken only by some rocky outcrops. Rising 160m from the valley floor, the mountain is thickly forested but with an open area near the summit that offers breathtaking views, including to Rennes-le-Château. Pech Cardou is a key point in several landscape geometries, such as that mapped out by Henry Lincoln, and there are claims that something of immense significance lies buried within the mountain, ranging from the Ark of the Covenant to the tomb of Jesus Christ! Magnetic anomalies have been reported by aircraft flying over the mountain, and visitors to its summit have experienced disorientation and the sense of losing time. Cardou can only be visited on foot. It's on three hiking trails and there are several paths leading up to the summit from Rennes-les-Bains (parking 42.9218, 2.3207, 4km), or the nearer village of Serres (parking 42.9459, 2.3229, 3km). Facing Pech Cardou and guarding the other side of the valley entrance is **Château Blanchefort** (42.9378, 2.3114). Although only the foundations and sections of the walls remain, a watchtower or small castle has stood on this perfect vantage point over the valley of the Sals since the 10th century. The château probably takes its name from the promontory of white rock on which it stands, although legend links it to the famed 13th-century Queen Blanche of Castile. Another popular but incorrect association is with Bertrand de Blancafort, Grand Master of the Knights Templar. However, a Templar connection does exist, at least in local lore, which relates that the Knights discovered a treasure beneath the castle. Blanchefort was captured by Simon de Montfort in 1209 during the Crusade against the Cathars. In the 13th century it became part of the lands of the Lords of Rennes-le-Château.

Getting to the ruins of Blanchefort through the forested hillside is difficult, but there's a trail leading up to it from the D14 north of **Rennes-les-Bains** (42.9274, 2.3159. 1.6km), although there isn't an easy parking place. A longer route starts in the village itself, beginning at the Chemin des Fangalots opposite the mairie (42.9183, 2.3190, 4km), but it's harder to follow as it intersects with other trails.

Rennes-les-Bains has found fame internationally owing to the mystery centring on the village priest, Abbé Henri Boudet. A contemporary and friend of Abbé Saunière of neighbouring Rennes-le-Château, Boudet oversaw the parish between 1872 and 1914. He was a renowned scholar, a member of several learned societies, and took an interest in many subjects from archaeology and languages to the then-new art of photography. In 1886 he published a very strange book, *La Vraie Langue Celtique et le Cromleck de Rennes-les-Bains* (*The True Celtic Language and the Cromlech of Rennes-les-Bains*), in which he put forward two apparently eccentric ideas. The first was that the original language of all humankind, from which all other languages are derived, was English! In support, Boudet offered many patently absurd examples of how place names in the area were derived from English words. However, not only was Boudet a historian but he also had a degree in English so was unlikely to make such errors. This has led many to see the text of his book as a code giving clues to a

11

11 Pech Cardou

11 Spring at Chair of Isis

11 La Roche Tremblante

hidden secret – the literary counterpart of Saunière's church decorations.

Boudet's second claim was that the mountains and other geological features around his village formed a natural stone circle. This is the cromlech of the book's title, measuring some 16–18km in circumference and with Rennes-le-Bains at its centre. The entrance to the cromlech is via the pass between Pech Cardou and Blanchefort. To ancient peoples, Boudet argued, this marked the land out as sacred, so they augmented it with standing stones and other megaliths. He provides examples but many consider these to be naturally eroded rock outcrops. Combined with the linguistic 'code', the whole book is regarded as a series of cryptic clues. When decoded, these point to a specific location and reveal Boudet's knowledge of an ancient landscape geometry.

The mysteries of the two Rennes have become entwined to the point that they are now seen as inseparable. Rennes-les-Bains also features in the ongoing controversy surrounding the secret society, the Prieuré de Sion, and its purported documents – the 'Dossiers secrets' as featured in both *The Holy Blood* and *The Da Vinci Code*. The names or pseudonyms of some of the alleged authors of the Dossiers are clearly intended to point to the village, such as Madeleine Blancasall (from the two rivers, the Blanque and Sals, that meet just to the south). Another, Walter Celse-Nazaire, comes from the two saints to which the parish church is dedicated, St Celse and St Nazaire.

Henri Boudet is buried in the church's graveyard, and there is a memorial to him inside. The graveyard holds another tomb that is caught up in the mystery. It is the resting place of Paul-Urbain de Fleury, who died in 1836. Like the tombstone of his grandmother, the last Dame of Rennes-le-Château, the inscription contains errors that are so glaring as to suggest that they are deliberate and have a coded meaning.

Whatever the truth of these modern mysteries, **Rennes-le-Bains** is surrounded by magical sites, both natural and manmade, that are well worth visiting. In the mid-19th century a well-known writer of the time, Auguste de Labouïsse-Rochefort, equated the village and its surroundings with the idyllic Arcadia of Greek myth. Today it is designated an area of ecological interest because the fusion of mild Mediterranean and mountain climates enables a wide variety of plant and animal life to flourish.

Numerous key alignments and geometric patterns formed by natural features and castles, churches, chapels and other man-made structures dating back millennia have been traced in the area. Many of them are centred on **Rennes-les-Bains**, indicating that it was regarded as a sacred place even before the Romans arrived. Some also think that the pattern of alignments around Rennes-les-Bains is similar to those centred on the oracle site of Delphi in Greece, which was considered a sacred centre by the ancient Greeks.

There are five hot springs feeding baths that have long been used for the relief of rheumatism, arthritis and other conditions. The main baths, the Thermes de Rennes-les-Bains, is a spa that charges for booked appointments and offers other therapies such as massage, but there is an open natural pool, **Les Bains Doux** (42.9219, 2.3177, parking 42.9218, 2.3207, 300m), beside the Sals and below the remains of the Roman spa. The pool, reached by a path down from the car park at the village's northern edge, is fed by a culvert from the rock face and the water is at a constant 37°C throughout the year. It is popular with locals and visitors.

In the forested hillside just to the south of the village is the **Chair of Isis** (42.9124, 2.3159), a large boulder with a stone seat carved out of it and more commonly known as Le Fauteuil du Diable (Devil's Armchair). In recent years the 'Isis' attribution has become popular with spiritual seekers who are attracted to the area. Were it not for the trees, anyone sitting in the boulder would have a grand view over the valley, suggesting it dates from a time when the hillside was unforested. Who carved it and when is a complete mystery, although it is thought to be very ancient. The connection with the Egyptian goddess, which was first proposed in the mid-1980s, comes from the throne being both one of her symbols and also part of her name when written in hieroglyphs.

Some have theorised that the demon statue that the Abbé Saunière placed in his church in Rennes-le-Château, which is crouching as if about to sit, was intended to point to this site. Similarly, the circle that the demon is making with his fingers could be a reference to the **Source du Cercle**, a small circular spring next to the Chair of Isis. A more crudely-shaped, natural rock not far above it is now referred to as the Male Chair, a counterpoint to the feminine Chair of Isis, and a little further south is a larger outcrop with a flat surface that has been called the **Altar stone** (42.9106, 2.3154). The site of these formations is reached by a trail heading up into the hills from the Chemin de Cercle, just south of **Rennes-les-Bains** off the main D14 road that runs through the village, with a car park opposite (42.9118, 2.3181, 300m). A few minutes' walk further along the trail from the Altar stone is the **Roche Tremblante** (Trembling Rock, 42.9100, 2.3148), a boulder balanced on a rock outcrop. According to local lore, although the stone could be rocked it wasn't possible to push it off its base. Less than a kilometre south of Rennes-les-Bains is one of several cold water springs, the evocatively named **Source Madeleine** (42.9072, 2.3195), perhaps in memory of Mary Magdalene's visit. It is also known as the Source de la Gode. At this very tranquil and popular spot, visitors have been carving their names and initials into the rock face by the spring since the late 1800s. Located off the D14 just by the river Blanque into which it flows, the spring is rich in iron and the water has tinted the rock red. A smaller nearby spring contains sulphur as well as iron. There's parking near the bridge at the junction of the D14 and D74 to Sougraine (42.9094, 2.3195, 300m), then follow the course of the Blanque.

Just over a kilometre further along the road to Sougraine is the enchanting **Fontaine des Amours** (42.9061, 2.3283; parking 42.9073, 2.3281, 100m), a rock pool carved out by the Sals that is large and deep enough for swimming. It is said that if you bathe there naked with your partner you will both fall in love for ever. Leave Rennes-les-Bains heading south, then turn left onto the D74 and look out for a small parking place on the right with a wooden sign pointing to the site.

Further along the D74, 3km past the village of Sougraine, is the road to the **Source Salée** (42.8921, 2.4000), which is the source of the river Sals. The spring water has a high concentration of salt ('sal'), which gradually diminishes as the river flows towards Rennes-les-Bains. A valued commodity throughout the ages, salt has been collected here since Roman times. Look out for the easy-to-miss signpost at the start of an unsurfaced road (42.8977, 2.3867), which leads to a car park by the spring. It is in an area of woodland, the Domaine de l'Eau Salée, noted for its wildlife and popular hiking trails.

Parking: 42.9218, 2.3207

12 Termes Castle

The most northerly of castles known as the 'five sons of **Carcassonne**', the **Château de Termes** was, like the others, a refuge for Cathars during the Crusade launched against them by the pope. Although nearly 500m above the Gorges de Termenet and protected

by steep cliffs on three sides, the castle was captured after a three-month siege in 1210. **Termes Castle** is open to the public every day from April to October, weekends only in March and November and closed during the winter months. Park in the town of Termes below and walk up.

43.0022, 2.5567 €; Parking: 43.0010, 2.5655, 1km

PYRÉNÉES-ORIENTALES

13 Cave of Mary Magdalene, Opoul-Périllos

Known locally as La Cauna ('The Cavern') this large atmospheric cave is 370m above sea level, and close to the abandoned village of Périllos with its ruined château. Accessed via an entrance in a prominent

13

outcrop, the cave opens out into a large circular space, around 50m in diameter and 15m high. It is well lit from a natural opening in the roof, particularly towards the end of the day. Several huge stalagmites rise dramatically from the floor like living columns of rock. Remains of pottery as far back as the Roman period have been found in the cave, as well as burials of unknown date outside the entrance. There are carved marks on the walls that some believe to be Neolithic, as well as some more modern graffiti.

It's been suggested that, during her legendary travels in the region, Mary Magdalene spent time in quiet contemplation in this cave. Whether true or not, visitors remark on the peaceful atmosphere within.

The cave is on one of the many popular hiking trails in the area and it can also be reached by road. Approaching Opoul-Périllos from the southwest on the D9, turn left at the 'Falaise d'Opoul' sign and carry on past the Château d'Opoul. Park opposite the short, rugged track (only suitable for 4x4s) to the cave.

42.9034, 2.8602; Parking: 42.8972, 2.8573, 1km

14 Hermitage of St Anthony of Galamus

The spectacular Gorges de Galamus, cut by the river Agly through the mountains between Cubières-sur-Cinoble and Saint-Paul-de-Fenouillet, is home to the dramatically-sited **Ermitage Saint-Antoine de Galamus**. Built on the side of a steep cliff, the secluded retreat consists of a grotto that was converted into a chapel in the 15th century by the Franciscan Order, with an adjacent building to house the friars. Dedicated to the patron saint of hermits, the chapel once held relics of the True Cross and St Victor. The site was abandoned during the French Revolution but revived in the 19th century. During the years of disuse, travellers from Paris described it as 'the most beautiful wonder of Roussillon'.

The inhabitants of the nearby town of Saint-Paul-de-Fenouillet credit the presence of the chapel and the protection of St Anthony with sparing them from the epidemic of sweating sickness that swept the region in 1782. There's a traditional pilgrimage to the chapel at Easter and Pentecost. The hermitage was used as a location in Roman Polanski's 1999 esoteric thriller *The Ninth Gate*.

A footpath leads down to the hermitage from a car park off the D7 that runs through the Gorges de Galamus.

42.8379, 2.4812; Parking: 42.8357, 2.4802, 500m.

Carcassonne
Trèbes
Lézignan-Corbières
Mirepoix
Limoux
Paris Meridian
Lavelanet
Quillan
Proposed route of Mary Magdalene
Estagel
Rivesaltes
Ax-les-Thermes
PERPIGNAN
1 2 3 4 5 6 7 8 9 10 11 12 13 14

PROVENCE AND MARY MAGDALENE

From the Mediterranean coast to the Alps, Provence has a rich variety of landscapes, including mountains, forests, plains and the extensive marshlands of the Carmargue. Before being incorporated into the Kingdom of France a little more than 500 years ago it was an independent land, and still retains its distinct culture and language.

Folktales about 'fées' (fairies) and other nature spirits are attached to water sources, caves and forests throughout the region. Ancient Greek and Roman settlers brought their own deities, and it is striking how many of their temples, later replaced by churches and cathedrals, were once dedicated to goddesses. A divine feminine presence seems to pervade the region and nowadays the most compelling spiritual sites are those associated with Marie-Madeleine – Mary Magdalene. There are deep-rooted legends of this mysterious disciple travelling to what was then a Roman province, bringing Christianity to France.

Early Provençal traditions present Mary Magdalene as an apostle, preaching and baptising, while later ones depict her as living out a life of penitence as a hermit. They tell of her coming ashore at Saintes-Maries-de-la-Mer in the Camargue, after having been cast adrift with others on a boat without sails or oars. She is said to have preached to and converted pagans in many places, such as Marseilles, before retiring to a life of solitude and prayer in Mary Magdalene's Cave in the Sainte-Baume mountains. When she died her body was said to have been entombed in Saint-Maximin-la-Sainte Baume, where her relics can be seen today in the Basilica of St Mary Magdalene. All these places are now centres of pilgrimage for both Christians and spiritual seekers alike.

In Provence, as in the Languedoc, the veneration of Mary Magdalene is a long-held tradition which became entwined with other mysterious and mystical beliefs. One of the most significant, though cryptic, connections is with Black Madonna statues that are frequently found at sites associated with the Magdalene legend, such as St Victor's Abbey in Marseilles, the Madonna of Fenestres Chapel and Our Lady of the Angels Sanctuary in the far west of Provence. Whatever secrets lie behind these interconnected traditions, Provence truly is 'Magdalene country'.

VAUCLUSE

1 Fontaine-de-Vaucluse

In a stunning location, amid rocky cliffs at the end of a valley and with the ruins of the medieval castle of the Bishops of Cavaillon looming over it, the village of **Fontaine-de-Vaucluse** (Spring of Vaucluse) is the setting for two potent legends. Both centre on the fast-flowing and turbulent river Sorgue that runs through the village. The river's source is the extraordinary chasm, the **Gouffre de Fontaine-de-Vaucluse** (43.9178, 5.1328, 1km walk upstream from the village). Unlike the small springs from which most rivers are born, this source is a deep, turquoise-blue pool in a yawning cavern at the base of a 230m-high cliff. How deep the pool is remains a mystery: there have been many attempts to find out by sending remote-controlled submersibles down into its depths, the furthest reaching 315m without touching the bottom. There's a legend of a nymph who is the guardian of the source. She appeared to a wandering minstrel named Basile who was sleeping near it, and led him to the pool. The waters then parted, allowing them to descend into an underground realm of meadows filled with dazzling flowers. The nymph showed Basile how she controlled the level of the Sorgue by removing or replacing diamonds covering seven springs. The other tale is of a female dragon, the Coulobre, which lived in the river Sorgue's network of underwater caves, emerging to terrorise the surrounding area. The townsfolk appealed for help to the hermit Saint Véran (St Veranus), a real 6th century holy man who became Bishop of Cavaillon. Saint Véran's Cathedral (43.8364, 5.0361) is located about 10km from **Fontaine-de-Vaucluse**. By his prayers he defeated the

Coulobre, and the dying dragon flew off, far up in the Alps where it expired on the site of the village of Saint-Véran (Haute-Alpes, 44.7008, 6.8683), 160km away. As it flew, it shed drops of blood, and wherever one fell a village was named in St Véran's honour. They include one close to **Lumières**, 12.5 km from Fontaine-de-Vaucluse. Another church dedicated to St Véran, 170km away in **Utelle**, lies due east of the scene of his battle with the dragon and the carvings on its doors feature an image of St Véran and the dragon.

The **Église Notre-Dame-et-Saint-Véran** (Our Lady and St Veranus' Church, 43.9215, 5.1267) in Fontaine-de-Vaucluse was built in the 11th century on the site of a pagan sanctuary. One of the sanctuary's original columns was used in the church's construction.

Parking: 43.9223, 5.1264

2 Lumières, Goult

The area surrounding this tiny village in the wide valley of the river Calavon has been a centre of mystery, sacred secrets and strange phenomena from ancient times to the present day.

Lumières ('Lights') gets its name from a mysterious nocturnal phenomenon seen regularly during the 1660s – the appearance of lights moving over and around the rock plateau, its cliffs rising 40m over the village. The lights were particularly associated with two small chapels, one up on the plateau and the other near the base of the cliffs. The lights were interpreted in religious terms, with visions of glowing figures, and the **Sanctuaire Notre-Dame-de-Lumières** (Our Lady of Lumières' Sanctuary, 43.8598, 5.2316) was built on the site of the lower chapel, which later became the current sanctuary's crypt and a famous place of pilgrimage in the region.

When the sanctuary was built in 1699 a Black Madonna, also named Notre-Dame de Lumières, was installed. Also known as the Santo Vierge Négro (Holy Black Virgin), the 40cm wooden statue of the standing Madonna holding her Child was believed to heal blindness. Sadly, the original was stolen in 1979 and today's statue is a replica.

The walls of the church are bedecked with old paintings of visionary experiences of glowing figures, while in the centre of the church, steps lead down to a remarkable crypt. At the end of the long painted tunnel stands a resplendent statue of a Madonna and Child, Notre-Dame de l'Eternelle Lumière (Eternal Light) surrounded by clouds and cherubs. Located in a side chapel

2 Chapelle Saint-Véran

2

2

2

2 Dolmen de l'Ubac

is the replica of the small Black Madonna statue. Confusingly, the larger statue, which was placed in the crypt in the mid-19th century, is sometimes also referred to as Notre-Dame de Lumières.

In a ceremony dating back to the sanctuary's origins, every year on 15 August the Black Madonna is carried in a procession up to the other ancient chapel linked with the mysterious lights, the **Chapelle Saint-Michel-de-la-Baume** (Chapel of St Michael of the Cave, 43.8619, 5.2305). The chapel has stood on the hill above Lumières since at least the 11th century and, like many hilltop sites that were re-dedicated to the Archangel Michael, it was previously sacred to the Roman god Mercury. The procession of the Black Madonna could therefore be a continuation of a pagan tradition repurposed as a Christian one.

2 Dolmen de l'Ubac

The trail to the chapel starts behind the Hôtel Notre-Dame de Lumières (43.8600, 5.2317), originally a monastery where monks ministered to the pilgrims.

The theft of the original Black Madonna may be linked to modern esoteric beliefs whose adherents continue to regard this particular icon and place as holding the key to a profound secret. In the early 20th century, one of the priests at the Sanctuary was the enigmatic Émile Hoffet. He was not only deeply involved in Paris' thriving occult scene but also turns up in the mystery that centres on another priest, Abbé Saunière of **Rennes-le-Château**. Perhaps for that reason the controversial secret society the Prieuré de Sion (Priory of Sion), which claims to hold the secret of the Rennes-le-Château affair, singles out this Black Madonna for special reverence. According to the society, 'Our Lady of the Lights' refers to the Egyptian goddess Isis, who was sometimes portrayed with a halo of lights.

Other signs of pagan worship include a fragment of a carved Neolithic stele bearing the face of a god that was found nearby, as well as an excavated Roman building featuring altars to nymphs and the god Sylvanus, the *genius loci* of forests. In Lumières' neighbouring hamlet of Goult (Parking: 43.8629 5.2434), less than 0.5km away on a small hill in the centre of the valley, the 12th-century **Église Saint-Sébastien** (St Sebastian, 43.8629, 5.2444) was built on the site of a pagan temple. In the Middle Ages, the valley was a centre of the Waldensian sect, also known as the Poor of Lyons, that was associated with the Cathars. It was declared heretical and its followers were persecuted by the papal inquisition but nevertheless the sect survived into the modern era.

Around 2.5km southeast of Lumières is Saint-Véran, one of the villages said to have been founded where a drop of blood from the Coulobre, the dragon defeated by St Véran at **Fontaine-de-Vaucluse**, fell. Just outside the village is the ancient **Chapelle Saint-Véran** (43.8444, 5.2437), which sits on a wooded mound.

On the opposite bank of the river Calavon lies the 5,000 year old **Dolmen de l'Ubac** (43.8564, 5.2314). Excavations in the 1990s removed the earth mound covering it and found the remains of around 50 people inside. Unusually, the dolmen and tumulus were constructed on a circular flat base of stones, which became visible once the mound had been completely removed, giving the dolmen the appearance of sitting at the centre of a sacred circle. The site is off a cycle/walking route that crosses the river. Just after the small bridge, there is a short, signposted path down to the dolmen.

Parking: 43.8593, 5.2301

BOUCHES-DU-RHÔNE

3 Église de la Madeleine, Aix-en-Provence

Considered one of the most beautiful churches in Provence, the Église de la Madeleine (Church of the Magdalene) was founded in 1272, although the one we see today is a rebuild from around 1700. It's dedicated to Mary Magdalene, Provence's patron saint who according to tradition lived the last part of her life in the region, then a Roman province. Tradition also says that the first Bishop of Aix was St Maximinus, one of Jesus' 72 disciples who was among those on the boat that miraculously brought Mary Magdalene to France.

The historical capital of Provence, Aix began as a Roman thermal spa town named Aquae Sextiae on the trade route between Rome and Massalia (Marseilles).

3

4

4

The Romans established the town in 123 BC after capturing the nearby Oppidum d'Entremont, the fortified capital of the Salyes, a Celto-Ligurian people. The foundations are open to visitors and are located on the northern edge of Aix (43.5522, 5.4392; Parking: 43.5531, 5.4364, 250m).

Aix's medieval **Cathédrale Saint-Sauveur** (Holy Saviour, 43.5319, 5.4472), 500m from the Church of the Magdalene, is on the foundations of the Roman temple to Apollo, where St Maximinus is said to have built a chapel. Its octagonal baptismal pool, built in the 5th or 6th century on the site of the Roman forum and fed by the waters from the hot spring, is one of the oldest in France.

Aix-en-Provence has many historic monuments and is known as the 'town of a hundred fountains' because of its many public fountains. It actually has around 250, so rather more than 100.

43.5294, 5.4514; Parking €: 45.5323, 5.4504, 400m

4 Saintes-Maries-de-la-Mer

This small and isolated harbour town is believed to be on the site where Mary Magdalene and her companions, Mary Salome and Mary Jacobi, first came ashore. According to others, the legend of the Three Marys was a Christianisation of the Three Matres, the triple-aspect goddess of

the Celts, to whom the site was previously dedicated. It was a centre of pilgrimage even before Christianity, and is today still considered sacred in Roma culture.

Saintes-Maries-de-la-Mer (Saint Marys of the Sea) lies within the Camargue, a huge area of marshland and saltwater lagoons ('étangs') where the river Rhône meets the Mediterranean. It is home to flocks of flamingos and a unique breed of semi-wild white horses. Located some 30km from the nearest town, **Arles**, in antiquity the place was a centre for trade across the Mediterranean, bringing together many cultures, and there were temples to the goddesses Artemis, Cybele and Isis. According to Roman sources, there was a fortress named after the Egyptian god Ra and there's evidence that it was a place of pilgrimage for the god Mithras and the goddess Diana.

Today, the spiritual heart of Saintes-Maries-de-la-Mer is the Romanesque church of **Notre-Dame-de-la-Mer** (Our Lady of the Sea, 43.4517, 4.4278). Built between the 9th and 11th centuries, the church was fortified because of the threat of coastal raids by Moors, Vikings and others. In the mid-15th century two sets of bones, taken to be those of Mary Jacobi and Mary Salome, were discovered beneath the church and are now preserved in a decorated chest in the high chapel. But most intriguing is the crypt dedicated to Sara la Noire (Sara the Black) whose statue – dark-skinned, crowned and dressed in sumptuous gowns – is honoured there. Sara is tantalisingly ambiguous. She is venerated by the Catholic Church as St Sarah, the Three Marys' servant girl who accompanied them on their voyage, or in another version she was a pagan princess who they converted to Christianity. She is also revered by the Roma as *Sara e Kali*, linking her to Kali, the Hindu goddess of time, creation and destruction. Saintes-Maries-de-la-Mer plays host to the largest Roma pilgrimage in Europe, an annual event during which the women elect their Queen. A result of the two traditions converging on Saintes-Maries-de-la-Mer is

that each year there are overlapping pilgrimages and festivals of Catholics celebrating Mary Salome and Mary Jacobi, and Roma people honouring Sara e Kali. On 24 May the Roma bring the statue of Sara from the crypt and carry it in procession to be immersed in the sea, and the following day there is a Catholic procession of the chest containing the relics of the Two Marys and a sculpture of them in the boat that brought them to France. Sara la Noire forms a bridge between the Hindu goddess Kali and the enigmatic Black Madonnas that are found throughout Provence and which are often associated with Mary Magdalene, pointing to an underlying if mysterious spiritual connection between these powerful feminine figures.

Parking: 43.4523, 4.4287

5 Arles Cathedral

The 12th-century cathedral, dedicated to St Trophimus the legendary first bishop of Arles, is at the southern end of an alignment of Gothic cathedrals that runs all the way through France to **Le Puy-en-Velay**, **Bourges** and **Chartres**. Like Le Puy-en-Velay, Arles is also one of the starting points for the pilgrimage to Santiago de Compostela. Before the arrival of Christianity, Arles was a centre for the goddess cults of Isis and Cybele, and the church of **Notre-Dame de la Major** (43.6778, 4.6325) was built over the site of the temple of Cybele. The Venus of Arles, now in the Louvre, is the most famous of many statues found in the ruins of the nearby Roman amphitheatre (43.6777, 4.6309), which has been restored and is now used for plays and concerts. Reinforcing Arles' strong divine feminine spirit, the Cathédrale Saint-Trophime once housed a famous Black Madonna statue, Notre-Dame de Grâces. During the French Revolution, when many churches and cathedrals were desecrated, the revolutionary who tried to topple the statue was thrown down and broke a leg, after which nobody dared to touch it. During a severe drought in 1868 the townspeople prayed to the Madonna for rain – and their prayers were answered. Sadly, the statue disappeared from the cathedral in 1915.

43.6767, 4.6281; Parking €: 43.6770, 4.6301, 250m

6 Abbaye Saint-Victor, Marseilles

The crypt of this important abbey in Marseille's Vieux-Port district houses one of Provence's many shrines to Mary Magdalene. It is in the chapel dedicated to St Lazarus her brother, where a relief depicts Mary on her knees praying to a crucifix in a cave – a reference to **Mary Magdalene's Cave** at La Sainte-Baume. Founded in

the 5th century, the abbey church is one of the earliest recorded Christian sites in France. Dedicated to the martyr St Victor of Marseille, it was an early pilgrimage site. With its solid walls and battlements it looks more like a castle than a church, but like **Saintes-Maries-de-la-Mer** it had to be fortified because of the danger of raiders arriving by sea. The abbey's importance is demonstrated by the lands that it possessed across southern France and even into Spain and Sardinia. They included the church of **Saint-Maximin-la-Sainte Baume**, a key Magdalene site.

The crypt also has a Black Madonna, Notre-Dame de Confession, a metre tall and carved from walnut. The statue is the focus of one of Marseilles' most popular festivals that takes place at Candlemas (2 February) when, dressed in a green mantle, she is carried in procession around the streets. It replaced a pre-Christian procession in honour of Persephone, the Greek goddess of spring and the underworld. During the celebration, it's customary to eat 'navettes', biscuits in the shape of a boat that represent the one that brought the Three Marys to Saintes-Maries-de-la-Mer. The festival effectively creates an association between the Black Madonna and the traditions of Mary Magdalene in France.

According to local lore, Mary Magdalene herself preached on the steps of the Temple of Diana, built on the site of what is now Marseilles' Place de Lenche (43.2975, 5.3656). The temple was replaced by a convent, which stood opposite **St Victor's Abbey** and was founded at the same time, but Moors destroyed it in the 8th century. Today this ancient site is a tree-lined square of restaurants and bars.

43.2906, 5.3656; Parking: 43.2908, 5.3661, 100m

VAR

7 Basilique Sainte-Marie-Madeleine, Saint-Maximin-la-Sainte-Baume

A major site connected with Mary Magdalene in Provence, the Basilica of St Mary Magdalene houses what are believed to be her body and tomb. Brought in antiquity from **Mary Magdalene's Cave**, the remains are venerated as holy relics by the Catholic Church. The Basilica dominates the town of **Saint-Maximin-la-Sainte-Baume** and is one of the most famous sacred buildings in France.

The town takes its name from the legendary first Bishop of **Aix-en-Provence**, St Maximinus. According to some versions of the legend of Mary Magdalene's arrival in France, he was among those who were cast adrift with her and the other women. 'La-Sainte-Baume' (The Holy Cave) was added to the town's name a century ago to emphasise its close connection with her cave shrine. Previously, before the arrival of Christianity, the town had been named after the Celtic mother goddess Matrona.

Mary Magdalene's tomb, along with that of Maximinus, was discovered beneath the Saint-Maximin church in 1279. According to a document found with her body, it had been hidden some five centuries earlier to safeguard it from raids by Moors from Spain who were targeting churches. Accounts relate that when Mary's sarcophagus was opened a sweet scent arose from it and a green shoot was found growing from her mouth. The search had been ordered by

Charles d'Anjou, Count of Provence, who was convinced that the Magdalene's body lay under the church, even though at the time it was believed to lie in the Abbey of St Mary Magdalene in **Vézelay**, Burgundy. A fierce dispute ensued between the two places, which was settled when the pope declared in favour of Saint-Maximin. Until then the church had been the property of **St Victor's Abbey** in Marseilles, but it was placed under the Dominican Order in the late 13th century, when the construction of the huge basilica seen today began.

The Magdalene's tomb was considered the third most important in Christianity, after the Holy Sepulchre in Jerusalem and St Peter's in Rome, and many kings and queens made the pilgrimage there. The relics were said to produce miraculous cures, even bringing people back from the dead. These, along with her sarcophagus, are now displayed in the crypt. The centrepiece is Mary Magdalene's skull, which is kept in a bronze reliquary with a crystal front. On her feast day of 22 July, the Magdalene's skull is covered by a cast of her face then paraded through the town in a procession. Another reliquary in the basilica holds a lock of her hair.

43.4528, 5.8633; Parking: 43.4523, 5.8683, 500m

8 Chapelle Sainte-Roseline, Les Arcs

This atmospheric medieval chapel is dedicated to St Roseline of Villeneuve (1263–1329), known as 'the rose without a thorn'. The daughter of the Lord of Villeneuve, she was raised in the Château de Villeneuve in Les Arcs and the 'miracle of the roses' is attributed to her. During a time of famine Roseline secretly took food from the castle's stores to give to the local people, but when confronted by her suspicious father she opened her apron to reveal not bread but roses. A medieval archway from the original castle in Les Arcs still stands and is known as the **Porte du Miracle** (43.4647, 6.4778). Roseline later became a Carthusian nun, entering the Abbey of Celle-Roubaud, 3km from Les Arcs and once the property of the Knights Templar who had dedicated it to St Catherine of Alexandria.

Many other miracles were attributed to Roseline, including power over demons and the ability to summon help from angels. In one account, she became so rapt in religious ecstasy that she forgot to prepare the communal meal, but when the nuns arrived at the table angels entered and laid out the food. A mosaic on the wall of the chapel, the *Repas des Anges* (Angels' Meal) by artist Marc Chagall depicts the scene.

Roseline's brother Hélion de Villeneuve was Grand Master of the military order of the Knights Hospitaller when the Hospitallers were taking over Templar property and assets, following the Templars' suppression on charges of blasphemy. A legend tells of Roseline rescuing Hélion who had been captured and imprisoned by the Turkish army on the island of Rhodes. Her prayers had a miraculous effect and transported Hélion from his dungeon back to Provence. Having risen to become Prioress of the Abbey, Roseline died on 17 January 1329 and five years later her body was exhumed and found to be preserved, especially her eyes which were still bright. Her body was displayed in a shrine in the chapel, which was then the abbey church but the eyes were removed and placed in their own reliquary. Pilgrims flocked to venerate the relics and many miraculous cures were reported. Roseline's body is said to be especially healing for children, and her eyes for problems with sight. Today Roseline's body is displayed in a glass casket and her eyes look out from their reliquary. One of the eyes was damaged after Louis XIV, visiting the chapel in 1660, had his physician pierce one of the eyeballs to prove it wasn't glass. In the 19th century the chapel was re-dedicated to St Roseline. It was restored in 1968 with contemporary artists, including Chagall and Giacometti, contributing to its decoration.

In the mid-19th century Roseline's saint's day was changed to the day of her death, 17 January. For reasons that remain obscure, that date recurs in connection with **Rennes-le-Château** and there are other tantalising links, including to the Merovingian dynasty and the Templars. Taken together with Roseline's extraordinary life in Provence, a region steeped in legends of Mary Magdalene, her story has mysterious associations and some even consider Roseline descended from the bloodline of Jesus and Mary Magdalene.

A cryptic association with the Paris Meridian (see **Paris Observatory**) recurs in the Rennes-le-Château mysteries, especially in connection with the Merovingian St Sulpice whose feast day is also 17 January. He was Bishop of **Bourges** which lies on the meridian, while the church of **Saint Sulpice** in Paris has its own meridian line. Because of these associations the name 'Roseline' (Rose Line) is now used to refer to the esoteric aspects of the Paris Meridian

The town of Les Arcs has many medieval remains in its scenic streets, including ramparts, gateways and vestiges of the Villeneuve's castle, including the 20m-high keep (43.4646, 6.4778).

The **Chapelle Sainte-Roseline** is part of a working monastery but is open to the public Tuesday–Sunday from 14.30 (closed mid-December to end of January).

43.4739, 6.5133; Parking 43.4748, 6.5143, 250m

9 Chapelle du Saint-Pilon

9

9

9

9 Mary Magdalene's Cave, Plan-d'Aups-Sainte-Baume

The most famous and evocative of the sites in France connected with Mary Magdalene is the remote Grotte de **La Sainte-Baume** (Holy Cave). This cave was, however, associated with feminine spirituality long before Mary Magdalene's legendary journey to **Saintes-Maries-de-la-Mer**, and at one time was sacred to the goddess Artemis. *Baumo* is Provençal for 'cave', and the spacious grotto, 30m deep by 20m wide, is near the bottom of the cliff face of the Sainte-Baume massif, a towering white ridge that rises from the dense and ancient Forest of La Sainte-Baume. A wall built across the cavern's yawning mouth has transformed the cave into a large chapel. Within the grotto is an altar and statues representing scenes from Magdalene's life. Behind and above the altar is the rock, the 'rocher de Marie Madeleine', where she is believed to have prayed. According to Christian tradition, Mary Magdalene retreated to the cave for the last 30 years of her life, spending her time alone in meditation, contemplation and prayer. Her clothing perished, so she lived naked for most of that time covered only by her long hair, and this image became part of her traditional iconography. However, the story has clear similarities with that of another repentant female saint, the 5th century Mary the Egyptian, a prostitute who converted to Christianity and then became a hermit in the desert. An element that is unique to the Magdalene legend is that she was sustained in this isolated place by angels. They raised her up to the top of a tall stone column seven times each day so she could be nourished by the music of heaven, which served her in place of food. The spot on the clifftop above the grotto where the column once stood is marked by the small **Chapelle du Saint-Pilon** (Holy Pillar, 43.3272, 5.7650). It's reached by a steep 1km track that branches off from the main trail to the grotto. Another legend, commemorated by a statue in the grotto, is that a dragon living in the cave was driven out by Archangel Michael. At the end of her life, Mary's body was said to have been taken by her one-time companion St Maximinus and buried in the church of **Saint-Maximin-la-Sainte-Baume**, where her relics are still on display.

9

9

Controversy surrounds Mary Magdalene's connection with the cave, which dates back only to the late 12th century. This is long after the Provençal traditions that portray her as playing an active part in bringing Christianity to France, travelling the region to preach and win converts. Some think that the image of her as a penitent hermit was created by the medieval Church to play down her important work as an Apostle, a role at that time considered exclusive to the male disciples. Whatever the truth of the legend's origins, in the Middle Ages La Sainte-Baume was considered the third most important pilgrimage in Western Europe after Rome and Santiago de Compostela, with kings, queens and popes among those who journeyed there. Today the sanctuary is in the care of Dominican monks, regular Catholic services take place inside, and it receives around half a million pilgrims and tourists each year. The cave can only be reached on foot. After a 1km walk along the Chemin des Roys (Kings' Path) through the enchanting ancient forest, there are 150 steps up to the sanctuary. Another site that is highly charged with feminine energy is the **Grotte aux Oeufs** (Cave of Eggs, 43.3250, 5.7546), also known as the Yoni Cave. Located on a forest trail that climbs up the face of the ridge and is tough going in places, the cave can be difficult to find because the entrance is obscured behind a large rock that's easy to miss. The cave is a deep cleft that penetrates the cliff and the narrow access passage suggests a vulva. Women often leave offerings of eggs and lighted candles inside. If visiting, be sure to take a torch.

Back on the main road is the Hostellerie (43.3356, 5.7569) built to house pilgrims and run by Dominican monks. Inside you can find visual displays and lots of information on the life of Mary Magdalene, including a map of a long-distance walking route tracing her journey from **Saintes-Maries-de-la-Mer** to **Saint-Maximin-la-Sainte-Baume**.

The surrounding area has a number of hiking trails that take in some wonderful springs, waterfalls and caves which, like similar sites throughout the region, are often associated with fairies and other nature spirits. A particularly captivating site is the **Sources de l'Huveaune** (43.3442, 5.7592), 1km north of the Hostellerie. Said to have sprung from the Magdalene's tears, the spring rises in a large grotto 600m up the valley, the Vallon de Castelette. The stream then flows down through the forest in a cascade of multicoloured step-like terraces, to become the river Huveaune that eventually empties into the Mediterranean at Marseilles, 50km away. The river is named after the Celtic goddess Ubelka. The official Sources de l'Huveaune trail begins in the village of

Nans-les-Pins (Parking: 43.3691, 5.7852, 3.5km; Trailhead 43.3551, 5.7771, 2km).
43.3272, 5.7647; Parking: 43.3355, 5.7655, 1km

10 Sanctuaire Notre-Dame-des-Anges, Pignans

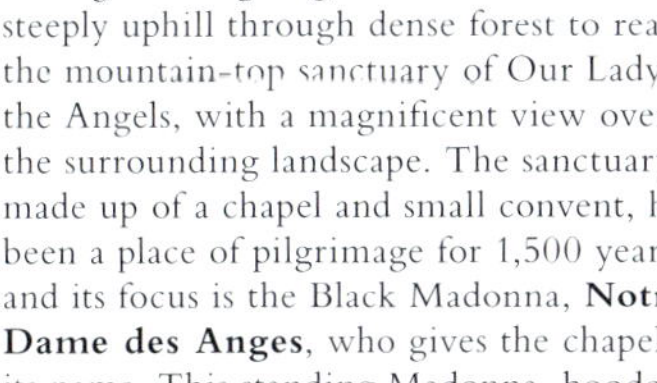

A long winding single track road leads steeply uphill through dense forest to reach the mountain-top sanctuary of Our Lady of the Angels, with a magnificent view over the surrounding landscape. The sanctuary, made up of a chapel and small convent, has been a place of pilgrimage for 1,500 years, and its focus is the Black Madonna, **Notre-Dame des Anges**, who gives the chapel its name. This standing Madonna, hooded and with hands together in prayer, is carved from dark wood and over the centuries her presence has been credited with saving Pignans from plague and drought.

Today's building dates from the mid-1800s but the original chapel was founded in the early 6th century by the Merovingian king, Thierry, to show gratitude following his victory over the Visigoths. During the Middle Ages it came under the control of the **Abbaye Saint-Victor** in Marseilles. Legends tell of the sanctuary's even earlier foundation by the sister of St Maximinus and servant of Mary Magdalene, who was among the group that came ashore at **Saintes-Maries-de-la-Mer**. Her name was Nymphe and she is said to have carved the Black Madonna. Later, the statue was venerated in the Merovingian chapel but was lost when the building was destroyed during invasions by the Moors in the 9th–10th centuries. Much later, in the 16th century, a sheepdog unearthed the staue from undergrowth and the shepherd took it to his parish church. However, the statue kept disappearing, only to turn up back at the spot where it had been found – a sign that a chapel had to be built there. Similar legends are found elsewhere in France in connection with Black Madonnas, such as **Notre-Dame de Marceille** in Aude. Black Madonna statues are sometimes associated with Mary Magdalene as well as with pagan forms of the sacred feminine. Such cryptic but potent connections are especially clear at Our Lady of the Angels Sanctuary, most obviously in the name of its founder Nymphe – a female nature spirit identified with rivers and streams, and especially their sources. It is perhaps no coincidence that a spring, the **Source de Notre-Dame** (42.2834, 6.2921) is located just 250m from the chapel. Set in a stone surround, the shrine where the spring emerges is on a bend in the lane leading up to the sanctuary.
43.2814, 6.2939

11 Pierre de la Fée, Draguignan

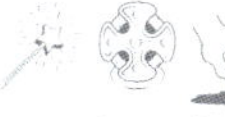

Standing on the outskirts of the town of Draguignan, the **Pierre de la Fée** (Fairy Stone) is one of the largest and most famous dolmens in Provence. It's 2.4m high and its capstone, 6m by 5m, weighs around 60 tonnes.

According to legend, the stone was the home of a fairy named Esterelle (from the Provençal *estello*, 'star'). The local women left offerings at the stone to invoke her help either with conceiving a child or, if they were pregnant, for a healthy birth. In some versions of the tale, Esterelle is a witch or wise woman rather than a fairy. The dolmen is on private property by a house but there is parking and respectful visitors are welcome.

Also associated with Draguignan is the tale of a winged dragon, a small but particularly fierce creature that was defeated by Saint Hermentaire (or Armentarius), a 5th-century Bishop of Antibes. The **Chapelle de Saint-Hermentaire** (St Hermentaire's Chapel, 43.5289, 6.4547) was built on the spot where the confrontation took place.

43.5447, 6.4531

ALPES-MARITIMES

12 Madonna of Fenestre Chapel, Saint-Martin-Vésubie

Home to one of the most important of the enigmatic Black Madonna statues found throughout Provence, the **Chapelle de la Madone de Fenestre** sits isolated in a powerful mountain location where the visitor feels the elemental forces of nature all around. The chapel is at the head of the Vésubie river valley and at an elevation of nearly 2000m. Here, the forests of the valley give way to the bare craggy peaks of the Alpes-Maritimes and the Col de Fenestre, the mountain pass that runs to the Italian border just 3km away. There is a feeling of being in a liminal place, which is reflected in the Madonna's alternative names of Madone des Frontières (Madonna of the Borders) and Madone du Bout de Monde (Madonna of the World's End). Although no longer black since being repainted in the 1970s, the statue and the story of the Madonna are charged with meaning.

Within the 50km-long Vésubie valley, the atmosphere is of a self-contained world, distinct from the rest of France and with a look and feel that isn't at all French. The area is called 'Suisse Niçoise' ('Switzerland of Nice') as the houses on the valley sides resemble Swiss chalets, and being so close to the border there's a strong Italian influence. Until 1860, Saint-Martin-Vésubie even had an Italian name, San Martino Lantosca. The valley's past is steeped in the hidden side of history, with some evidence that alchemists and other practitioners of the esoteric arts lived there. In the Middle Ages the Knights Templar were a major presence with much of the valley being under their control, and that enigmatic order of warrior-monks played a significant part in the story of the Black Madonna.

The wooden statue is of a standing Madonna and Child, 75cm high, and it has two homes. At the end of September, the Madonna of Fenestre is carried in procession 10km down to Saint-Martin-Vésubie, the largest town in the Vésubie valley, to spend the autumn and winter displayed above the altar of the **Église de Notre-Dame-de-l'Assomption** (Church of Our Lady of the Assumption, 44.0681, 7.2558; Parking: 44.0694, 7.2547, 200m). The 17th-century church with its ornate Baroque interior replaced a medieval original that was a possession of the Templars. In July, the Madonna of Fenestre is carried back to her chapel in another festive procession.

According to legend, the statue was made by St Luke and brought to France by Mary Magdelene when she arrived at **Saintes-Maries-de-la-Mer**. It was kept in Marseilles, where the Templars later acquired it. Whatever the truth of the legend, a Middle Eastern origin is likely as it's carved from Lebanese cedar. The icon's name comes from *fenêtre* ('window'), after a rectangular window-like opening in a prominent peak on the skyline, the Grand Cayre (Great Rock, 44.0986, 7.3822), also known as the Cayre de la Madone (Madonna's Rock). In the 1200s there was an apparition of the Virgin Mary on this mountain, and in acknowledgement the Templars rebuilt the chapel that had been destroyed by the Moors centuries before, installing the Black Madonna on the altar. According to some, the original chapel was built on the site of a Roman temple to the god Jupiter.

In 1308, during the suppression of the Order of the Temple, a group of Templar knights were slaughtered in the chapel.

In the centuries that followed so many misfortunes and tragedies, including earthquakes, plagues and famines, hit the area that the inhabitants came to believe that the massacre had placed the land under a curse. There were accounts of ghostly Templar knights, taken to be the spirits of the victims, seen wandering the mountains. There were even attempts to exorcise the entire valley.

The chapel and the road up to it are closed during the winter months and even sometimes in summer due to bad weather and landslides.

44.0955, 7.3561

13 **Sanctuaire de Notre-Dame de Bon-Port, Antibes**

This site on the Plateau de la Garoupe, the highest point of the Cap d'Antibes, with superb views over the Mediterranean and the French Riviera, has been sacred throughout its known history. The ancient Ligurian peoples who settled on the Mediterranean coast worshipped an unknown deity who was most likely a goddess, because when the Romans subsequently occupied this plateau they built a temple to their moon goddess, Selene, on it. The site then became a place of Christian worship and was dedicated to the mother of Emperor Constantine, St Helena, to whom many attribute her son's conversion to Christianity. According to local legend, around the year 300 Helena visited the town, then called Antipolis, and climbed up to the plateau. A simple oratory was built there and Helena's route is said to be the trail now known as the Chemin de Calvaire (Calvary Path).

14

Further change took place when the Église Notre-Dame de la Garoupe was built on the plateau in the late Middle Ages. Later, the church was enlarged and the sanctuary of **Notre-Dame de Bon Port** (Our Lady of the Good Harbour) was incorporated within it to house the icon after which it is named The sanctuary is located in one of the church's two naves. St Helena's oratory, with its well, is against the church's western wall, while the church itself is entered through its attached gift shop.

Set in front of a niche, the 1.2m high statue of Notre-Dame de Bon Port, carved from the wood of a fig tree, is a Madonna and Child resplendent in gold robes and wearing silver crowns. She holds a sailing ship in one hand, signifying that she is the protectress of the sailors of Antibes. Devotional model ships are hung all around the nave, which is decorated with frescoes portraying angelic beings engaged in nautical activities. On the first Tuesday in July the statue, carried by 10 barefoot sailors, is taken in procession down the Chemin de Calvaire on the 3km journey to **Antibes Cathedral** (43.5811, 7.1283) where it is left until the following Sunday before being carried back.

43.5642, 7.1319

14

14 **Utelle**

A former Templar possession 20km down the valley from **Saint-Martin-Vésubie,** the village of Utelle is dramatically sited atop a ridge giving expansive views of the Alps and the valley below. The medieval houses still bear carvings of the Templar seal and

14

14

other symbols including the Masonic square and compass, while those on the great oak doors of the ornately decorated 10th-century **Église Saint-Véran** (St Veranus, 43.9167, 7.2481) depict scenes from the saint's life, including his battle with the Coulobre dragon at **Fontaine-de-Vaucluse**. On the plateau above the village, the **Chapelle de Madone d'Utelle** (43.9114, 7.2314) has been a place of sanctuary, pilgrimage and miraculous healing since the 9th century. The original chapel was built by Spanish sailors in gratitude to the Virgin Mary after she saved them from shipwreck during a tempest, and the Virgin herself is said to have specified its location. The rock around the chapel contains many fossilised marine creatures in the shape of five-pointed stars, said to have been scattered from heaven by Mary as a blessing to pilgrims.

43.9168, 7.2481

INDEX

Main locations in bold
Sub-locations and cross references in light
Towns and villages in italics

GLOSSARY

French	English
Artus	Arthur (King)
abbaye, abbatiale	abbey
allée couverte	passage grave
ange	angel
baie	bay
basilique	basilica
bête	beast
butte	small hill
cap	cape
champ	field
chemin	path
chapelle	chapel
château	castle
citadelle	citadel
col	mountain pass
côte	coast
crypte	crypt
département	county
diable	devil
église	church
étang	pool, lake
fontaine	fountain
fée	fairy
forêt	forest
géant	giant
gouffre	chasm
grotte	cave, grotto
île	island
lavoir	washhouse
Madeleine	Magdalene
mare	pool
Marie-Madeleine	Mary Magdalene
Marie-Morgane	seawater fairy
mégalithique	megalithic
mont, montagne	mount, mountain
moulin	mill
musée	museum
Notre Dame	Our Lady
palais	palace
pierre	stone
pointe	point
porte	door, gateway
prieuré	priory
rivière	river
roche	rock
ruisseau	stream
sanctuaire	sanctuary
source	spring
Templier, Templière	Templar
tour	tower
tombeau	tomb
val	valley

Prehistoric features

cairn: pile of rocks, sometimes covering a grave

cromlech: an altar tomb similar to a dolmen ii) large stone circle (Brittany)

dolmen: tomb with a large flat stone supported by upright ones

megalith: large monumental stone

menhir: upright standing stone

passage grave: burial chamber covered by earth or stone with a narrow entry

stele: upright stone slab, often carved with images or text

tumulus: mound of earth or stones covering one or more graves

Long distance alignments

Please see map on right for main alignments

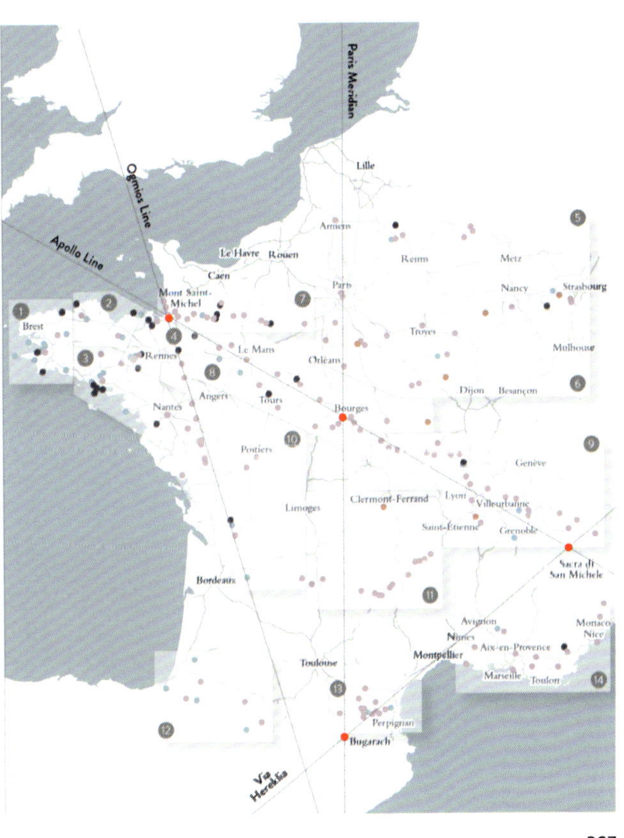

Magical France
500 Enchanted and Mystical Sites

Words:
Rob Wildwood

Photos:
Rob Wildwood

Additional research & writing:
Clive Prince

Editing:
Anna Kruger

Layout & design:
Gary Nickolls
Rhiannon Batten

Illustrations:
Dan Bright (symbols)

Proofreading:
Bethany Williams

Author acknowledgements:
With thanks to my travel companions: Este Cann, Alphedia Arara, Alison Gillies & Miananda.

Photo credits:
Carcassonne & Puilaurens - Michael Tingle.

Bibliography / Further Reading:

A Guide to Mystical France, *Inman*
A Mystic's Journey to the Sacred Sites of France, *Abbott*
A Traveller's Guide to the Mystery of Rennes-le-Chateau, *Lawlor & McLean*
Atlas des Chemins de Compostelle, *Mérienne*
Broceliande et l'énigme du Graal, *Markale*
Broceliande Forest's Guide Book, *Rasson*
Cathedral of the Black Madonna, *Markale*
Celtic Sacred Landscapes, *Penwick*
Echoes of the Goddess, *Brighton & Welbourn*
Fées, *Korrigans & Autres Créatures Fantastiques de Bretangne, Le Stum*
Guardians of the Dragon Path, *Williams*
Le Mont Saint-Michel et l'énigme du dragon, *Markale*
Le Mur Paien du Mont Sainte-Odile, *Fischer*
Les Mystères de la cathédrale de Chartres, *Charpentier*
Les Sites magiques de Provence, *Tarade & Barani*
Lieux Magiques et Sacrés de France, *Alternbach & Legrais*
Lieux Mystérieux en Bretagne, *Roger*
Melusine of Lusignan, *Knight*
Mythologie française, *Dontenville*
Rocamadour – Great Pilgrimage Centre, *Poux*
The Ancient Paths, *Robb*
The Church of Mary Magdalene, *Markale*
The Cult of the Black Virgin, *Begg*
The Dance of the Dragon, *Broadhurst & Miller*
The Discovery of King Arthur, *Ashe*
The Earth Spirit, *Michell*
The Holy Blood and the Holy Grail, *Baigent, Leigh & Lincoln*
The Holy Place, *Lincoln*
The Map and the Manuscript: Journeys in the Mysteries of the Two Rennes, *Miles*
The Nine Maidens, *McHardy*
The Paths of King Dagobert, *Bousigues*
The Sacred Journey, *Wineyard*
The Templar Revelation, *Picknett & Prince*
The Treasure of Montségur, *Birks & Gilbert*
Tous les Secrets de Bretagne,Ouest France
Voices Out Of Stone, Hoffman & North

Distribution:
Central Books Ltd
50, Freshwater Road
Dagenham, RM8 1RX
020 8525 8800
orders@centralbooks.com

Published by:
Wild Things Publishing Ltd.
Freshford, Bath, BA2 7WG

Contact:
hello@
wildthingspublishing.com